Urban Homesteading

Urban Homesteading

James W. Hughes
Kenneth D. Bleakly, Jr.

THE CENTER FOR URBAN POLICY RESEARCH
RUTGERS UNIVERSITY
BUILDING 4051—KILMER CAMPUS
NEW BRUNSWICK, NEW JERSEY 08903

Cover design by Francis G. Mullen
Interior illustrations by Kenneth D. Bleakly, Jr.

Copyright 1975, Rutgers—The State University of New Jersey

All rights reserved. Published in the United States by the Center for Urban
Policy Research, New Brunswick, New Jersey 08903.

ISBN: 0-88285-026-1

Library of Congress Cataloging in Publication data:

   Hughes, James W
      Urban homesteading.

      Bibliography: p.
1. Housing—United States—Case studies 2.
2. Dwellings—United States—Maintenance and repair—Case studies. 3. Urban
renewal—United States—Case studies.
   I. Bleakly, Kenneth D., 1950- joint author.
   II. Title.
   HD7293.H83   301.5'4   75-29148

To

Connie and Barb

Contents

APPENDICES AND BIBLIOGRAPHY

Illustrations And Exhibits

Acknowledgments

A statement of mere acknowledgment does not do justice to the debts owed to Professor George Sternlieb in making this study possible. His pioneering conceptualization of urban homesteading, and the critical factors upon which its success ultimately hinges, weighed heavily in the design of this undertaking. Where his ideas leave off, and ours begin, we will never know. But we certainly cannot overemphasize the degree to which his concepts permeate this work.

Our field research was greatly assisted by the cooperation of officials in the various homesteading programs studied. A critical review by Dr. Jack Lane of the chapter on the evolution of the homesteading concept provided us with several valuable insights.

The authors are also indebted to Ms. Carol Rosen, whose editing and shaping of the manuscript deserve special tribute, and to Ms. Connie Michaelson, who carried out almost every aspect of the manuscript preparation. Mrs. Mary Picarella, Mrs. Joan Frantz, Mrs. Lydia Lombardi, Mrs. Anne Hummel, and Ms. Elizabeth Batchelder, the mainstays of the Center for Urban Policy Research administrative and typing staff, all provided invaluable assistance.

Preface

In an era of uncertainty, promising new programs are often overloaded by their own proponents. The lust for cure-alls can, as in the proverbial life boat situation, swamp concepts as bewildered bureaucrats cling to them as last hope efforts. Currently urban homesteading is in precisely that position.

The failure, whether programmatic or administrative, of so many central city renewal and housing programs, has left a policy vacuum. On the one hand, there are the doom-sayers suggesting that an attitude of not so benign neglect is the only one that makes actuarial sense for many of our urban core areas. On the other hand, there are a number of locally based movements which look to nonconventional management and ownership approaches as providing potential for stabilization and ultimately recoupment.

Can urban homesteading be made a useful part of the armory in the battle against the submerging neighborhood? Does it have a potential in terms of securing for its participants, not merely shelter, but also most significantly, capital accumulation? Will the sweat and personal involvement required of the homesteader pay off?

Given the changed realities of housing costs versus consumers' means, the study presented here by the Rutgers Center for Urban Policy Research provides insight into the resolution of these important questions. The track record is far from clear, the program still more verbal than physical. The significance of the problems addressed are so important, however, that we felt it essential to provide a study base.

George Sternlieb
Director, Center for
Urban Policy Research

Introduction

Urban homesteading burst upon the urban scene in early 1973 with much fanfare; expectations were great that the vast wilderness of abandoned housing in the far reaches of America's cities would be reclaimed by a new breed of frontiersman—the urban homesteader. Reinforced by the glamour of historical analogy, the basic concept saw the transformation of gutted shells and hostile neighborhoods into pioneering urban colonies through the offering of free "claims" to vacant housing by enterprising young households of the 1970s. The development of the homestead grants into valuable assets was to take place through the settlers' own initiative, drive, and sweat. "Go urban, young man" became the updated dictum of Horace Greeley's famous advice "Go west, young man!" Pliers, not plows, were to be the tools for peopling not a continent, but our older central cities, which, with accelerating decay and residential abandonment, presented the prospect of emerging ghost towns in the very hearts of metropolitan regions.[1] Given the complementary failure of a generation of centrally directed urban redevelopment programming aimed at stemming this deterioration, it is not surprising that this new rhetoric, entertaining visions of a successful policy of the past, should have quickly gained the fancy of the mass media.[2] The unique local noninstitutional orientation, with prime emphasis not on a centrally directed bureaucracy but on the *individual* fortitude of American households, became the ideal virtue to be promulgated.[3]

Early documentations of urban homesteading read like public relations handouts, dwelling inordinately on very shallow historical analogies. Such catch phrases as "the homesteader of 1975 having to cope with rats and vandals rather than Indians and vegetable blights" proliferated into a multitude of vignettes.[4] Yet while this focus was fostered by those grappling to create a program out of a phrase, one should not simply decry it as blatant opportunism. In 1970s America, the potency of the phrase is great, and wise program administrators must pyramid every public relations gimmick into prominence until substantial accomplishments permit the endeavor to stand on firm foundations.[5] As George

Sternlieb has emphasized, a program may depend upon the anecdote as it makes its way through the tortuous political maze leading to operationalization—the phrase must be parleyed as a merchandizing tool. But ultimately the rhetoric must yield to an operational system which can deliver results.[6] And now the lack of substantial accomplishments has started to weigh heavily on the potency of historical analogy.

In the three cities where it has been struggling the longest—Wilmington, Baltimore, and Philadelphia—at this writing a total of less than 200 families have become active homesteaders. These homesteading programs have yet to make a significant dent in the abandonment problems of their respective settings; nor have they had an impact on housing shortages. Why these difficulties?

THE REALITIES SET IN

Undoubtedly, the noninstitutional flavor of homesteading has contributed to its rapidly rising appeal; the failure of the centralized redevelopment efforts of the past 20 years to deliver success stories has made attractive indeed a new individualized approach to program design.[7] But those intimately involved in day-to-day homestead operations quickly grasp the complexities of modern urban society. The frontiersman "go it alone" vision quickly yields to institutional and legislative encumberances, and ever-present market realities. Substantial support mechanisms are recognized as indispensible to meet the demands of code enforcement standards, fiscal realities, and financial exigencies. So the pure individualistic approach has fallen victim to the necessary institutional strictures that characterize American life today.

The recent followup literature has markedly shifted position, displaying cynicism and decrying bureaucratic slowness. This new fashion may be premature, however, since there may be a substantial lapse between program initiation and results. As the case studies in this book strongly emphasize, urban homesteading needs a sophisticated operational framework, as well as substantial support systems, if the concept is to reach its potential. The most immediate danger facing homesteading is that it will become a hostage to the verbiage advanced in securing its political acceptance; the time lag between operational field set up, as well as the practical requirements which go along with it, and the delivery of substantive results may doom the approach.[8] This is the situation in which homesteading finds itself now; the shakedown period is still in process. We only hope that the forces which initially promulgated its virtues do not serve to sour the image of homesteading before it has a chance to prove its mettle.[9]

But at the same time, even the popular media are becoming increasingly sophisticated about the manifold complexities of homesteading. Added to the historical romanticisms are the more precise languages of fast taking mechanisms, service costs, title encumberances, financing vehicles, and institutional redlining. Some realization is emerging about the burden placed on the homesteader by society and rewards accruing to society through the homesteaders' efforts.[10] While the great potential of homesteading is still recognized, the realization of this potential is no longer thought to be painless.

Moreover, the phenomena homesteading is intended to combat—housing abandonment—has confounded the welter of observers, both scholars and practitioners alike. Homesteading cannot combat this infection by itself, but must be part of a much broader offensive, encompassing a whole system of positive actions. Nevertheless, it has become one of the few implementable forces put into the battle against abandonment.

ABANDONMENT

The abandonment of housing has become widespread throughout this nation's urban areas. While it has become a basic entry on the balance sheet of national housing accounting, its most serious effects are felt at the local level. Its appearance has been documented in most major population centers, yet it is little understood and its very definition is subject to a variety of interpretations.[11] Despite the confusion surrounding the abandonment process, it is clear that the many urban ills of our society have reached their endpoint in the wholesale abandonment of residential parcels.[12] Abandoned housing units attract social undesirables who vandalize the property; they provide alluring opportunities for crimes of property and violence; and they establish a clear cut social and physical hazard to any neighborhood citizen. Residents in the immediate vicinity who can move out of the affected area are likely to do so as neighborhood confidence is undermined. The high vacancy rates which then result from those fleeing the process cause reduced rental incomes and ultimately further abandonments as the process feeds upon itself. The fiscal plights of municipalities are exacerbated and the problems of the recipient neighborhoods are intensified. Neighborhood decline toward nonviability is rapidly accelerated.

Local, state, and federal officials are often bewildered as seemingly sound structures are transformed into empty shells in relatively short periods of time. Many times this phenomenon is concentrated in what appear to be down-and-out neighborhoods, but it also affects areas of seeming viability. Thus, abandonment is not the sole province of our worst slums, but can be found in many places along the continuum of neighborhood types. The policy response should be dictated by the characteristics of the affected area. (See Chapter 2.)

HOMESTEADING: THE WORKING CONCEPT

This book focuses on one of the most highly publicized and widely discussed policy responses in regard to the reuse of abandoned housing in urban areas—urban homesteading. The concept is a simple one which borrows from past experience. The homesteader "purchases" his parcel by the agreement to reside in the unit and improve it over a certain period of time. For this he receives title to the property free, or for a nominal charge. The central thesis underlying this program is that homeownership fosters a higher degree of parcel maintenance and specific attachment. The objective is to make previously unattractive units available to qualified owners for little or no initial cost, with the result that parcels which have been economically nonviable can come back on the market simply for the cost of rehabilitation. Implied, but not stated, it is the hope that new residents will be young, upwardly mobile people whose present income does not really reflect their potential. Ideally the program will draw these people back into the central city where, through hard work and a large amount of "sweat equity," the homesteaders will rebuild their homes and, indirectly, the city. Thus, by increasing the number of homeowners, especially in a mix of income brackets, improvements can be made in the quality of life in urban areas.

It is the goal of this book to examine the urban homesteading phenomenon as it has evolved and to look at its operational realities in four major cities. Out of the experience to date, the critical success factors are isolated by applying a common framework for evaluation in the four case studies. We then attempt to weave these elements into coherent statements of effective homesteading formats. While the substance of the final document would make valid the label of handbook, we have also sought to provide a wider scope of inquiry. Given significant attention are the historical homesteading efforts and their linkages to present efforts (including a detailed case study of Roosevelt, N.J., a 1930s subsistence homestead); the role of homesteading in the abandonment response process is also closely examined; and a neighborhood decline reference framework is provided with which to coordinate various housing policies. While these additional avenues of inquiry may appear somewhat abstract, we hope they make the overall document that much more readable, while not detracting from the work's utility as an operational document.

THE POLICY CONTEXT

Urban homesteading may be interpreted as an expression of a shifting national policy which has resulted in the troubles of the cities being given relatively low priority.[13] It has been almost a decade since the urban situation occupied the time and attention of a nervous capital, when outbreaks of urban racial violence were one of the nation's most worrisome maladies. Its role as a critical national issue, at least in the minds of recent Administrations, is now over. Urban conservation is the phrase of the moment, and the propositions and platitudes of the 1960s, of a massive rebuilding of the cities to their perceived former glories, retain little credibility. A visible reduction of the federal role in local affairs and greatly reduced commitments to the final vestiges of the massive Great Society programs of the last decade provide tangible evidence of the federal belief that the urban crisis is over.

Sensing the evolution of federal policy, and finally coming to grips with the firmly embedded trends of long-term diminution of central city population and traditional economic activities, some urban policymakers have come to the conclusion that their basic overall strategy cannot be encouraging regeneration so much as ensuring continued livability.[14] While there is far less glamour and certainly far less visibility of success in a maintenance program than in a regenerative one, homesteading may well be a last grasp at the regeneration strategy, as well as the first stage of a maintenance strategy.[15] Maintaining the extant housing stock, while appearing under the guise of a regenerative phraseology, is homesteading's task. It is clearly a stability mechanism of the last resort, an effort not to prevent urban neighborhoods from changing, but to prevent them from drowning.

Two threads of the homesteading fabric—the shift in federal commitments and the trend toward stabilization and conservation rather than renewal—have been joined by a third strand, a clearer understanding of the market realities of low-income residential realty. The conventional tools of the 1960s, targeted to ameliorate the housing woes in urban America, were predicated on the assumption that moderate rental rates were sufficient to support adequate rates of return along with improved parcel maintenance.[16] All that had to be done, it was assumed, was to reallocate the portions of the rental income inordinately weighted to landlord requirements, through mechanisms such as code enforcement, rent control, and receivership.[17] Even if the landlords' rate of return were diminished, an adequate profit margin would remain while the housing stock could be substantially improved.

However, the track record of these mechanisms has shown that the rent dollar is more finite than had been perceived.[18] The strength of this belief has grown in concert with the recognition—spurred by the energy crisis and the dollar flow to the petroleum exporters—that we have a finite level of resources at our disposal. In the housing sphere, suspicions mount that the older notions of unlimited reserves served to increase the cycle of decay and abandonment in the urban setting.

At the same time, evidence has piled up that the one major variable that could directly be linked to housing maintenance and positive attitudes toward residential realty in the central city was homeownership.[19] But attempts to operationalize an expansion of homeownership produced the enormous series of scandals under Section 235 of the 1968 Housing Act. The concept may have been valid but its program manifestation reflected serious flaws. This large scale centralized effort, which was not merely insensitive but oblivious to market realities, contributed to the disfavor and eventually to the bankruptcy of the traditional institutionized approach to regeneration.[20]

And so, homesteading grew out of the shifting federal commitments and program failures, the growing realization of the need for stabilization and conservation in the central city, a recognition of the market realities of core housing, and the benefits of resident ownership. Yet compared with the halcyon days of the mid-sixties, financial commitments to this new approach to housing are meager indeed.

THE ORGANIZATIONAL SCHEME

The first section of this study, which comprises two chapters, is entitled "Urban Homesteading: A Historical Perspective and Policy Concept." The first traces the historical development of the homesteading concept to its present manifestation. This step backward is important for grasping the appeal of modern homesteading programs; yet a critical examination of historical efforts provides some sobering facts which should enable a more realistic evaluation of our case areas to be made. The second chapter, entitled "Housing Abandonment, Neighborhood Decline, and Urban Homesteading," provides a paradigm of neighborhood evolution based on identifiable stages of decline within which both housing abandonment and urban homesteading are subsequently examined. These two chapters suggest both a long-range and wide-range perspective with which to view the operational manifestations of urban homesteading.

The second section of the book, "Urban Homesteading: Operational Realities," comprises five chapters. The first, "The Evaluative Framework," presents the ten major subject areas which are subsequently investigated in the case observations. Each of the homestead ventures is evaluated in terms of this standardized format; these evaluations constitute the next four chapters, specifically focusing on the homesteading programs developed respectively in Baltimore, Maryland; Wilmington, Delaware; Philadelphia, Pennsylvania; and Newark, New Jersey.

The final section, "Program Synthesis and Evaluation," uses the comparative framework presented earlier to analyze the procedures followed in the different cities, and offers policy recommendations based on a synthesis of the most successful procedures.

A series of technical appendices are provided to clarify some of the operational processes necessary for an effective homesteading program, particularly as a response to housing abandonment. The first appendix provides an operational definition of abandonment, perhaps the first step in having buildings declared legally abandoned, and a proposed monitoring and reporting system. The second reviews the municipal cost-revenue methodology which is employed in each of the detailed case studies. The third presents a summary in matrix form of the program requirements in each of the case studies. The final appendix provides some of the relevant local and state ordinances pertinent to urban homesteading efforts.

NOTES

1. "From Plows to Pliers—Urban Homesteading in America," *Fordham Urban Law Journal*, Vol. 2, Winter 1974, pp. 273-304.

2. George Sternlieb, "The Myth and Potential Reality of Urban Homesteading," paper presented at Confer-In 1974, American Institute of Planners, p. 1.

3. *Ibid.*, p. 5.

4. Sophie Douglass Pfeiffer, " 'Go Urban Young Man!'—American Homesteading 1862-1974," *Historic Preservation*, July-September 1974, pp. 16-22.

5. Sternlieb, "The Myth and Potential of Homesteading," p. 2.

6. *Ibid.*

7. *Ibid.*, p. 1.

8. *Ibid.*, p. 2.

9. *Ibid.*, p. 3.

10. *Ibid.*, p. 9.

11. George Sternlieb and Robert Burchell, *Residential Abandonment: The Tenement Landlord Revisited* (New Brunswick, N.J.: Center for Urban Policy Research, 1973).

12. *Ibid.*, chapter 7.

13. Sternlieb, "The Myth and Potential of Homesteading," pp. 2-3.

14. *Ibid.*

15. *Ibid.*, p. 8.

16. *Ibid.*, pp. 3-4.

17. *Ibid.*, p. 2.

18. *Ibid.*

19. *Ibid.*, p. 3.

20. *Ibid.*, p. 5.

Urban Homesteading

Section I

Urban Homesteading: A Historical Perspective And Policy Concept

Chapter 1

Urban Homesteading: A Historical Perspective

INTRODUCTION: FOLLOWING THE TRAIL

From its earliest origins, this nation has clung to the notion that home or land ownership is something to be revered and sought by rational men. While the sanctity of the home and the corollary dogma of the nobility of landed yeomanry may have lost their relevance with the industrialization and immigration that has buffeted America, they have not lost their potency among the chief folk myths of society.

As George Sternlieb has observed:

> Generations of movie-going have imbued the American public with a positive concept of the homesteader. Who ever saw the homesteader as the bad guy or ultimate loser? True, as in the classic wrestling match, he may take his thumps in the first couple of acts. But ultimately he wins, (sometimes indeed, in a general amnesty with the cowpunchers and other forms of exurbanites). The phrase, given its overtones of private ownership, self-help, and the anticipated doing away with the so-called bureaucracy of the poor, is one which has at least a rhetorical appeal both to the left and to the right, though with perhaps more vigor to the latter group.[1]

An equally significant undercurrent in America's history has included various attempts to redistribute population to areas which were unable to attract a significant number of persons on their own, because of remote location or hostile environment. In an attempt to overcome these disincentives to settlement under regular market conditions, the national government offered new settlers the enticements of free land and, in the 1930s, of very low cost housing and land. This concept has come to be called "homesteading."

Its origins date back to the pre-revolutionary era. Early colonists to

Virginia were attracted by a "head right" which guaranteed a minimum acreage to any settlers willing to face the hardships and uncertainties of life in the wilds of America.

From 1804 on, pleas were heard in Congress for some type of free land policy in the West. After a protracted legislative battle during the 1850s and early 1860s, President Lincoln signed the first homesteading act on May 20, 1862. Under its provisions any settler could claim 160 acres of land for a $26 claiming fee provided he was willing to live on and improve the land for 5 years.[2]

One of the cherished beliefs behind the homesteading concept was "land to the landless." The popular feeling was that if free land were made available in the West, an escape valve would be provided to immigrants overflowing the eastern cities. In fact, no such thing occurred. Although the land was offered at almost no cost, most immigrants lacked the money to provision themselves both for the long migration or for subsistence during the first few years. This meant homesteading was left to those of more substantial, if modest incomes.[3]

The Great Depression supplied the impetus for the next major evolutionary step in homesteading. Drawing support from the back-to-the-land movement during that period, the federal government instituted a new form of resettlement called the Subsistence Homesteads Program. This effort derived its philosophical rationale from the belief that the causes of the depression could be traced to the overly diversified and mechanized economy which had developed with the coming of the Industrial Revolution. This movement had caused the vast majority of citizens to lose control over the production of the essentials of life: food, clothing, and shelter. The subsistence homestead program attempted to redress this imbalance by resettling land and retraining low-income persons to become more self-sufficient.

The most recent form of homesteading has taken on the role of drawing "settlers" to abandoned structures in urban core areas. A free granting of title is provided in return for a promise of residency and rehabilitation. Urban homesteading had been discussed for several years by national housing experts as a method of both returning abandoned structures to the housing supply system and increasing homeownership in core areas. One of the earliest proponents of the concept was George Sternlieb, who suggested in 1971 both an operational format and a framework of necessary supportive services for a program of homeownership and housing rehabilitation under the umbrella of urban homesteading.[4] The first real stirrings for the creation of such a program soon followed.

Myth or Reality?

Homesteading conjures potent historical images—images which have been used to promote the current urban-oriented programs. But how do these images compare to the actual experience of modern homesteading's main antecedents: the headright provisions of colonial times, the frontier homestead of the western migration, and the community settlements of the Depression? While we cannot, in the scope of this work, undertake a complete history of these developments, we believe that a survey of their conflicting philosophies, operational difficulties, and administrative shortcomings and accomplishments provides a valuable perspective from which to view present homesteading efforts.

In the following sections of this chapter, we will discuss the historical antecedents of homesteading in detail, focusing on both their operational achievements and limitations. Moreover, we will suggest analogies between the past and the present, in terms of the philosophic orientation and functional goals of the programs. And, perhaps most significantly, we will note areas where the analogies break down—in particular, the disparities between homesteading a fertile tract of farmland, which has at least a modest potential for economic return, and an abandoned building in the central city, which may not have any substantial market value.

SECURING A HEADRIGHT

> ... (All Settlers) will be entered as adventurers in the present voyage to Virginia, where they will have houses to live in, vegetable gardens and orchards and also food and clothing at the expense of the Company and besides this, a share of all products and profits that may result from their labor, each in proportion, and *they will also secure a share in the division of the land for themselves and their heirs for evermore* ... (Author's emphasis)[5]

The Virginia Company's broadside promotion of the settlement of American lands in the year 1609 had established a basic policy which was to determine the shape of land ownership in a majority of the American colonies. This announcement was the first acknowledgment of a major system for enticing new settlers to the colonies—the "headright."

Under the headright concept, the proprietor and later the state in most of the colonies would make grants of land to immigrants and their servants. Under feudal land systems, ownership remained in the hands of the nobility with encumberances forever clouding the title held by the peasants. Headrights were a bridging mechanism between this feudal method of land tenure and the development of fee simple ownership and the free alienation of land, thereby permitting greater ease in the securing and transfer of its ownership.

While this procedure was common in Virginia, New York, New Jersey, Maryland, Pennsylvania, Delaware, the Carolinas, and Georgia, the size of the grants varied greatly by location, time of settlement, and the group immigrating.

As with the homesteading laws of a later generation, the headright was a mechanism for inducing settlement in areas which otherwise might not develop because of their hostile environs. It also served as an equalization mechanism by bringing surplus land into the hands of the land-hungry masses of Europe through the use of the wealth concentrated in the upper class who, in return for their speculation, received a monetary reward in the form of feudal tithes.[6]

Typically in the colonies which granted headrights, each person who paid his own passage or that of another person from Europe could receive a grant of land. For example, under the ruling issued by the Virginia Company in 1620 "Ancient Adventurers and Planters," meaning those who were shareholders in the company and who had paid their own way to the colony and resided there for three years by the year 1618, were entitled to 100 acres on the first public division of the land. When a second division occurred, they would also receive an additional 100 acres provided the land received on the first division was sufficiently peopled.[7] (Every man who came as a tenant or servant of the company before 1618, was allowed 100 acres of land at the expiration of his period of servitude.)

Adventurers, both for their own passage and for every person for whom they paid passage between 1618 and 1625 received 50 acres in fee simple with no feudal charges on the first and second division of land. Settlers who were non-shareholders in the Virginia Company but transported themselves and/or others during this period were also granted 50 acres, but after a seven year abatement period their quitrents were to resume at 12 cents per year.[8]

While the great majority of allotments were from 50 to 200 acres, which would account for the average landowner and a servant or two, more substantial tracts of land were often given to corporations which represented large commercial interests. However, a significant number of the large allotments were held by individuals.

When the original grant of what is today New Jersey was given to Berkeley and Carteret in 1665, they established conditions which would decrease the amount of land available by headright. Those male settlers who had arrived before January 1, 1666 and had met the Governor received 150 acres for themselves and for each male servant in their possession. Persons arriving between January 1, 1666 and January 1, 1667 could receive 90 acres and after January 1, 1667, 60 acres. In 1684, the headright was even further decreased in East Jersey to 25 acres by the group of 12 investors who had purchased the land from Carteret.[9]

Under the provision of the headright most proprietors required a feudal tax known as a quitrent. This was a small annual charge usually paid on an acreage basis to the proprietor either in the form of money or goods. This was the most obvious link between the headright and feudal land tenure systems, binding the settler in fealty to the proprietor and depriving him of fee simple ownership of the land. Another encumbrance on the title of the headrighter was the "planting and seating" provision which required that a certain degree of improvements be made on the land to realize full ownership.[10]

Prior to 1666 in Virginia, "sufficient" planting and seating was required within three years of the allotment, but the term sufficient was not defined. However, in that year the legislature declared the seating requirement satisfied if a house and stock were kept on the land for one year and the planting requirement satisfied if one acre of ground was cleared, planted, and tended for one year. Three years were allotted for carrying out these provisions unless the owner had been molested by Indians in which case he would be allowed seven years.[11]

The headright system had both advantages and disadvantages. It provided a mechanism by which any person, regardless of economic background, or race, could immigrate to the colonies and obtain a parcel of land in return for labor.[12] Certainly, the headright made colonial land ownership accessible to most socioeconomic classes. It offered to the settler who was willing to accept some modest conditions the 17th century's most prized possession, land, and during the period of conditional ownership, the proprietors were assured of an income flow. Furthermore, the competition between colonies for settlers eventually reduced ownership requirements.[13]

As a major undertaking, however, it was beset with problems. Because of the vastness of available land and the disjointed organization of most colonial governments, many irregularities occurred in the administration of the program. Frequently the same person would be granted more than one allotment either through erroneous recordkeeping or outright fraud. It was not uncommon to see a great similarity in the names of the owners of headrights in a particular area, often with one or two letters being the only difference in thier spelling.[14] Another common practice was the granting of headrights to persons making return trips back from England. Thus, wealthy owners with business in England often received several grants based on their commutation.[15] A particularly effective deception was for more than one person to claim a headright on an individual. Shipmasters often claimed they had provided passage for individuals, when the latter had either been sailors or paying passengers. It was also common for a shipmaster to claim he had paid the passage of a person, only to have a merchant who actually paid the person's way also claim his headright; then if the person were indentured to a planter for a period of time, the planter would claim a headright, with the immigrant receiving his headright at the end of his servitude.[16] All the possible fraudulent combinations made equitable enforcement extremely difficult.

In Virginia and New York, the use of headrights declined soon after 1700, and in most of the other colonies that had offered headrights, the practice had been eclipsed as a major means of land tenure by the more direct land sale methods by the end of the 18th century.

Nonetheless, the headright concept had far-reaching implications for national land use patterns. Unlike New England, which developed around small settlements carefully surveyed and somewhat planned by the dictates of the settling corporation, the headright states exhibited a more "individualistic" and random land use pattern that was derived from the speculative nature of the land's acquisition. Since surveys were rare and multiple headrights easy to obtain either through honest or dishonest means, the land quickly took a spread-out and disjointed pattern.[17] Those patterns would later play a major part in determining the socioeconomic fabric which developed in the different areas of colonial America.

The headright system, then, was widely used by both corporations and individuals to obtain multiple titles to vast tracts of land beyond the original intentions of the proprietary companies. The grants did, however, establish the first workings of a land system which offered an avenue to land ownership and economic independence to the poor and indigent willing to come to the colonies—something which they had been denied in Europe.

WESTERN HOMESTEADS

Homesteading evokes no more vivid picture than the sodbuster eeking out an existence amid the rolling sea of prairie grass in the western plains of 19th century America. This image has spurred present interest by association in urban America; the independence and tenacity of those early settlers is what many city governments, plagued by burgeoning bureaucracies and stagnant budgets, hope to evoke from their homesteaders.

Yet this popular image does not directly correspond to the historical reality. This section will examine the disparity between the myth and the reality of western homesteading to gain perspective in judging current efforts.

The homesteading concept grew during the first half of the 19th century from a welter of competing interests, each desiring free land in the West but for far different reasons. The Democratic Party's Jeffersonian and Jacksonian elements both saw free land as a necessity for preserving the democracy they cherished. Their beliefs echoed those of Jefferson when he said:

> Those who labor in the earth are God's chosen people ... whose breasts He has made His peculiar deposit for substantial and genuine virtue. It is the focus in which He keeps alive the sacred fire, which otherwise might escape from the face of the earth.[18]

or on another occasion when he espoused the sanctity of the yeoman class:

> ... generally speaking, the proportion which the aggregate of the other classes of citizens bears in any state to that of its husbandmen, is a good enough barometer whereby to measure its degree of corruption .... The mobs of the great cities add just so much to the support of pure government, as sores do to the strength of the body.[19]

Such an attitude implies a liberal land tenure policy to foster yeomanry and preserve a perceived delicate balance between farm and city.

Urban laborers also favored a liberal land policy, not as a sanctuary for an exalted class of yeoman farmers, as the Jeffersonians perceived it, but as an escape valve from the increasing hostility and pressures of the growing urban centers.

The Westerners themselves saw the further settlement of their territories as a positive development for the nation, with future financial reward to themselves; a free land movement would increase their power and prestige considerably.

Perhaps the most influential group of homestead lobbyists comprised speculators who, at first blush, would appear as homesteading's logical enemies. If all the designated lands were settled by homesteaders who held their titles to maturity, this would be true. But, in an imperfect world, the speculator knew there would be untold profit-making opportunities once a loosely administered government land program was established.

So a coalition of agrarian philosophers, western boosters, urban laborers, and shrewd speculators joined forces in the early 19th century to bring their wishes to fruition.

The government's early land policy was contrary to the interests of these free land groups. The Act of 1796 established the federal public land auction with a minimum acreage set at 640, and a price of $2.00 per acre, with half of the price payable at the time of purchase and the remainder in one year.[20] The price and acreage stipulation was intended to discourage land speculation; it also effectively discouraged settlement.

In 1800, the minimum acreage was lowered to 320 with the payment period extended to 4 years, increasing the program's attractiveness to settler and speculator alike. Farming 640 acres was beyond the capabilities of the early 19th century farmer who had to clear by hand heavily forested land, and the one-year payment period conflicted with the difficulty of obtaining any kind of immediate return from the land. With the conclusion of the War of 1812, a renewed movement west brought the first widescale application of the federal land auction system.

Three key variables in the new system—transfer of land from federal title, actual settlement, and economic development—were substantially independent and not interrelated as the free land proponents first supposed.[21] The first major settlements under the modification of the Act of 1796 showed that a great deal of land was moving from federal title but was never improved because of its purchase by speculators; other sections were never purchased but were in fact settled by squatters; still other parcels, neither settled nor bought, were ravaged by exploiters who sapped the land to feed cattle and cut lumber. Very little land was purchased by settlers and subsequently developed, a factor that must be kept in focus in any evaluation of the federal land distribution schemes.

The widespread settlement of federal lands by squatters in the early 1800s illustrated the deficiencies of extant land systems. Land contained the necessary resources for development; settlers could provide the necessary labor to create that development; however, the third essential element, capital, was lacking, thereby necessitating the taking of the land to permit development. The colonials had been able to solve the problem of bringing capital to the underdeveloped regions by offering investments to the wealthy. The squatters approach was a taking of the land.

Preemption: Prelude to Homesteading

The attempt by squatters to lessen capital requirements reached its zenith in the fight for preemption laws. Under such a policy the squatters sought governmental validation of their claim in return for a $1.25 per acre payment. Their argument focussed on their demonstrated ability to develop the land and to produce sufficient capital to pay $1.25 per acre after the land's settlement; thus they desired to legalize their claim to their squatted land. The government concurred and in 1841 passed the Preemption Act authorizing the purchase of up to 160 acres by persons not already owning more than 320 acres on previously surveyed land.[22]

With its enactment, widespread abuses immediately emerged. Since the only requirement for obtaining title was to swear that improvements and occupancy of the land had occured, perjury prevailed.[23]

Favorite settlers' tactics included "claims clubs" or "squatters organizations." Long revered in folklore as a tool for preventing speculators from driving up land prices, these organizations actually played a far different role. Since the settler had to place a bid on his land at the time of government auction, the "claims clubs" attempted either to prevent the auction from being held or insure the price remained at the minimum $1.25 per acre. This in and of itself was not an inappropriate procedure for circumventing the upbidding done by speculators on the 160 acres to which the settler was entitled; however, this practice was often used to keep artificially low the price of land on *additional* quarter sections, so it was not uncommon for the settlers to obtain 320, 480 or even 640 acres at the minimum price, thereby exceeding their legal limit through pressure tactics.[24]

Preemption was especially abused in the late 1870s and 1880s by timber and mineral interests, amassing great tracts of valuable land by using false claims and dummy corporations.[25] By 1882 the General Land Office, in no uncertain terms, called for the end of preemption citing the aforementioned abuses; Congress finally acted on this request in 1891.

Preemption, while having little support outside the western states, did, however, open the door for a land policy more oriented toward settlement. The primary objective—protecting the settler from the outside speculation—was accomplished, but at the cost of allowing the settlers themselves to become speculators. Morever, it established the precedence of settlement over speculation and, as such, served as the logical prelude to the homesteading concept.[26]

The Beginnings of Homesteading

With the signature of President Lincoln, homesteading became a reality on May 20, 1862, culminating the many attempts at obtaining free land for those willing to settle upon it.

This policy's first vestiges were the land bonuses given to veterans. While specific tracts were never designated, veterans received warrants entitling them to a specific number of acres. All told warrants for 61 million acres were issued; after 1852 the warrants became fully negotiable and could be traded on the open market like any other government obligations.[27] As could be expected, they quickly became the prey of speculators and the number of soldiers who used the land bonuses to settle in the West was quite small.[28] Their total land area was not. Forty percent of Iowa and large sections of Minnesota, Kansas, Nebraska, and Illinois were distributed in this manner.[29] Consequently, the land sold at public auction was made less attractive, since the warrants generally sold for less than $1.25 per acre, further adding to the malaise of the federal land policies. The actions of the speculators were so widely perceived prior to the passage of these bonuses that some concluded that Congress was far less interested in either the soldiers or the settlers than in the speculators.[30]

Horace Greeley tartly summed up the public reaction to the government's land bonus policy:

> By these Bills, (The Land Bonus Legislation) a little money has been secured to the discharged soldiers, and a great deal more to claim agents, warrant speculators, attorneys, brokers, etc., all at the expense of the future pioneers of our new state.[31]

While the land bonus system was problem-laden, it did serve, as did preemption, as a major prelude to the homesteading laws which soon followed. Most importantly, it established the principle of *free* lands to settlers, if only to those of a special class, i.e., soldiers.

The pressure in the West for even more liberal federal land policies never ceased. While preemption allowed vast tracts of land to be settled at low cost this was not enough. At the same time, the land bonuses were despised by the Westerners once they became assignable because of their boon to speculation.[32] The dream of the Westerners was a free land policy open to all willing to settle and develop the land.

Such a policy had already been tried in several territories. In 1842, Congress offered free homesteads to settlers willing to move to Florida, cultivate five acres, and remain five years. Parenthetically, this act was a complete failure and even the government's lifting of the cultivation requirement could not attract enough participants.[33]

The Oregon Donation Act of 1850 created a more successful model for early homesteading efforts. Every male settler arriving in Oregon before 1850 could receive 320 acres, with an additional 320 acres allotted to his wife, provided the land was occupied for four years. Persons arriving between 1850 and 1853 could qualify for half this amount.[34] The majority of the settlers found little use for such large parcels but petitioned the government for a quick means of obtaining negotiable title. Congress subsequently permitted them to purchase the land after 2 years at $1.25 per acre. A full 72 percent of the settlers opted for the special quick purchase arrangement,[35] demonstrating once again the principle first made obvious under the preemption law: the settlers were more interested in becoming speculators themselves rather than in abolishing speculation. While the desire for free land goes back to the nation's founding and the first settlements over the Appalachian mountains, the chief obstacle to this policy was the different perception of the issue in the East and in the West. The prevailing attitude among Easterners was that western lands were bringing in good prices and as such provided substantial revenues to the country; thus they saw it as a legitimate policy of government to sell the land to the highest bidder be he settler or speculator.

The Westerners, not surprisingly, saw this issue in a different light. To them the land was a public domain which required a great deal of effort to develop.[36] Thus, any price was an undue burden on those willing to make the tremendous sacrifices necessary to develop the land. Because of the political dominance of the eastern seaboard and the relative political impotence of the western states the free land advocates never really had any hope of success in the early 19th century. The first major bill to create homesteading on a national scale was introduced by Senator Thomas Hart Benton of Missouri in 1825; nothing substantial came of this early effort, however.[37]

One of the major forces in legitimizing the homesteading concept was a report by the Committee on Public Lands of the House of Representatives issued in 1825, which called for the creation of a program that would grant 80 acres to the heads of families willing "to cultivate, improve, and reside" on the same for five years.[38]

Its rationale was argued as follows:

> ... The poor furnish soldiers, and an experience shows that the patriotism which exists apart from an interested love of country cannot be relied upon. The affections of good citizens are always mingled with their homes and placed upon the country which contains these fields and gardens.[39]

It is interesting to note that while the federal government is emphasized in the development and creation of homesteading programs, Arkansas and Indiana had already established homesteading by 1830. The requirements and the size of the grants, 5 years residence and 160 acres, anticipated the basic requirements of the Federal Homesteading Program.[40]

Free western land was initially the clarion call of the western states, but with the great immigrations of the 1840s and '50s and the resultant rise in the power of the labor movement, the cry for free land was heard also from the teaming slums of the East.

The notion of free public lands quickly spread among the urban working classes, largely as a result of the efforts of publicists such as Horace Greeley. Greeley and many of his followers believed, though events later proved them wrong, that free land could act as an escape valve for overcrowded cities and help control what they saw as rapidly rising "pauper class," suffering chiefly because they were landless.[41]

Homesteading was buoyed by this support, and by 1852 a bill was passed by a two-to-one majority in the House, only to fail in the Senate.[42] The failure of the bill in the Senate was important in the legislation's history, for the previous coalition of Westerners and urban labor votes verses the coastal states had now shifted to an issue of North verses South.[43]

The South, after the Compromise of 1850 and the passage of the Wilmot Proviso, feared its political power would decrease if a large amount of settlement occurred in the Northwestern free states. Since homesteading would encourage such a power transfer, they opposed it.

In 1859, with a large number of recently elected Republicans pledged to the homesteading concept, the bill seemed assured of passage. And as in 1852, it passed the House easily by a margin of 120 to 76. It was the Senate which proved the stumbling block once again. The issue became embroiled in a battle by the Southern representatives to pass a law annexing Cuba as a slave state. When action on that bill was postponed until a vote was taken on homesteading, the Southerners became enraged. Their anger drew an equally partisan response from their Northern colleagues. This animosity on both sides made homesteading the political football of the day.

In 1862, with a new President in power, one who was more disposed to the concept from a philosophical perspective and equally aware of its strategic importance in gaining support for the Northern cause, homesteading became a reality. Under the law, the persons included under the Preemption Act of 1841 had a right to a homestead of 160 acres on surveyed public domain. They could acquire title by continuous residence and improvement for five years and payment of a filing fee. After a period of 6 months of residence and improvement, the claimant might "commute" his homestead entry to full title simply by the payment of $1.25 per acre. Any improvement to the extent of an acre or more entitled the claimant to commutation. No lands acquired under the act could become future payment for the satisfaction of a debt contracted prior to the issuing of the patent. The claimant was required to swear in an affidavit that he or she was the head of a family, was over 21 years of age, and had not borne arms against the United States. Also, the claim was to be "for his or her exclusive use and benefit" and that the claim was "for the purpose of actual settlement and cultivation; and not, either directly or indirectly, for the use or benefit of any other person or persons whomever."[44]

Aid to the Homesteader

An equally important piece of legislation benefiting the early homesteaders, and their ancestors, was passed several months after the homesteading law, the Morrill Act.

Under its provisions, public grants of land were to be made to the states to establish colleges for the benefit of agricultural and mechanical arts.[45] Each state was granted 30,000 acres for each senator and representative it sent to

Congress. Should sufficient acreage be unavailable, "land scrip" could be issued and sold to private individuals to apply to unoccupied western lands.[46] The proceeds from the sale of scrip was to go to the support of an existing college:

> ... where the leading subjects should be, not excluding other scientific and classical studies, and including military tactics, such branches of learning as are related to agriculture and mechanic arts, in such manner as the legislatures of the states may prescribe in order to promote the liberal and practical education of the industrial classes in the permanent pursuits and professions of life.[47]

Thus, the Congress had established the need for institutions of higher learning to train settlers in the best methods of farming and living on their newly acquired lands. The Morrill Act provided a means of assisting the homesteaders through the dissemination of new technologies.

Homesteading in Practice

The Homesteading Law in practice was not always the great boon to the settlement of the West that common mythology would have us believe. For example, the legislation permitted the settler to "commute" his homestead into a negotiable title very quickly by paying the regular price for the land any time after the first six months of filing his claim.[48] From the time of the law's inception until 1880 only about four percent of the settlers did this. After that date a great change occurred. From 1881 to 1904, 23 percent of all the acreage claimed was commuted.[49] This shift towards increased commutation can be attributed to the rise of speculation and the decline of actual settlement on the homestead claims. Many persons, entertaining little thought of settling, saw commutation, like preemption, as a device for obtaining quick cash by overtly selling their lands to other settlers seeking larger properties, and to other speculators.[50] The use of the commutation privilege by non-settlers was documented by the chief of special agents of the U.S. Land Office at the time:

> ... They (the commuters) are usually merchants, professional people, school teachers, clerks, journeymen working at trades, cow punchers, or sheep herders. Generally, the lands are sold immediately after final proof.[51]

A device which reduced commutation's impact on homesteading was the lowering of the residence requirement to three years, making it easier to stay the required period than pay the fee per acre.[52] This did not, however, alter the basic problem of persons filing a homesteading claim strictly for speculative reasons. It is also important to note that homesteading occurred on only a small segment of the available public domain, with railroad, timber, and mineral claims and lands for public sale eventually constituting a larger share of all acreage passing into private ownership.[53] By way of illustration, more land was sold by the government between 1862 and 1891 than was homesteaded between 1862 and 1899.[54] This land was often purchased by the homesteader himself who expanded his holdings through preemption or purchase from the state, railroads, or timber interests.[55]

Once the homesteader settled on his land, it was not uncommon for him to expand his holdings often beyond the boundaries he could hope to utilize. This has led some commentators to question whether the first occupation of the pioneers was farming or land speculation.[56] With so many opportunities available to cash in on their claims it is not surprising that many choose to do so.

The degree of success of the homesteading program also varied with the location and suitability of the area for farming. While the national average of homestead claims carried to patent was 50 percent, 58 percent were patented in Kansas, 61 percent in Nebraska, and 52 percent in Dakotas.[57] While the most successful homesteads were in the heart of the Midwest, claims occurred all over the country. Twenty-three percent of all homesteads were located east of the Mississippi, with the highest concentrations in Alabama, Florida, Mississippi, Michigan and Wisconsin.[58] The largest number of initial homestead claims occurred in Kansas; however, Minnesota which had the next highest number of claims had the highest percentage of those claims settled for the mandatory five year period and matured into private ownership.

The success of the homesteading concept is best measured in the period from its passage until 1880. It was during this time that most of the good farmland in the Midwest was settled. The record for the settlers of that period is most impressive, with 55 percent finally receiving title to their lands. Afterward, homesteading became a device for ranching, mining, and timber interests to obtain vast tracts of land. As proof, the ratio between homestead entries and actual farms in the far western states is instructive. Idaho, which had 60,000 final entries, only had 40,000 farms. Colorado had 107,000 final entries but only 57,000 farms; Arizona had 20,000 final entries and 9,000 farms; and Wyoming 67,000 final entries and 15,000 farms.[59]

Federal homesteading was greatly curtailed in 1935 when President Roosevelt issued an order withdrawing 165,695,000 acres from claimable unfarmed lands. This was done so that the land might be preserved while studies were undertaken to determine its best use.[60] This act by the President largely signaled an end to the public domain as a conduit for private ownership. As historian Roy Robbins has observed, "For over forty years historians had been heralding the passing of the frontier; without a doubt the old frontier had now passed."[61] A very limited amount of homesteading has continued up to the present day, with 193 homesteads awarded by the U.S. Department of Interior in 1972. The major remaining arable land available for homesteading was in Alaska, but even this was withdrawn from the category of open land under Public Land Order 5418 by the Bureau of Land Management in March 1974.[62]

Western homesteading established the principle of a free grant of land to citizens by the government rather than through proprietary interest as occurred in the colonial era. Homesteading, like its counterpart the headright, brought together the three tools necessary to stimulate development—capital, labor, and land. Chiefly this was accomplished through the provision of capital incentives in the form of free land, to settlers willing to locate on lands where free market forces alone were insufficient to encourage development. Like the headright, too, the lax administration of the homesteading program could not prevent speculative practices which undermined the democratic goals of the program itself. While vast numbers of settlers did stake and develop their homestead claims, an equally significant development of the program was the illegal speculation and acquisition of vast tracts of land by timber, cattle, mineral, and railroad interests. Homesteading in the West provides an excellent example of the need for a strong and vigilant monitoring agency to prevent widespread abuse of any such open-ended land distribution scheme.

It is interesting to note in hindsight the relatively small benefit free lands were to the western settlers in terms of the necessary capital to start a farm. Assuming a 160 acre tract at the prevailing preemption price of $1.25 per acre, a homestead would cost the settler $200. This could be paid for over a four year period; thus $50 per year was necessary to insure land ownership. Much has been made of the burden this amount proved to the average settler, but compared with the costs of moving West—even just the basic equipment and necessary provisions—the amount seems minimal. If the government believed enough in the need to develop the West to offer land, it became legitimate to be caught up in the euphoria and take a chance on a homestead. It became a colossal dare—too tempting for many of that era to resist.

Homesteading therefore was as much an attitude and spirit as it was a concrete program. The aura of enterprise and the mystique of rural life created by the government and the popular press were as important in the decision of many settlers to move west as was the offer of free land.[63]

In operation the romantic hopes of homesteading's proponents failed to sustain many of the settlers. Proclamations about the sanctity of the life of the soil and the great benefits derived from location in a healthy agrarian environment offered little comfort to the lonely, weary, and often destitute settlers out on the prairie. Clearly the mere free granting of land was not sufficient. If the virtues of the new life on the western lands were to be obtained more help was needed from the government. It would take another 50 years before this fact would be acted upon. And at that time, it would result from a new set of pressures for a return to the land, one induced by a weakened economy. Thus, it is the Subsistence Homesteads Program of the New Deal which we now turn our attention.

SUBSISTENCE HOMESTEADS

As the world wide depression dragged on into the years 1932 and 1933, the centers of urban concentration, which had drawn millions of farmers into their orbit during the 1920s, had begun rapidly to lose much of their attraction.

The dismal economic situation caused many individuals to turn their eyes back to the land; rekindled were the notions of security and the old homestead. While rural America in the depression era was impacted as much as the urban centers, the vision of a rural haven persisted. In the cities the unemployed still spoke of their dreams on the land. A back-to-the-land sentiment billowed, with subsistence farming and subsistence homesteads the general operational notion. A host of individuals of different persuasions and philosophies all evolved schemes for moving the unemployed and discontented back to the land. While many widely divergent viewpoints were expressed, somehow out of the confusion which resulted came the first New Deal communities. As historian Paul Conkin has noted:

> A few men took a term, "subsistence homesteads," converted it into a physical reality and in so doing led the national government into the role of community building. The reality could please only a few of those who had acclaimed a term, or an abstract concept, but nevertheless it was their advocacy of the term that made the reality possible.[64]

While the actual implementation of the ultimate homestead programs retained little of the directions indicated by the numerous back-to-the-land movements, it should be remembered that without the overall impetus of the back-to-the-land sentiments, there probably would not have been any subsistence homesteads legislation. So while little of the ultimate operational reality of the homesteading endeavors was congruent with the formulations of back-to-the-land movement, the latter was a significant factor in the federal government's entry into the field of community building. The ultimate programs thus flowed in the wake of a broad trend.

Several subsistence homestead bills were proposed as separate entities, but the final legislation was a small section of a larger act, the National Industrial Recovery Act, passed in May 1933. Established as Section 208 of Title 2 of this act, the legislation read:

> To provide for aiding in the redistribution of the overbalance of population in industrial centers $25,000,000 is hereby made available to the President, to be used by him through such agencies as he may establish and under such regulations as he may make, for making loans for and otherwise aiding in the purchase of *subsistence homesteads*. The monies collected as repayment of said loans shall constitute a revolving fund to be administered as directed by the President for the purposes of this section.[65] (Emphasis added)

As can be seen, the language of the act is very general and a number of ways of dispersing funds could probably be made, from planned communities to loans to individual homesteads. The Subsistence Homesteads Program was to be worked out by the implementing agency without any clear mandate from the Congress as to its preferred direction. Emergency legislation of this type was not unusual during the Depression, and the planning of the program was left in the hands of the Executive. Subsequently, President Roosevelt placed the responsibility of carrying out the provisions of Section 208 with Harold L. Ickes, Secretary of the Interior. With little guidance given by Section 208 as to how to disperse the $25,000,000 allotted for subsistence homesteads, Ickes created a separate program to handle them.

Thus, a Division of Subsistence Homesteads was eventually organized in the Department of Interior, headed by M. L. Wilson, who came from the Department of Agriculture. Three main programmatic thrusts were decided upon. First, there would be communities of part-time farmers situated near industrial employment opportunities. A second effort would concentrate on the resettlement of sub-marginal farmers into all-rural colonies. In the third and most controversial proposal, several colonies would be established with newly decentralized industry. A Federal Subsistence Homesteads Corporation was formed to make loans, not grants, with repayment over a 30-year period at 4 percent interest, to local corporations.[66] Under this institutional arrangement, 23 industrial type subsistence homesteads were eventually completed. This type of colony, located within commuting distance of some type of economic employment center while at the same time providing the opportunity to earn a partial subsistence from the land, were generally much more successful than either the purely rural colony or the decentralized industry type.[67] However, out of the latter came perhaps the most interesting subsistence homestead, Jersey Homesteads near Hightstown, N.J., an endeavor we will subsequently examine in much more depth.

In any case, all of the homestead attempts were related to the following general scheme: The colony was to contain between 25 and 100 families; the housing units were to be moderately priced but had to conform to preset standards of sanitation, convenience, structural characteristics, and utility provisions. Each of these units was to be placed on a lot varying in size between one and five acres, large enough to permit subsistence agricultural activities. The homesteaders were to be drawn from low-income groups and their selection was to be based on such criteria as personal character, potential employability, agricultural knowledge, and similar factors.[68] The selection was essentially made at the local level, and the homesteaders were to eventually own their own homesteads.

The first major policy and administrative change in the Subsistence Homesteads Program focused upon the question of local versus federal control. The outcome of a series of disagreements led Ickes to abolish all effective control by local corporations and as a result the Subsistence Homesteads Program was completely federalized.[69] Under the new organizational scheme construction work continued on the originally selected projects. Eventually Roosevelt created a new Resettlement Administration, which would consolidate several extant agencies. This move was occasioned by the nullification of the

National Industrial Recovery Act by the United States Supreme Court. It was into this newly created Resettlement Administration that the Division of Subsistence Homesteads was transferred, a shift which alienated homestead administrators and sponsors, and the homesteaders themselves. Moreover, during the year previous to this shift, Ickes had replaced Wilson with Charles E. Pynchon as head of the Division of Subsistence Homesteads, a man less identified with the agrarian homesteading concept.

One important consequence of the federalization was that now homesteaders were selected by a board in Washington based upon the recommendations from the local communities. The criteria employed resembled those discussed above, but with added emphasis on families with children or families young enough to have children, and those with incomes not exceeding $1,200 a year. However, the income ceiling was often exceeded in implementation of the projects. In fact, at one project, over half the homesteaders had incomes in excess of $1,200.[70] Since it was in the government's and the local sponsor's interest to ensure the project's success and viability, selections tended to favor homesteaders who could financially meet the desired payments and who were of such character as to ensure a strong contribution to the ultimate success of the community. The program's evolved focus then, was not the direct aiding of the poor, but the creation of viable communities, regardless perhaps of those most in need of financial assistance.

The community aspects of the program were always heavily emphasized along with its educative aspects. There was a conscious attempt to create something more than a group of individualized homesteads through the provision of a range of community services. The community development section contained specialists in education, co-operatives, insurance, home management, gardening, agriculture, and industry.[71]

The Resettlement Administration, which subsumed the Division of Subsistence Homesteads in May 1935, was headed by Rexford G. Tugwell, Undersecretary of Agriculture. The initial year and a half of this new organization represented the apex of the New Deal's community building program. Public opposition to Tugwell and growing controversy surrounding planned communities resulted in the stabilization of the entire program by 1937, after which a long period ensued in which the communities already planned were completed and then ultimately disbanded. However, the Resettlement Administration did initiate further new towns programs to rehouse low-income families living in city slums. Tugwell established a Surburban Resettlement Division which created the now famous Greenbelt Towns, a homesteading precursor which we will look at in more depth after a detailed examination of Jersey Homesteads, later known as Roosevelt.

In a fashion similar to that of its predecessors, the Resettlement Administration was continually plagued with legal and congressional obstacles.[72] One significant limitation was the Resettlement Administration's inability to pay local taxes or to make payments in lieu of taxes. But an

amendment to permit the latter enabled certain legal opposition to be eliminated. Since a prerequisite for success of current homesteading efforts appears to rest on property tax abatements, one should be aware of potential resentment of this aspect of the program as its use becomes more widespread.

In any case, the resignation of Tugwell at the end of 1936 led to an Executive Order which transferred the Resettlement Administration to the Department of Agriculture. The next year the Secretary of Agriculture was limited in regard to this program, being only able to perform such functions necessary for the completion and administration of the Resettlement program. This marked the end of experimentation in community building by the federal government in the first half of the 20th century.

ROOSEVELT: A SUBSISTENCE HOMESTEAD

In order to gain a better perspective on present homesteading efforts, it is extremely valuable to examine in some detail the difficulties and controversies surrounding an actual subsistence homestead project as well as some of the reasons for the latter's success. Roosevelt, N.J. is a case in point. This is a project which encountered severe difficulties and controversies, yet today is a viable community that stands almost as a tranquil residential oasis in what are now the burgeoning suburbs of central New Jersey. At present it is difficult not to conclude that the remnants of this early homesteading effort are a major contribution to the life and heritage of the flat plains of western Monmouth County, New Jersey. We will examine the turmoil which surrounded this endeavor from its inception, with the hope of establishing a frame of reference with which to evaluate current homesteading attempts.

One of the critical elements in Roosevelt's success has turned out to be spatial location, which was in line with the major shifts in population and jobs occurring in the last 40 years. The value of its location in terms of access to employment and propinquity to population concentrations has tended to improve with time as nearby metropolitan centers have expanded. Particularly in the 1960s and early 1970s a number of industries decentralized along the New Jersey Turnpike and along Interstate 287, the latter constituting the metropolitan circumferential beltway of the New York region; these shifts have served to increase the viability of any residential complex located in its vicinity. Additionally, an important lasting element of the settlement originally known as Jersey Homesteads is the viable community structure that it fostered and maintained to this present day. Obviously, the size of the project, approximately 200 families, was such to facilitate a sense of community and to permit the dynamics of community to be self-generating. These two factors, location within the metropolitan region and the cohesive community which eventually evolved, have permitted Roosevelt to flourish for four decades.

Perspective and Origins

Now famous for its impressive restored mural and memorial sculpture of Roosevelt by Ben Shahn and its artist colony atmosphere, this homesteading effort renamed in honor of Roosevelt after his death reflects the continuity of historical resettlement programs and reveals the unique difficulties and stumbling blocks that can befall any such attempt.

The present village, now feeling the encroachment of the burgeoning suburban development of central New Jersey, began as a vision of a cooperative community.[73] Its roots are embedded in the long-term endeavors of Jewish leaders to develop a strong Jewish agricultural community and of past attempts by Jewish immigrants to move onto the land; it principally represents the culmination of the long history of Jewish agricultural and industrial colonization in America which originated in the late 19th century.[74] Various rural colonies were established during this period, with the New Jersey efforts representing the most successful attempts. To aid these colonies, a Jewish Agricultural and Industrial Aid Society was formed for the purposes of the "removal of those working in crowded metropolitan sections to agricultural and industrial districts, the granting of loans to artisans seeking suburban homes, the decentralization of industry, and the encouragement of co-operatives."[75] The back-to-the-land idea fired the imagination of many idle New York City garment workers during the Depression, and the flowering of Jersey Homesteads was the result of the seeds of these ideas. The creation of the federal Subsistence Homesteads Program in 1933 allowed their planting and fertilizing. The initial plan, proposed by Benjamin Brown, an enthusiastic organizer of rural co-operatives, was for

> a colony of 200 skilled Jewish needleworkers, who were to become self-sustaining through subsistence farming combined with seasonal employment in a co-operative garment factory. Small individual homestead plots were to be supplemented by a community truck garden, dairy, and poultry plant, all operated co-operatively. Completing the circle of co-operative activities was to be a community store to sell the community-produced products. The cost of such a colony, including the factory, was estimated at $600,000, with $100,000 to be provided by the 200 homesteaders, who were to contribute $500 each.[76]

With co-operative stores, farm, and factory, Jersey Homesteads was planned as the first triple co-operative in the new world.[77] Everything was co-operative except homeownership and garden production. Moving from the urban blight of New York City, immigrant Jewish garment workers from Russia and Poland were to work part-time both on co-operative farms and in a co-operative garment factory. This utopian dream was to take place on approximately 1,200 acres in the flat wilderness of central New Jersey's Monmouth County. Bussed from the teeming Manhattan slums to see the land

and the foundations, the pioneer residents experienced the hardships and discrimination seemingly endemic to all resettlement movements.

The Manifold Difficulties

Goldie Rosenzweig is getting old. She's had to stop working at her trade in a nearby garment factory. Now she's on social security and rents a room to our only policeman. When she walks to her son's house to visit her grandchildren, you can tell that her feet are giving out. . . . "We came in 1936, . . . The houses weren't finished. The roads weren't finished. Nothing. I used to cry every minute . . . . We didn't make a living. We suffered here . . . . No libraries here, no movies here, no friends here, no cars here. Nothing here . . . . We walked so many times the four miles to Hightstown. We had to go shop . . . . Some stores wouldn't let you in. In one of them I went to buy something that year. So the man said: 'From where you come?' I said from Jersey Homesteads. He said: 'I'm not going to sell you . . . Because its communist there I won't sell you.' "

Prejudice is two-sided. But only the big formless majority has the power to practice discrimination. In the thirties the countryside hereabouts and especially the centers, such as Hightstown, four miles away, were part of the South. The Klan was a fact of life like the bank on Main Street and the potatoes in the fields . . . . "It was Mississippi exactly . . . the Homesteads, that was the place for the Jews."[78]

Suspicions over the New Deal, the "communist" image of the co-operative idea, the Russian heritage and the Jewish religion of the residents, all in the context of a depression era mentality, provided a hostile social milieu for the settlers. Moreover, technical and physical shortcomings dealing with actual construction and implementation of the homesteading effort abounded.

As was to be expected, the screw-ups were innumerable. It was decided, for instance, that the houses were going to be the first prefabricated concrete dwellings, with whole walls precast in a slab plant. The scheme was ambitious: the entire side of a house was going to move through a series of buildings, with all the equipment in place, the window frames, the pipes and the electric lines, and with the concrete curing as it moved. There was only one trouble with the idea: it didn't work. The walls wouldn't stand up, they couldn't take the strain. Besides, before the procedure could be improved, an inventor turned up with a patent, a little detail nobody had taken the trouble to check. So there was nothing to do with the big slab plant except use it to produce cement blocks . . .

Unfortunately they cost four times as much as the same blocks
bought in the open market. And so, after a while, the slab plant was
dismantled. It was only a temporary structure anyway.[79]

While the concrete slabs were eventually to be used for the roofs, the
unfavorable publicity led to the exclusion of all visitors from the construction
area and the establishment of security posts at the project entrances.[80] The
attempt at construction innovations, coupled with the inefficiency of relief
labor, led to fairly severe cost overruns, which in turn led to charges of
extravagance and other controversies.

As construction was underway, further obstacles emerged. The first
involved problems of coordination and timing of the various project sectors. The
garment factory depended upon the homesteaders being settled and forming a
co-operative. Until this could be done, it was felt that a private manufacturer
could operate the endeavor. However, the International Ladies' Garment
Workers Union opposed the subsidized removal of jobs and a firm from the
struggling New York City scene. Eventually the Resettlement Administration
obtained approval for the factory, provided it was a co-operative venture from
the start.

> The factory building was 100 feet by 220 feet, mostly all windows,
> air-conditioned, and declared to be the most modern in the East.
> Present at the dedication were union officials, sales organization
> executives, fashion models, and an orchestra. Large orders for coats
> were announced. Benjamin Brown, who presided at the dedication,
> defended Jersey Homesteads against charges of communism,
> declaring instead that it was "common sense-ism" and in line with
> the Constitution and the American way. The trade name of the
> factory product was to be "Tripod," standing for the triple
> co-operative foundation of the colony. Brown said: "On this tripod
> we will not only bring back craftmanship and pride of achievement,
> together with security, but we will bring back prosperity based on
> abundance and not on curtailment."[81]

The factory failed in its first year of operation. Many reasons have been
put forth for its lack of success—inexperienced management, inefficient
production, high labor costs, ill-defined markets, and production surpluses.[82]
However, most relevant to current homesteading efforts were the attitudes of
the Jersey Homesteaders. Their motivations, described below, are not unique but
endemic to programmatic endeavors:

> Even though many of the homesteaders felt that the failure was the
> fault of the government, they would have been more realistic if they
> had placed the blame on themselves and their own attitudes.
> Habituated to highly competitive endeavors, they were frankly

seeking more wages and a better job for themselves rather than a new way of life. Co-operation meant benefits to the exclusion of sacrifice.[83]

The factory was eventually sold and rented to a private women's hatmaking operation. And while the co-op store was the strongest, but by no means highly successful, element of the tripod, the co-operative agriculture attempts never employed more than 13 people and rarely did they turn a profit.

Ultimately, the finished residential portion of Jersey Homesteads contained 200 homes containing five to seven rooms. Designed by a German architect trained in the Bauhaus tradition, they reflected the spare functionalism—concrete boxes with floor to ceiling windows and flat roofs—and rectilinear purity of LeCorbusier.[84] Such structures were totally at variance with the dreams and expectations of the homesteaders. With visions shaped by American folk mythology—rural landscapes, cozy cottages, gingerbread trim, gabled roofs, clapboard walks, and operable shutters—the settlers experienced what amounted to cultural shock.[85]

It was really a lot to ask of them: that they should fit themselves into the bare and undecorated functionalism that was modern at the time. It was, in fact, the imposition of one culture on another, a minor rape of minds, to demand of them that they make themselves over in an image that was in no way their own. Because, as immigrants—early refugees, if you like—they had at least one wrench behind them: from Poland or Russia to Brooklyn or the Bronx, from the stetl to the great, the incomprehensible, the American city. They had made this step, at a cost varying with individuals. And each in his own way had learned to visualize the Promised Land (which this country was to them) in a composite of the ideal derived from the illustrations in the Saturday Evening Post.[86]

But the people adapted to the concrete boxes, perhaps admitting they were not so bad after all, and some 40 years later these same block residences, softened by landscaping and foliage, look very attractive indeed. In this case, then, the ultimate success or viability of the homesteading effort apparently did not hinge on a decorative style consistent with the occupants initial values.

The earliest homesteaders were selected with the approval of the Division of Subsistence Homesteads. Specific requirements hinged on union membership, required skill levels to insure economic success, an understanding of the co-operative approach, a stable family situation which reflected good home management, and perhaps most significant, the possession of $500, since the screened applicants had to contribute this amount of money to the project.[87] To leave their jobs and to raise this amount of money entailed great sacrifices for many of the original colonists.

What was originally envisioned as a housing shortfall, eventually turned into a surplus. The Resettlement Administration attempted to restrict entry so that new arrivals and economic opportunities would dovetail. However, after the initial surge of applicants, few families could be found who would be willing to pay $500 for a venture whose economic base was a demonstrated failure. So at no time did the homesteads ever contain more than 120 member Jewish households.[88]

Eventually, the Resettlement Administration leased the balance of the vacant units to non-participating families. This perhaps signified the beginning of the end of the Jersey Homesteads experiment. Subsequently, the farm, poultry plant, and related economic activities were auctioned off. Nevertheless, a community had been created, one whose tradition is evident in the current residents and atmosphere of Roosevelt.

Predominant Criticism

The element most subject to criticism, and the one which can be fully documented, concerns the cost figures which were maintained by the Resettlement Administration. Some critics claim that the price of the entire Jersey Homesteads project came to more than $4 million.[89] This figure is at slight variance with that accounted for by the Farm Security Administration, whose cost estimate was in the vicinity of $3.4 million. An average cost per unit then would exceed $16,500 if the total amount were divided among the 206 homesteads, which includes farm housing units.[90] Alternatively, if the 120 participating Jewish households in the project were used as the true estimate of the people who shared in the community facilities, then the total unit cost would be in excess of $20,000.[91] Of course, the attempts at innovative construction, the use of inefficient relief labor, and the money poured into the operation of the co-operative factories, all served to escalate the cost figures to $20,000 or $16,000 per unit level. However, even discounting these various elements, there appears to be no question that the total cost of Jersey Homesteads exceeded its actual value by at least a factor of three.[92]

Summary

The lessons of Roosevelt are manifold. The project encountered many severe difficulties, yet it evolved into a stable and attractive community. The failure of the co-operative economic activities, the hostility exhibited by the surrounding residents to the new homesteaders, the bleakness of the modernistic houses, the impracticality of innovative construction techniques, the inefficiency of relief labor which ultimately drove up costs beyond all reasonable bounds, the self-conscious attitudes of many new residents, and the scarcity of households willing to make the $500 down payment—these were all notable defects in the development of Roosevelt as a social experiment. However, Roosevelt did develop as a community, one which is at least in part maintained to the present day. Why this success? The initial social cohesion of the settlement kept it from coming unglued during the early difficult years. Yet, spatial setting has been the most critical factor in the long-term success of the project. Situated in line with the main locational dynamics operating within the New York metropolitan region, the settlers found that other job opportunities were readily available after those within the project had disappeared. This factor, coupled with the proximity of various educational institutions, insured the continued residential attractiveness of the project. Academics from nearby Rutgers and Princeton, artisans drawn to the area's bucolic setting, and workers employed in the growing industrial bands along the New Jersey Turnpike and Interstate 287 are the mainstays of modern Roosevelt.

GREENBELT TOWNS

As director of the newly formed Resettlement Administration, Rexford Tugwell implemented some of his ideas for satellite cities and new towns. Aware of the currents of planning thought both in America and abroad, he sought "to go just outside centers of population, pick up cheap land, build a whole community and entice people into it. Then go back to the cities and tear down whole slums and make parks of them."[9-3] This grandiose idea did not yield any new park areas to replace massive slum sections in any of America's cities nor did it ever redirect the spatial structure of America's urban areas, but the Greenbelt Towns which eventually resulted probably were indicative of the way planners envisioned millions of this nation's citizens would prefer to live.[9-4]

The Greenbelt Towns were founded upon a base of solid economic and demographic analyses. To select sites for resettlement areas, planners studied the 100 largest cities in the United States, evaluating such items as standards of local government, civic attitudes, labor policies, and growth patterns, attempting to isolate those areas which experienced steady growth and were not subject to cyclical booms and busts.[9-5] The Greenbelt Town idea was also predicated on studies of contemporary population movements, which showed strong growth in the peripheral and outlying sectors of metropolitan areas. Greenbelt Town planners recognized the thrust of suburbanization and sought to take advantage of it. They argued that the towns should be built in line with this major social force in order to achieve a viable working and living environment. This attitude was expressed in the arguments used to defend and publicize the Greenbelt Towns: a suburban lifestyle, the advantages of country and city living, an escape from the city with its congestion and undesirable environment, a demonstration of the practicability of the garden city idea and a new type of community planning. Many of these elements had become established dogma to American citizenry in the post-World War II era.

Eight metropolitan areas were initially selected as sites for Greenbelt Towns, but limitations of funding eventually reduced the number to four—Greenhills, a town near Cincinnati; Greendale, which was near Milwaukee; Greenbelt, located in the capital district in Maryland; and Greenbrook, located at a site in the outer reaches of the New York metropolitan area in Franklin

Township, New Jersey. However, legal opposition to the latter placed the entire Greenbelt and Suburban Resettlement Programs in jeopardy by challenging its constitutionality. Although the circuit court of the District of Columbia upheld the challenge, the United States Attorney General ruled that this decision applied only to the New Jersey Greenbrook project. This ruling essentially saved the three other Greenbelt projects, and the Resettlement Administration was satisfied to sacrifice one to ensure the successful completion of the other three.

The Greenbelt Towns evolved into small, well planned, garden suburbs, lacking any self-contained industrial base. With an average size of 700 families when completed, their most distinctive feature was a green belt protecting the residential area from external encroachments while providing spaces for agricultural activities. What relevant lessons can be drawn from this program? First of all, the projects when evaluated today certainly represent successful residential communities. As with the case of Roosevelt, New Jersey, they presently appear as oases of good design in a desert of haphazard suburban development. Certainly the care and sensitivity which went into the design of these projects has been a major contributing element to their success. However,their long-term success may have been ensured by locations in congruence with the dynamics of modern population redistribution. They were located in the path of suburban development, and as in the case of Roosevelt, their residential utility over time certainly increased.

This housing effort represented a community-wide approach, with the size of each garden colony having a sufficient critical mass to allow a sense of community to develop. Certainly the residents of these towns did not feel like isolated pioneers in a hostile environment. These were factors which were important to the overall success.

But deficiencies were certainly not absent from these projects. As in the case of subsistence homesteads, the use of relief labor construction increased construction costs and raised charges of waste and extravagance. Perhaps more important, their high costs—some estimates range up to $15-16,000 per unit—restricted their clientele to those with at least a middle class background and financial level.

HOMESTEADING TODAY:
RELATION TO HISTORICAL PRECEDENTS

While the threads of these earlier homestead efforts are difficult to weave into a consistent pattern, they nevertheless provide us with a backdrop against which to view current programmatic formats. One continuous thread has been the strong emphasis on self-determination and self-help, along with the advocacy of land for the landless. Additionally, a cooperative atmosphere permeated the Depression Era adaptations. Moreover, all the precedents discussed here reflected the theme of population redistribution under the auspices of the federal government; this redistribution was targeted to areas unable to attract a significant number of persons on their own, either because of remote location or other disincentive pressures. Federal programs were designed to boost the incentive—by offering land or housing free, or at relatively low cost, or within the context of attractive community services.

But, as we have emphasized earlier, many of the early attempts, ranging through the subsistence homesteads in the 1930s, were in areas whose growth potential and future habitability were almost insured by the major trends of their respective time periods; even if the territories of colonization were not able to attract ownership under regular market conditions, they represented images consistent with the ultimate desire of much of America at that time. Current urban homesteading, also an attempt to overcome disincentive pressures to a somewhat hostile and perhaps non-marketable location, may be at variance with the lifestyle preferences of 1970s America. The overwhelming trends of suburbanization and urban decay are forces which urban homesteading must confront head on.[96] So, while modern homesteading programs do represent an attempt by government to redistribute population, the redistribution appears to be against the current direction of market forces. However, given a state of recession/depression, and renewed increases in energy costs, it is not inconceivable that market demand could increase again in this nation's urban areas. This would be analogous to the back-to-the-land movement which emerged strongly during the Hoover-Roosevelt era. Add in such factors as the myriad growth controls[97] in prized suburban territories and a growing trend toward educational funding reform, which would enhance somewhat the troubled fiscal conditions of most urban areas, and a mild back-to-the-city sentiment becomes at least a potential scenario, however difficult its achievement.

Historical homestead efforts were invariably tied to a subsistence effort; the homestead itself offered at least a partial economic base rooted in agriculture. Colonists of limited means would therefore not only be provided with land and homeownership, they would be offered means of self-support. The Homesteading Act of 1862 provided for plots of 160 acres of land, certainly a start at minimum economic self-sufficiency. This theme also runs through the Subsistence Homesteads of the 1930s which were located either in purely rural areas with agricultural base, or were located near employment centers, or were part and parcel of a community with decentralized industry. In the latter situations, the agricultural sector took second place and was represented by a subsistence garden. In sharp contrast, present homestead programs are purely residential in nature, and are somewhat out of line with the dominant employment location trend.[98] The long-term residential utility of the current homestead is certainly much more questionable than the projects of the 1930s.

Homesteading historically has emphasized both the individualistic pioneering aspect of settlement, as well as thrusts toward a united community effort. In settling large portions of the West, the former predominated, although many homesteaders were drawn to frontier areas by the promise of financial gain through speculation in towns which were to emerge concurrently with the arrival of new settlers.[99] Intimately tied to real estate promotional schemes, the new towns represented a sentiment for community linkages as well as the opportunity to own land and be economically self-sufficient.

The subsistence homesteads attempted much more extensive community development, arising from the co-operative nature of many of the endeavors. This conscious attempt at non-individualized efforts may have been a significant factor in the success or failure of many of these communities. The myriad of community services offered to inhabitants, however, certainly increased their chances of survival. In contrast, urban homesteading efforts represent a potpourri of approaches, ranging from highly individualistic thrusts to much more coordinated formats. The latter try to generate that critical mass which may be an important ingredient in the development of valid urban communities and the long-term value of the homesteaded properties.

Much of the earlier homestead legislation did not particularly benefit the nation's citizenry in most dire economic straits—vast western homesteads were acquired by business interests and the Depression projects were aimed essentially at the middle class. Reasoning from historical analogy, we should be surprised if current programs really did benefit the urban poor. The latest eligibility criteria, which will be reviewed later in this study, appear analogous to those set up for the subsistence homesteads and the Greenbelt Towns. Such criteria are intended to ensure that highly motivated households are drawn into the program, families which are economically self-sustaining and extremely stable. However, if the goal of homesteading is to attract new population to the central cities and to eventually return abandoned properties to the tax rolls, rather than to directly improve the lot of the poor, such criteria may be unavoidable.

Current resettlement efforts also reflect wide variances in the degree of community services provided to the homesteaders. Due to the complicated nature of many of the present programs—and modern society—such supplemental services may be essential to the homesteading programs' chances of long-term success. The present movements seem to encourage the household to follow the individualistic philosophy of the western homesteads in renovating their urban homestead, while at the same time requiring them to comply with very high building code and sanitation standards that are integral to modern day urban society. Much of the construction and rehabilitation work is left up to the household head either as a self help effort or through the mandated responsibility to act as a general contractor. This involves not a small degree of technical sophistication on the part of the homesteader. Moreover, certain tasks can only be undertaken by licensed craftsmen. This makes it imperative that a number of technical services be available to households engaging in such a process, such as assistance in finding certified contractors, aid in costing out the necessary rehabilitation work and projecting this amount into monthly carrying costs, inspections to see that contracted work is up to code standards, and if the work is undertaken by the individual homesteader, provision of various tools and supplies for the more difficult and complex tasks. In any case, the individualistic approach to the processes of settlement and creation of a suitable living environment is difficult in the complexity of present day urban society and demands a great deal of effort from and assistance for the homesteader.

When the government was directly involved in the homestead construction process during the 1930s, cost overruns became a way of life. Significantly it was the government itself which bore the burden of any cash shortfalls, while those passed on to the homesteader were indeed minimal. Today the problem is still with us and the homesteader must bear these costs, despite serious attempts at their valid estimation by the program sponsors. While this may be a fair proposition, it may prove fatal considering the uncertainties of the processes involved.

A Final Word

From the first settlers seeking their headright, the early colonists were fleeing, rather than seeking to reform, a repressive political system in the hope of finding financial rewards barred to them at home. Later, the increasing urban pressures of the rapidly industrializing cities forced many to move westerly with the same goals in mind. Still others took advantage of the speculative gains available to them through the various land programs. This propensity is manifested in the creation of the western homesteading program.

The present flight from the urban center shares similar motivations. It is not a new development but a long-term demographic pattern which has accelerated with the advance of the automobile age and has become more noticeable with the decline in immigration which tended to mask the magnitude of the outmigration from the central cities.[100]

Today's homesteader is asked to make a stand against the historical escapism that has characterized earlier resettlement efforts. The necessary motivation for those willing to homestead is a commitment to, not a fleeing from, our urban centers.

The difficulties discussed earlier are all borne out when the individual case studies are presented. Before we direct our attention to them, however, it is useful to examine some of the underlying forces defining the settings of urban homesteading. In particular, the dynamics of neighborhood decline and housing abandonment, which have given rise to urban homesteading, deserve considerable attention. This is the task of the next chapter.

NOTES

1. George Sternlieb, *Toward an Urban Homestead Act.* Mimeograph (New Brunswick, New Jersey: Center for Urban Policy Research, Rutgers University, 1971).

2. Roy M. Robbins, *Our Landed Heritage: The Public Domain, 1776-1936*, 3rd ed. (Lincoln: University of Nebraska Press, 1962), pp. 206-207.

3. Fred A. Shannon, "The Homestead Act and the Labor Surplus" in *The Public Lands*, ed. by Vernon Carstensen (Madison: University of Wisconsin Press, 1963), p. 306.

4. Sternlieb, *Toward an Urban Homestead Act.*

5. Marshall Harris, *Origin of the Land Tenure System in the United States* (Ames: Iowa State College Press, 1953), p. 194.

6. *Ibid.*, p. 194.

7. *Ibid.*, p. 200.

8. *Ibid.*, pp. 200-201.

9. *Ibid.*, pp. 224-225.

10. *Ibid.*, p. 204.

11. *Ibid.*, p. 204-205.

12. *Ibid.*, p. 195.

13. *Ibid.*, p. 199.

14. *Ibid.*, pp. 207-208.

15. *Ibid.*, p. 207.

16. *Ibid.*, p. 196.

17. Marion Clawson, *The Land System of the United States* (Lincoln, Nebraska: University of Nebraska Press, 1968), pp. 20-21.

18. John M. Brewster, "The Relevance of the Jeffersonian Dream Today" in *Land Use Policy and Problems in the United States*, 2nd ed., ed. by Howard W. Ottoson (Lincoln, Nebraska: University of Nebraska Press, 1964), p. 98.

19. *Ibid.*

20. Thomas Le Duc, "History and Appraisal of U.S. Land Policy to 1962" in Ottoson, *Land Use Policy and Problems*, p. 7.

21. *Ibid.*, p. 8.

22. *Ibid.*, p. 14.

23. Benjamin H. Hibbard, *The History of the Public Land Policies*, 2nd ed. (Madison, Wisconsin: University of Wisconsin Press, 1965), p. 458.

24. Le Duc, "History and Appraisal," pp. 14-15.

25. Hibbard, *Public Land Policies*, p. 169.

26. George M. Stephenson, *The Political History of the Public Lands: From 1840 to 1862*, 2nd ed. (New York: Russell and Russell, 1967), p. 72.

27. Le Duc, "History and Appraisal," p. 17.

28. Hibbard, *Public Land Policies*, p. 128.

29. Le Duc, "History and Appraisal," p. 18.

30. *Ibid.*

31. Hibbard, *Public Land Policies*, p. 126.

32. Stephenson, *Political History of Public Lands*, p. 102.

33. Le Duc, "History and Appraisal," p. 18.

34. *Ibid.*

35. *Ibid.*

36. Hibbard, *Public Land Policies*, p. 348.

37. *Ibid.*, p. 350.

38. *Ibid.*, p. 351.

39. *Ibid.*, pp. 351-352.

40. *Ibid.*, p. 352.

41. Stephenson, *Political History of Public Lands*, p. 111.

42. *Ibid* , p. 144.

43. *Ibid.*, p. 143.

44. Robbins, *Our Landed Heritage*, p. 207.

45. Hibbard, *Public Land Policies*, p. 331.

46. *Ibid.*, p. 328.

47. *Ibid.*, p. 322.

48. *Ibid.*, p. 386.

49. *Ibid.*

50. *Ibid.*, p. 388.

51. *Ibid.*, pp. 360-361.

52. *Ibid.*, p. 388.

53. Robbins, *Our Landed Heritage*, p. 369.

54. Paul W. Gates, "The Homestead Act: Free Land Policy in Operation, 1862-1935" in Ottoson, *Land Use Policy and Problems, p. 30.*

55. *Ibid.*

56. *Ibid.*, p. 34.

57. *Ibid.*, p. 37.

58. *Ibid.*

59. *Ibid.*, p. 42.

60. Robbins, *Our Landed Heritage*, p. 422.

61. *Ibid.*, p. 423.

62. Sophie Douglas Pfeiffer, "Go Urban Young Man", *Historic Preservation* (July-September 1974), p. 17.

63. See generally, Robbins, *Our Landed Heritage* and Paul W. Gates, "The Homestead Act."

64. Paul K. Conkin, *Tomorrow a New World: The New Deal Community Program* (Ithaca, New York: Cornell University Press, 1959), p. 12.

65. United States, *Statutes at Large*, XLVII, pt. 1, pp. 205-206, and Conkin, *Tomorrow a New World*, p. 88.

66. Conkin, *Tomorrow a New World*, p. 106.

67. *Ibid.*, pp. 104-108.

68. *Ibid.*, p. 106.

69. *Ibid.*, p. 120. The Division of Subsistence Homesteads from its inception was continually plagued by legal and administrative entaglements. The many permutations and combinations of difficulties which evolved present a complex narrative beyond that required for this work. Many of the complexities

are reported in Paul K. Conkin, *Tomorrow a New World*.

70. *Ibid.*, p. 125.

71. *Ibid.*, p. 128.

72. *Ibid.*, 173.

73. Edwin Rosskam, *Roosevelt, New Jersey: Big Dreams in a Small Town and What Time Did to Them* (New York: Grossman Publishers, 1972).

74. Conkin, *Tomorrow a New World*, p. 256.

75. *Ibid.*, p. 259.

76. *Ibid.*, p. 262.

77. *Ibid.*, p. 267.

78. Rosskam, *Roosevelt, New Jersey*, pp. 1-6.

79. *Ibid.*, p. 22.

80. Conkin, *Tommorrow a New World*, p. 265.

81. *Ibid.*, p. 268.

82. *Ibid.*, p. 271.

83. *Ibid.*

84. Rosskam, *Roosevelt, New Jersey* p. 41.

85. *Ibid.*, p. 42.

86. *Ibid.*

87. *Ibid.*, p. 264.

88. *Ibid.*, pp. 269-270.

89. *Ibid.*, p. 275.

90. Select Committee of the House Committee on Agriculture, Hearings on the Farm Security Administration, 78th Congress, 1st Session, 1943-1944, p. 1118, and Conkin, *Tomorrow a New World* p. 275.

91. Conkin, *Tomorrow a New World*.

92. *Ibid.*

93. Mel Scott, *American City Planning Since 1890* (Berkeley and Los Angeles, California: University of California Press, 1969), p. 337.

94. *Ibid.*

95. Conkin, *Tomorrow a New World*, p. 307, and Scott, *American City Planning.*, p. 337.

96. James W. Hughes, *Suburbanization Dynamics and the Future of the City* (New Brunswick; New Jersey: Center for Urban Policy Research, Rutgers University, 1974).

97. James W. Hughes, *New Dimensions in Urban Planning: Growth Controls* (New Brunswick, New Jersey: Center for Urban Policy Research, Rutgers University, 1974).

98. *Ibid.*

99. An amusing historical reconstruction of speculative towns and homesteading can be found in James Michner, *Centennial* (New York: Random House, 1974).

100. George Sternlieb and James W. Hughes, eds., *Post-Industrial America: Metropolitan Decline and Inter-Regional Job Shifts* (New Brunswick, N.J.: Center for Urban Policy Research, forthcoming).

Chapter 2

Housing Abandonment, Neighborhood Decline And Urban Homesteading

INTRODUCTION

Urban homesteading has been basically conceptualized as one response to the problem of abandoned housing in urban areas. In reality such a response must be calibrated to the magnitude of the abandonment phenomenon and the level of decline or viability in the desired area or neighborhood. For example, an isolated abandoned structure in a relatively healthy neighborhood certainly offers immediate potential for an individual homestead. However, a neighborhood which is in the late stages of decline and is experiencing heavy abandonment does not lend itself to an individualistic approach, but requires a substantial homesteading program with supporting elements.

In other words, ameliorative action must be tailored to the specific area or neighborhood of focus. It is thus necessary to examine quite closely the macrodynamics of residential abandonment and the available neighborhood typologies to guide legislative administrative action. We must also consider the interrelationship between housing abandonment and its effect on neighborhood decline. It is this reference frame which must be the backdrop for any serious program of urban homesteading.

ORGANIZATION

The web of forces enveloping urban change generates such momentum as to overwhelm programs not designed in reference to their formal appraisal. The fear of self-fulfilling prophecy, of dooming a neighborhood by realistically appraising its potential payoff, has often inhibited such analysis. But, it has not retarded de facto abandonment by government as well as by households. Moreover, neighborhood stabilization and preservation efforts, including urban homesteading, may become the major thrust of urban action programs. If an urban homesteading program is to be successful, extremely difficult decisions have to be made on areas of application, since the lack of a realistic appraisal of the basic parameters of urban neighborhoods may severely inhibit success potential, and in fact may reinforce the cycle of decline.

Is there a neighborhood typology to guide legislative and administrative action? This chapter begins with an attempt to define a "stable" neighborhood, one which is considered to provide a good residential environment. The factors establishing this stability are important, since their response to the broader forces of neighborhood change directly influences the decline or viability of local residential communities. The forces which tend to work towards a neighborhood's deterioration are then examined, viewing the neighborhood both as an isolated entity and as part of a broader system within which it has a specific function. And finally, there is a summary of the levels of decline through which a local area passes as it is impacted by these forces.

THE STABLE NEIGHBORHOOD

Our definition of a stable, "good and viable" neighborhood is admittedly impressionistic at the cost of scholarly rigor. But we have chosen to simplify here for analytical purposes, elaborating upon the dynamics as we proceed through the balance of the chapter. We have therefore focused exclusively upon those characteristics of good neighborhoods that are universally applicable, leaving the unique and select elements to be brought in at a later time.

Good neighborhoods do not have to be of high socioeconomic status nor do they have to be new, although, in many cases, they meet one or both of these conditions. But a good neighborhood does imply that residents are not burdened by severe economic problems, that they have a psychological sense of satisfaction, comfort, and control. Generally pleased with the level of community services they receive, the residents tend not to impose excessive burdens on the municipality. They are content with their schools and educational facilities, which provide an effective outlet for the social control and socialization of their children, while barring the introduction of "alien" norms of behavior. The pervasive sense of security in their neighborhoods is often related to the fact that their residents are very much alike.[1]

Furthermore, the residents are prepared to defend their territory, possessing both the economic and social vigor to fight off the inroads of blight and to resist any encroachment affecting their homes or their immediate environment. Fully aware of the increasing value and desirability of their homes, they confidently anticipate recouping their expenses for home improvements.

Although population stability is a defining characteristic of good neighborhoods, it does not preclude a degree of mobility and changing boundaries. Rather, the stability of such neighborhoods derives from a condition of "steady state": even though families are frequently moving in and out of the neighborhood, its social status tends to remain constant. In fact, neighborhood vigor may be in part attributable to this constant exchange of households, which sustains a high level of energy and enthusiasm for home maintenance and improvement. Some of this zeal tends to dissipate over time, particularly with the aging of residents. A flow of families in and out of a neighborhood may therefore be a precondition of long-range stability. It is only when the gap widens between the socioeconomic characteristics of incoming and outmoving households that neighborhood change is initiated; depending upon the respective statures, this change can result in neighborhood improvement or deterioration.

Our definition of a viable neighborhood does not assume socioeconomic homogeneity. Differing population groups—defined either by race, social or family status—can coexist in a good neighborhood but, again, only in a condition of balance or upward shift. Lower status groups cannot expand rapidly in proportion to the remaining residents. If they are the sole replacements for outmoving higher status families, for example, the neighborhood balance is upset and neighborhood confidence and security undermined.

A general component of a viable neighborhood, then, is a steady balance of the overall area as well as a continued equilibrium between member groups. In a viable, mixed neighborhood, this balance is very fragile indeed.

Good neighborhoods tend to be free from invasions of nonresidential land uses, higher density housing types, and new residents of radically different socioeconomic levels. There are many cases of such neighborhoods remaining "good" for many years, be they blue-collar working class or exclusive high status enclaves. Our subsequent analysis of long range viability will attempt to isolate the contributing factors.

THE DYNAMICS OF NEIGHBORHOOD DECLINE

The forces for neighborhood deterioration are separable into those internal and those external to the neighborhood itself. The distinction may not always be clear-cut, however, especially since we must view a neighborhood as part of a broader system within which it has a specific function. But this classification has some merit, at least as a starting point for giving structure to our analysis.

Internal Forces of Decline

To impart a degree of order to our examination of internal forces, we can subdivide them into those of a physical nature and those whose origin is social or psychological. Although these are highly interrelated, the distinction may be useful to keep in mind.

A neighborhood comprising new, well-equipped housing inhabited by young, family-raising households is usually at its peak.[2] Similarly, older stable areas can provide superior residential environments through sustained structural maintenance and constant vigilance against unwanted intrusions. Residents are predominantly concerned with maintaining their homes and preserving the most favorable environment for raising their families. And the structures, themselves, containing up-to-date amenities and design features, compete very favorably in the housing market; under normal conditions, they are marketable for at least their reproduction cost, i.e., the cost of building an identical unit at the present time.

But as structures grow old and depreciate, and as the children of resident families reach adulthood, there is a sharp reduction in the neighborhood's vigor and in its ability to resist physical and social encroachments. Combined with increasing housing maintenance costs resulting from the structure's age, there is the threat of obsolescence as newer, more fashionable residential options become available. As older residents gradually relinquish the constant struggle to preserve the neighborhood intact, a process of owner disinvestment may be set in motion. With physical and social maturation, therefore, the neighborhood becomes more and more susceptible to disease and infection.

Neighborhood decline may be further affected by several factors growing out of neighborhood specialization according to the social status of its residents, their stage in family raising, and their racial/ethnic status.[3] One such factor—obsolescence—affects housing built in a previous era for a special income class (social status) and for a specific family raising period (stage in life cycle). These structures may be totally out of date and unsuitable for the analogous functions today. The great bulk of central city housing, especially in northeastern cities, was constructed in the first part of this century. We are just now beginning to feel the impact of a massive supply of outmoded housing, with more units entering the obsolescence stage than at any previous time.

As a structure's reuse value decreases, its depreciation accelerates, thereby reducing resident confidence in the neighborhood's future and reputation. The waning morale may discourage potential newcomers from moving in, which in turn reduces the relative desirability of the area. Moreover, the confidence of investors and financial institutions, a vital prerequisite to long-term neighborhood stability, may be undermined.

Although all of these internal physical and social processes—obsolescence, aging, depreciation, and declining morale—are significant determinants of neighborhood decline, they do not represent the entire picture. The influence of external forces is at least as critical.

External Forces of Decline

In the process of growth, the city forms specialized residential neighborhoods, whose functions and roles are defined in terms of the total urban system. Since neighborhoods are thus integral parts of a larger functioning whole, they cannot be evaluated in isolation. Changes in the larger context require internal readjustments that force functional changes in neighborhoods. These are caused largely by the invasions of alien populations and land uses and the departure of the original inhabitants.[4]

These invasions directly affect neighborhood specialization. If the population and activities flowing into the neighborhood are markedly different from those presently included, rapid change may be precipitated.

What triggers these invasions? One cause may originate with the neighborhood itself. A once-fashionable area, for example, may age and lose prestige, thereby facilitating the entry of lower status groups who are eager to improve their housing position. This particular process is usually initiated by the upper income population which tends to define the "best" areas of residence in the metropolis,[5] thereby setting the standard for upward mobility. The resultant pull tends to drain less affluent neighborhoods of their more mobile inhabitants, who seek more prestigious addresses.

A push process frequently operates simultaneously. The urban immigration of a new depressed population at the bottom level neighborhoods sets in motion a whole series of successive neighborhood adjustments. Although the pattern is analogous to that resulting from the magnetic pull of the emerging high status, suburban zones, here households are pushed and shoved, rather than drawn, into new residential environments.

One of the major historic forces of urban expansion is the spread of the central business district through continual pulses of growth pushing out from the center. Commerical land uses invade adjacent residential neighborhoods creating undesirable living environments, and causing many households to move to more viable residential settings. Their vacated houses then become available to poorer new migrants.

But the significance of "push" factors has declined over the years, at least in many older metropolitan areas. As economic activities decentralize, growth at the urban center is almost nonexistent. And migration to the city is limited compared to historic magnitudes, with the absence of new immigrant groups to replace blacks and Puerto Ricans.[6] At the same time, the lure of outer suburbia with its promise of a better life, has, if anything, increased significantly. It is no wonder, then, that many areas geared to the central business district are no longer viable and that abandonment of structures is commonplace in the oldest and least serviceable urban neighborhoods.

Differential Effects

When an urban area is subjected to these forces of decline, the resultant changes vary according to neighborhood characteristics; the most important of these, obviously, is socioeconomic level, which tends to fall into three different categories. Each of the three responds differently to the forces for decline.

Formerly high-grade neighborhoods are subject to extraordinarily rapid obsolescence, since there are few takers for the aging and oversized dwellings vacated by the departing elite. Their prohibitive purchase price and maintenance expense rule out their availability to successively lower income groups and their continued use as single-family homes. Their subsequent conversion into boarding houses, offices, clubs, and the like, creates further neighborhood deterioration and further decline in property values.

In contast, houses of intermediate socioeconomic status, designed for use by families of moderate size and income, are readily transferable to successive groups as the structures age. Although there may be some depreciation, perhaps only relative, in their value, the buildings are still suitable for their original purposes. And the steady supply of prospective residents for intermediate rental neighborhoods assures a certain level of value stability. These mid-level areas are prime candidates for policies governing future residential maintenance.

Finally, the deterioration of low-rent neighborhoods leads to great change. Inhabited largely by the poorest, unskilled or unemployed persons, these sectors evidence the highest vacancy rates.

The worst structures are demolished, and, unless subsequent waves of poor immigrants enter the city to create a new demand, many obsolete structures are destined for removal from the market. This is particularly accentuated in our own time by the increased minimum level of operating expenses as a function of health and building codes, municipal taxes, heating costs, and the like. Thus low rent as well as high rent areas have the least stability over time.

General Thresholds and Areas of Viability

The evaluation of neighborhood decline must also be based upon several considerations involving general thresholds. First, one must analyze the potential of the broader metropolitan region: Is the city a vital link in the regional economy or has it lost many of its significant functions? Then, the viability of the central business district must be determined in relation to suburban economic growth. One index of the vigor of the central business district is its commercial density, which depends largely upon the status of commuter railroads and rapid transit. (It is difficult, for example, to conceive of New York or Chicago supporting their central area economic functions without these special transportation facilities.)[7] In areas where economic viability is uncertain, the degree of commercial concentration or dispersion will have an important bearing upon future neighborhood usefulness. Finally, one must consider the level of immigration by racial/ethnic groups and other specialized subpopulations. The interplay of these general thresholds provides an essential framework for evaluating neighborhood growth and change.

THE STAGES OF NEIGHBORHOOD DECLINE

The most ordered conceptions of neighborhood evolution focus upon distinct, identifiable stages in the decline process. Edgar Hoover and Raymond Vernon analyzed sequential patterns of development in specific areas, ultimately delineating five stages of neighborhood evolution.[8] This framework appears to have provided the foundation for futher attempts to classify levels of neighborhood change.[9] The following is a synthesis of these decline paradigms.[10]

Stage 1

Stage 1 neighborhoods are areas which are thriving and relatively free of social, economic, and physical problems. (Their detailed characteristics have already been examined in the section on stable neighborhoods.) These areas are thus free of invasions of nonresidential land uses, higher density housing types, and new residents of radically different socioeconomic characteristics. Many neighborhoods, be they blue collar working class or older, prestige areas, remain at the Stage 1 level for many years.

Stage 2

Stage 2 neighborhoods have aged both physically and socially. As the structures mature and approach functional obsolescence, there are few serious efforts to improve them. The limited maintenance may be a function of the replacement of maturing families, whose children are grown, by newcomers who are unable to commit the resources necessary to combat obsolescence. In cases where the more mature family remains, the family's needs no longer match the size of the structure and it eventually becomes difficult for the occupants to sustain the high maintenance necessary to keep it a Stage 1 residence. Whatever the cause—aging households or less affluent newcomers—the neighborhood's level of energy and vigilance slowly seeps away.

The neighborhood slips into a transition stage in which invasions of more intensive land uses and new populations become commonplace. Most new construction is concentrated in apartments, causing a significant increase in average densities. Since much of this apartment construction replaces older and larger single-family homes located in the inner urban zones, there is a change in the life cycle stage of residents and a declining proportion of owner occupancy. As a less affluent population takes over the single-family units, confidence in the area as a family-raising environment wanes and maintenance outlays decrease. The neighborhood's increased density, exerting greater pressure on the neighborhood's infrastructure, thereby reinforces the downward trend.

Minority group inroads appear at this stage, probably due to the less restrictive practices of new rental units and to the new availability of older, single-family homes. These incursions create a critical unknown. Will the presence of the newcomers make older residents want to flee? Will the neighborhood lose its reputation as a desirable place to live? Will a game of musical chairs ensue?

Stage 3

Stage 3 neighborhoods have realized all the fears hinted at by the changes initiated in Stage 2. Structural defects which began to appear in the previous stage increase, while minor deficiencies become ubiquitous. This downgrading period is typical of areas undergoing slum invasion. Older housing is increasingly adapted to higher density usage as its viability and economic rationale as single-family dwellings decline. Population and density growth are the outgrowth of conversion and crowding of existing structures rather than of new construction.

As overall confidence in the neighborhood slackens, the decline in its social status continues, bringing in poorer households and accelerating racial/ethnic change. And as the neighborhood increasingly becomes predominated by renters rather than owners, there are increasing discontinuities between housing needs and services. The widening gulf between owners/investors and tenants generates landlord disinterest in tenant problems, and the deteriorating relationships between the two result in rising management and operation costs. The latter adds a further spur to the cycle of decay.

Stage 4

Stage 4 neighborhoods, rapidly entering the final stages of decline, experience a thinning out process wherein household size and dwelling unit occupancy levels are sharply reduced. Housing becomes progressively deteriorated and dilapidated and physical decline becomes pervasive. As the minority inroads expand into full-scale social invasions, the neighborhood becomes marketable only to those of the lowest socioeconomic rank even at the risk of uncertain payment. The resultant decline in cash flow encourages owner disinvestment and places further strains upon the landlord/tenant relationship. The average household, existing at subsistence level, has social problems that are often so severe as to threaten the general safety and well-being of the neighborhood community. Pessimism about the neighborhood's future becomes endemic.

Stage 5

Stage 5 neighborhoods, at the bottom rung of the urban hierarchy, have little remaining utility as residential environments. Their residents have the lowest social status, the least economic means, and the weakest political leverage with which to improve the area. The worst of the buildings will be abandoned unless a new economic rationale is introduced, such as a new wave of poor immigrants entering the city. The resultant gaps among the inhabited structures lead to the eventual abandonment of the few remaining sound buildings in this declining environment. Adjacent areas are susceptible to infection from neighborhoods in such straits. Total renewal or total elimination becomes the sole remaining public policy option.

INDICATORS OF DECLINE

Given this hypothetical set of evolutionary stages, how can it be operationalized? What indices are useful to gauge or predict a neighborhood's status? A review of the historical literature on urban change and neighborhood decline reveals, unfortunately, a relative paucity of empirical and theoretical developments on advanced indicators of decay. Perhaps the most significant characteristic of impending deterioration is the presence of minority group members of low socioeconomic status. Neighborhoods of the city showing the highest concentrations of this subpopulation ten years ago most likely would be the most heavily abandoned today in the absence of substantial new immigration.

Also closely related to these parameters are the structure characteristics of owner occupancy and unit value. Areas of low unit value, or rental, and low degrees of owner occupancy would appear to be particularly susceptible to decay over time. In fact, neighborhoods with low unit values, low owner occupancy percentages, and an intermediate level of minority group presence would appear to have the secondary threshold characteristics for decay in the immediate period, and abandonment over the long range.

In contrast, ethnic persistence may provide a toehold for stabilization efforts. In such instances, the demographic characteristics of the neighborhood would remain relatively constant, as would socioeconomic status. However, declining proportions of ethnic residents, changing age parameters, and declining socioeconomic status give evidence of a declining urban neighborhood.

The tabular summary in Exhibit 2-1 presents a more structured review of the parameters which have been isolated in the literature and in the empirical review of indicators of neighborhood decline.

To move from the conceptual level to the operational, a more rigorous methodological base must be formulated. Work conducted under HUD auspices in Newark by the Center for Urban Policy Research is a first cut, providing the key indicators of empirical evidence leading to the development of predictors of decline.[11] Effort along these lines complements the development of a classification scheme which will permit the appropriate choice of housing and community development interventions.

Required Characteristics of an
Advanced Indicator System

For the purposes of broad national overview, it is essential that any system of advanced indicators be structured on universally available data. A particular series, specific to only one community, may be of great value and great interest to that community, but it cannot provide the kind of measurement which supports broader strategies. Our key here, therefore, is the use of census data, employment data. and the like to provide this typology and advanced indicator system. Such a system does not now exist. It is obvious, however, that we are well on our way toward this goal. Proper calibration of the basic algorithms currently available can be undertaken in relatively short order.[12] Our present state-of-the-art, subject to this development, lags behind the facts of life. By the time we have identified the area of incipient blight (given the time lapse in the application of meliorative programs), the ultimate scene may be altered beyond recall.

EXHIBIT 2-1

INDICATORS OF DECLINE OR STABILITY

Variable	*Concept*
1. Socioeconomic Status Income Education Occupation	A neighborhood's change in the specific variable in relation to change in the city as a whole serves to identify the evacuation of an area by the more affluent populations and the in-migration of poorer groups.
2. Ethnic Persistence Ethnic groups	Maintenance of ethnic preserves in the face of socioeconomic/racial change may be a pressure point for stabilization efforts. Declining ethnic concentrations are an early warning of impending decline.
3. Demographics Household age Household size School enrollment	Changing age characteristics indicate invasions of young family-raising groups and evacuation of older foreign-born households. Increasing stress is therefore placed on neighborhood infrastructure.
4. Racial-Ethnic Minorities of low social status Racial groups	This variable reveals the path of diffusion of ghetto concentrations or the vacation of a neighborhood by white subpopulations.
5. Structure Characteristics Owner occupancy Unit value	A high degree of owner occupancy may indicate a potential for a high degree of maintenance; declining occupancy rates may signal impending decline. Unit values can either indicate persistence or change.

HOUSING ABANDONMENT AND
NEIGHBORHOOD DECLINE

It is difficult to interpret residential abandonment and public policy responses to it such as homesteading in isolation from the scheme of neighborhood evolution discussed earlier. In fact, abandonment is both affected by a neighborhood's maturation and decline, and it can be a prime causal mechanism in this evolution. Alternatively, it is both an indicator of broad neighborhood deterioration, and an index of an obsolete housing type that may not be directly associated with a neighborhood's level of decline.

In the following analysis, we will attempt to evaluate the effects and significance of isolated, scattered incidents of abandonment in terms of the neighborhood decline scheme; the secondary effects of abandonment, such as vandalism, fires, and the like; and finally, the contagion effect generated by rampant abandonment.

Isolated Abandonment

Isolated abandonment is often a function of an economically nonviable housing type. We tend to see such abandonments as associated with specific conditions attendant to the buildings concerned rather than generic to the neighborhoods where they are located. An aging structure, subject to inflationary maintenance cost rises, demands economic rents beyond the means of lower income families. What abandonment challenges, then, is the conventional wisdom that there will always be people to live in the inner city and it will be profitable to house them. The costs of housing services—property taxes, fuel, mortgage interest rates, maintenance costs, and the like—may be increasing faster than the tenant's ability to pay. Thus, a problem of insufficient demand is evident. But rising costs of ownership are not simply a function of inflation. Absentee ownership, which may lead to general structure neglect; physical aging, which leads to expensive requirements for electrical, heating, and plumbing replacement and the like; inefficient heating systems in a time of rising energy costs; and problem tenants all lead to rapidly rising costs for the owner. When the rent levels cannot be increased to adequately cover these costs—due to the inability of tenants to bear the increased load—the landlord has little recourse but to abandon the parcel. In many cases, he will stop paying taxes on the structure for a period of time before abandonment. This can be interpreted as the owner "selling" the parcel to the city, that is, pocketing the tax payment as profit, and eventually leaving the building to the city.

Isolated incidences of abandonment are most commonly found in Stage 3 and Stage 2 neighborhoods. These are areas where the level of urban degeneration has not gone so far and where there are significant pockets of deeply rooted citizenry who can serve as an anchor for the maintenance of whole neighborhoods. But abandoned structures certainly would tend to weaken the confidence of such groups. It is in such areas that homesteading appears to have a maximum success potential.

An abandoned building not only becomes a physical eyesore to a neighborhood, but it may become a significant health hazard. Periods of time often elapse between actual owner disengagement and the municipality's recognition and response; the latter may be an ineffectual sealing of the building, consequently the structure is accessible to children with all its attendant dangers. In more dense urban areas, abandoned buildings may provide suitable accomodations for junkies and the like, fostering a deleterious social nuisance. (Casual entry by either children or more socially destructive elements can result in such vandalism as to render the parcel completely inoperative as an effective housing unit unless substantial capital improvements are made.) Events such as these can effectively undermine neighborhood confidence and stability. Certainly residents adjacent to parcels affected by these conditions would not be anxious to devote significant resources into the maintenance and long-term major improvements that are commonplace in viable residential communities.

Thus the beliefs and behavior engendered by isolated abandoned parcels on a neighborhood's citizens may be a catalyst in hastening the evolution of a neighborhood along the decline continuum. Stage 2 and Stage 3 neighborhoods, fragile at best, can very easily be undermined by isolated incidences of abandonment. It is vitally important that their identification by municipal authorities be fast enough so that the abandoned building can be reclaimed while it is still salvageable. Swift policy responses demand legal mechanisms which would enable a municipality to obtain title to such buildings and ultimately dispose of them—either a direct return to the housing supply system or demolition to prevent contagion.

Secondary Effects of Housing Abandonment

It was suggested above that even isolated abandoned buildings can establish themselves as a serious physical nuisance or hazard. One type of hazard, aggravated by those who congregate in abandoned buildings, is fire. Approximately 21 percent of all severe fires in Newark in 1970 and 1971 occurred in vacant structures, putting a severe strain on municipal resources.[13] Not only is the direct cost high to the municipality, but the adjacent buildings which are caught up in the conflagration add to the erosion of any remaining neighborhood integrity and stability.

A second type of public hazard is crime. Detailed analysis in Newark has shown that abandonment occurs in the same geographic areas as high crime.[14] While it is difficult to draw causal relationships in this regard, it can be safely said that abandoned structures provide the opportunities for crime; even if they do not inspire crime they undoubtedly facilitate it.

While the above two effects of abandonment focus on public safety, there exist less hazardous consequences which entail substantial diminution of municipal finances, housing stock, and private resources. The fiscal plight of many urban communities is a well-disseminated fact. Often, a landlord stops paying property taxes when he decides to abandon his building, perhaps even a year or two prior to the actual disengagement from the parcel. Tax delinquency has been used by certain landlords as a means of regaining invested equity and for investment capitalization. But the rest of the community must make up the revenues lost through such a practice. And when the property has in fact been abandoned, it will not generate any tax revenue until the dubious time when it will be returned to productive use. (And may reuses, such as homesteading, have some form of property tax abatement.) Thus abandonment may cause a large loss of revenue to a municipality, in fact lessening the resources to deal with the problem itself.

A second loss represented by abandonment is that of basic housing resources. To the extent that what is being lost is sound housing or housing that, given adequate financial means, could be maintained, then the loss truly represents a substantial waste of needed housing units. Many abandoned units, while out of fashion and obsolete in terms of consumer preference and perhaps location, were at the time of abandonment structurally sound. The abandoned unit which actually deserved to be removed from the housing stock is rare.

A third loss is that experienced by the owners and creditors of abandoned parcels. Financial institutions holding mortgages are direct losers, but the municipality of record may ultimately be the victim of a reduction in the flow of credit by such institutions as they sour upon lending in areas where they experienced losses due to abandonment. This makes public efforts at neighborhood stabilization that much more difficult, and jeopardizes the future of such "redlined" areas. This may be one of the more important dynamic forces engendered by housing abandonment.

The sum total of these secondary forces, as they emanate from isolated incidences of housing abandonment, is a macro-level force which has been labeled alternatively the "domino" effect or the "contagion" effect.

The Contagion Effect

Abandonment can become an infectious disease which may attack sound as well as bad housing. A kind of premature pessimism starts a snowballing process which speeds housing from deterioration to dilapidation to abandonment. Usually this occurs in Stage 3 and Stage 4 neighborhoods, hastening their evolution to the next level of decline.

The effects of contagious abandonment are both quantitative and qualitiative. In the former, the contagion takes the form of a geographic spread within the neighborhood; in the latter, the process causes the rapid decline and ultimate abandonment of relatively sound structures. Thus the problem shifts from one attendant to an individual building to a neighborhood problem. Not only are economically nonviable buildings affected, but habitable, occupied structures become enveloped by the social and physical deterioration, and the conditions of poverty, attendant to residential abandonment. The problems of hostility, crime, vandalism, and other poverty conditions create a very undesirable living environment in the neighborhood. This social environmental degradation drives out the remaining moderate or middle income residents, while it may overpower any individual attempts to rehabilitate or effectively manage parcels in the contagion area. Owners of the remaining sound structures are not only affected directly by a declining social milieu, but they also become victims of a depressed investment psychology. There is no one to whom they can sell their parcel, and they find themselves redlined by banking institutions, home improvers, and the like.

Thus abandonment can become a critical aspect of a socially destructive process that can make an entire neighborhood uninhabitable or nonviable (Stage 5), providing the final symbol to drive away stable residents, owners, and investors. Viable individual parcels thus become swept up in the tide of events. At this level of decline, the treatment of abandoned buildings per se becomes an ineffectual action indeed.

The subsequent effects on the housing supply system are the cessation of shelter functions of a number of potentially viable structures. Because they are in an area of active or potentially contagious abandonment, investors and owners see such buildings as having little future, regardless of current housing demand or vacancy rates. So, even in areas of tight housing markets, the housing supply system can be affected quite adversely by residential abandonment.

MATCHING PROGRAMS AND NEIGHBORHOOD TYPES

The Nonviable Neighborhood: Stage 5 and Late Stage 4

The concept of a nonviable neighborhood is not a novelty. It is essentially the descendent of the experience of the private market embodied for generations in areas which were simply redlined by banks and similar lending institutions. The recognition by our society as a whole of the unfairness which sometimes characterized the determination of these areas, which came forth in the late 1960s, swept away not merely the prejudices of the previous generation, but also some of the basic wisdom in terms of the facts of life of nonviable neighborhoods. It is essential that we recoup the latter while firmly resisting the former elements which have victimized significant elements of our citizenry.

The characteristics of such neighborhoods now are all too evident. Specifically, they are neighborhoods of high gross vacancy rates—though little of the vacancies may truly be usable by normal standards. Typically, it is an area of shrinking population, of high welfare occupancy, possessing all of the negative attributes of urban America—high crime rate, disease, etc. It is the home of those people who have no choice.

In no way should this situation be considered synonymous with an area of specific ethnic occupancy. While this zone of coming abandonment may largely be occupied by minority groups, certainly not all areas which are simply occupied by equivalent ethnic groups partake of this characteristic. It may be a great   tribute   to   our   society   that   these   abandonment   areas,   the bottom-of-the-barrel areas, are losing population. It suggests that the filtering down mechanism, and all of the other machinery of public and private housing, may be delivering alternate facilities for the former occupants of core areas. What is required here is much more in the way of clearance mechanisms. It is absolutely shocking that we have now a number of cities which will, for greater or lesser stretches of time, simply run out of demolition money. Both Chicago and Newark have been in this circumstance within the past year.

Bulldozer clearance is required for areas which are radically thinned out. The prevalence of fires, of abandoned structures serving as a haven for a variety of antisocial activities, makes this an essential to protect both the remaining occupants of the area as well as peripheral sections of the city. For the moment, then, there may be little in the way of ultimate use for the land cleared by such operations. It is very important, however, that, rather than fritter away this land through sales at giveaway prices to speculators who have no intention of building anything, it be preserved as a potential land bank for future redevelopment (which, given current energy and environmental conditions, may come upon us much sooner than we presently realize). HUD, in this particular setting, should develop a series of model codes to permit fast, efficient taking of clear title by local governmental jurisdictions of such troubled parcels. This kind of effective take-out mechanism, particularly if coupled with relocation of individuals who are living in semi-vacant structures and crumbling accommodations, can serve to generate increased market vigor within other units and in peripheral areas which will experience a stronger housing demand as a function of taking out the slack. These are not areas in which complete neglect can be viewed as benign. Their poisonous impact is difficult to exaggerate on peripheral areas. And to attempt homesteading in such areas is to jeopardize the entire concept, since its chance of success here is indeed minimal.

Stage 4 Neighborhoods

It is Stage 4, the area on the edge of abrupt population decline, which perhaps has the least clear-cut set of strategies attached to it. Typically, in terms of location, this is a high risk situation for homesteading and rehabilitation. Similarly, transfer of ownership to new minority group holders may be good for society, but probably not very good for the holders themselves, given the limited potential of this area for revitalization in terms of housing values. The levels of subsidy required to bring it up to standard are very substantial—the payoff is not at all clear. We think it is possible here to allow the natural market mechanisms to do their work. Neglect in this instance is not nearly so onerous as in Stage 5 areas. Certainly, given limited resources, not merely of money but administrative talent, it is Stages 2 and 3 which have a far higher payoff for almost all concerned parties.

Stage 2 and 3 Neighborhoods

It is in these areas that urban homesteading and housing rehabilitation programs—particularly relatively light efforts—can play a very major role. The level of urban degeneration has not gone as far, and there are significant pockets of deeply rooted citizenry who can be identified by specific programs and can serve as an anchor for the maintenance of whole neighborhoods. We have specific reference here to older ethnic groups, the provision of housing for the elderly, and substantial efforts towards homeownership for lower middle class minority groups and others of the same economic strata. Concentrated code enforcement, if applied sensibly, can work here, while in Stage 4 areas of decline, it can only lead to speeding up the abandonment process and risking the contagion of peripheral areas which are still sound. Moreover, this line of attack should also consider community development funds as well as specific housing trusts.

It is essential, however, that interventionary mechanisms on the urban scene be undertaken within an overall context of national growth policies. Where are the jobs going to be? What is the role and function of the central city, both in housing and employment opportunities? What goals does our society really want to endorse? If, for example, we want to secure very substantial financing for whole new towns and planned unit developments and embark on major developments which compete with older facilities, the entire approach towards the central city would have to be altered.

The present population drain on the central city is no longer one merely of middle class whites, but also of their equivalents in minority groups. With the substantial decline of population migration from the South, we are essentially dealing with a closed environment. If we add more sit-down places to our game of musical chairs, more and more facilities are going to be vacant—the number of players simply is not expanding commensurate with the level of accommodation.

Goals of the Central City

If we assume a straight-line projection of the trends which have dominated our society in the years since World War II, it is quite evident that we face a substantial diminishing of central city population and traditional economic activities. Certainly, this extrapolation is subject to a broad host of governmental programs and policies, as well as the environmental factors mentioned above. But if, for the moment, this scenario is maintained, then a basic overall strategy cannot be regenerating neighborhoods, but rather ensuring continued livability.

Regardless of the validity of the scenario, certainly for the next generation our central cities and much of their gray areas will continue to be the residence place of a very substantial number of people. There is far less glamour and certainly far less visibility of success in a maintenance program than in a regenerative one. This does not, however, diminish the importance of the former. Maintaining the basic housing stock, consequently, is an absolute sine qua non, and this is a task for urban homesteading. Coupled with this must be a continuous pruning mechanism. In this last regard, the combination of code enforcement and selective clearance and recompaction of population is required.

Our society has evolved in a fashion which has made the housing accommodations offered Americans the envy of the world. What is required is an orderly approach to make these accomplishments accessible for those who choose to live in the central city, or, for the moment, who cannot live in alternate accommodations. We have no clear-cut goal here. Is our program one of stabilizing neighborhoods, possibly at the cost of blocking the upward mobility to better facilities of those people emerging from the core? Or do we prefer continuously to provide new facilities for the more fortunate in our society and house poor groups through the process of filtering upward?

Certainly, stability-making mechanisms (homesteading, rehabilitation, code enforcement, and the like) and new housing production are rivals here. But they are only rivals if we do not comprehend both housing and neighborhood viability as part of a complete system. It is the pace of transition which is the key function which government must effect. We simply do not have mechanisms which will permit the kinds and pace of neighborhood transitions which have taken place, and still insure the viability of infrastructure and housing amenity which the new entrants are seeking.

URBAN HOMESTEADING: A RESPONSE TO ABANDONMENT

The many urban ills of our society have reached their endpoint in the wholesale abandonment of residential parcels. Urban homesteading has received much publicity in the news media as an attempt to recycle such units back into the housing supply system. Obviously, homesteading is not the only program aimed at combating abandonment. It is perhaps valuable then to look at a theoretical schematic flow of the potential disposition of abandoned units, and see where homesteading fits into this decision flow. This abandonment response process is detailed in Exhibit 2-2.[15]

The act of abandonment of a residential structure by its owner is the first step in a potential flow of abandoned housing. In order to inventory such structures, an operational definition of the phenomenon must be present. If the structure meets the criteria set forth in the definition, then specific public actions can be taken subsequently. A proposed operational definition of abandonment is presented in Appendix A.

Between the time of abandonment and the divestiture of the structure through tax sale procedures, extreme physical devastation can take place, rendering the parcel a useless shell. Under normal circumstances periods averaging two years in length must pass before a tax sale can be initiated. However, other approaches are available, the basic framework of which seems to be either an accelerated fast taking procedure, generally following the legal requirements of the long method with the essential difference being only a lessening of the waiting period before tax sale may be instituted or, new

EXHIBIT 2-2
ABANDONMENT RESPONSE PROCESS:
POTENTIAL DISPOSITION FLOW
OF ABANDONED HOUSING

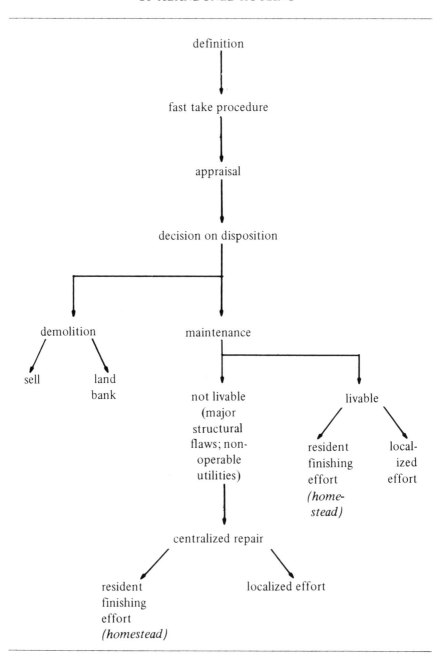

procedures which avoid the lengthy tax sale requirements.

Once title is taken to an abandoned building, it is necessary to have realistic estimates of the costs for returning the parcel to an operational living unit. What this means in reality is estimates of the costs of meeting code enforcement standards for each acquired parcel. This appraisal must be a preliminary action in any homestead program.

After the building is appraised, a decision must be made on its ultimate disposition. An important input into this decision must be its neighborhood location relative to the neighborhood decline model which we have discussed and any associated neighborhood preservation programs. The decision itself will be of the "go/no-go" genre: demolition or maintenance. Thus, the decision is either to terminate the life of the abandoned parcel or to try to enter it back into the housing supply system. The former course of action will normally be taken if the cost of bringing the parcel up to standards and habitability is not economically feasible, and/or the parcel is located in a Stage 4 or 5 neighborhood and would not be part of a concerted neighborhood-wide preservation effort. The decision may be made to demolish the parcel in order to prevent contagion to adjacent structures. Post-demolition choices range from either selling the resulting land package or banking the land parcel for future public use and/or development potential. This latter decision rests upon broader municipal policy and essentially terminates the flow emanating from the demolition course of action.

If the decision has been to maintain the structure, then a second decision must be made based on the cost appraisal functions and on the building's condition. These revolve about the immediate livability of the acquired units. Structures designated as not livable, based on findings of major structural flaws or inoperable utilities, are not desirable parcels for future homesteading. Structures so designated can either go directly to a localized rehabilitation effort or pass through a centralized repair agency. If the latter choice is made, it is possible to institute a form of homesteading as a finishing effort by the resident after the structure has been rendered structurally sound and the major utility systems operational. However, most homesteading would probably not be of this specific form.

If the evaluation of the parcel reveals that it is still in livable condition, and would not be overwhelmed by neighborhood conditions, the parcel could be then homesteaded or turned over to a localized rehabilitation program. It is this point in the disposition flow of abandoned housing that homesteading then comes into being.

It should be evident that a homesteading program does not exist in isolation from a host of other factors, and it is not a decision that can be made without substantial evaluation, both of a socioeconomic nature, (concerning the neighborhood within which the homestead is located) and a technical nature (concerning the costs necessary to return the parcel to habitability). And, while not couched in the specific phraseology used here, many of the subsequent homesteading efforts that we will be looking at actually follow a procedure not unlike the scheme depicted in Exhibit 2-2.

SUMMARY

The most critical decision which must be made in any effective homesteading system concerns the ultimate disposition of the available land parcels—should the abandoned structures be homesteaded or should more drastic actions be taken, such as demolition or land banking? Such a decision should be based not only on a realistic estimate of the costs of rehabilitating the individual unit, but, more importantly, on an appraisal of the neighborhood as a whole. A neighborhood decline typology, as outlined above, aids immeasurably in this critical appraisal.

NOTES

Note: Portions of this chapter have been extracted from George Sternlieb and James W. Hughes, *Analysis of Neighborhood Decline in Urban Areas*, a policy paper prepared for the United States Department of Housing and Urban Development, 1973.

1. A counter-argument could validly suggest that extremely viable areas, such as the Upper West Side of Manhattan, would prove counter to this assertion. In such instances, many of the residents may be homogeneous in terms of their desire for a varied, heterogeneous social environment. Nevertheless, we recognize the possible exceptions to our statement.

2. Again, we must put forth some qualifications. We are referring here to new neighborhoods, designed for at least moderate income households. We are not discussing areas constructed as tenements for low income families. Moreover the presence of young family-raising households does not imply a neighborhood at its peak. For example, the lower East Side of Manhattan is inhabited by young Puerto Rican families, yet the area, composing obsolete and decaying tenements, cannot be considered anywhere near a satisfactory environment.

3. See James W. Hughes, *Urban Indicators, Metropolitan Evolution, and Public Policy* (New Brunswick, New Jersey: Center for Urban Policy Research, Rutgers University, 1973), pp. 20-42.

4. The significance of invasions was recognized by the urban ecologists in the 1920s. See Roderick D. McKenzie, "The Ecological Approach," in Robert E. Park, Ernest W. Burgess, and Roderick D. McKenzie (eds.), *The City* (Chicago: University of Chicago Press, 1925), pp. 73-77.

5. See Homer Hoyt, *The Structure and Growth of Residential Neighborhoods in American Cities* (Washington, D.C.: Federal Housing Administration, 1939).

6. U.S. Bureau of the Census, "Mobility of the Population of the United States: March 1970 to March 1973," Current Population Reports, Series P-20,

No. 262 (Washington, D.C.: U.S. Government Printing Office, 1974).

7. Certainly, the rebirth of Brooklyn Heights, for example, and other areas of Brooklyn are predicated at least partly upon their superior access to Manhattan and its massive job market. Lacking this factor, their regeneration may have been much more questionable.

8. Edgar M. Hoover and Raymond Vernon, *Anatomy of a Metropolis* (New York: Doubleday Anchor, 1962).

9. Public Affairs Counseling, *HUD Experimental Program for Preserving the Declining Neighborhood: An Analysis of the Abandonment Process* (San Francisco, California: Public Affairs Counseling, 1973).

10. See also Real Estate Research Corporation, *Possible Program for Counteracting Housing Abandonment* (Chicago, Illinois: Real Estate Research Corporation, 1971). This decline model is essentially in reference to the evolution of city or inlying suburban neighborhoods which were constructed initially for non-poor households.

11. See George Sternlieb and Robert Burchell, *Residential Abandonment: The Tenement Landlord Revisited* (New Brunswick, New Jersey: Center for Urban Policy Research, 1973), and George Sternlieb, Robert W. Burchell, James W. Hughes, and Franklin J. James, "Housing Abandonment in the Urban Core," *Journal of the American Institute of Planners*, Vol. 40, No. 6, September 1974, pp. 321-332.

12. See Hughes, *Urban Indicators.*

13. See George Sternlieb and Robert W. Burchell, *Residential Abandonment.*

14. *Ibid.*

15. See also: George Sternlieb, James W. Hughes, Kenneth D. Bleakly, and David Listokin, *Housing Abandonment in Pennsylvania.* Mimeographed (New Brunswick, N.J.: Center for Urban Policy Research, Rutgers University, 1974).

Section II

Urban Homesteading: Operational Realities

Chapter 3

The Evaluative Framework

INTRODUCTION

The next four chapters focus on examples of urban homesteading. What we attempt to do is to evaluate these programs in a fashion which will enable us to synthesize the most desirable elements and ultimately derive typologies of alternative homesteading procedures. The methods we use are often qualitative, because of the difficulties inherent in attempting a quantitative analysis of a socioeconomic system. In the ideal, one would attempt to isolate a program's goals—a goal being defined as a very general statement depicting some desired future end—and then objectives—measurable attainable short-range targets.[1] Inherent in the latter is the assumption that we would be able to identify the program's output in quantifiable terms, and have the capacity to so measure them. A subsequent step in the analysis would be the isolation of the system structure whose function is to achieve the output state specified by the aforementioned objectives. Within the systems analysis, we would not only identify the critical features of the program which act causally to determine the desired ends, but also the main features of the environment that the program does not control, which also interact with the program and its objectives. By modeling such a programmatic system, we would be able to examine the net program benefits in relation to the stated goals and be able to determine a cost-effectiveness ratio or a cost-benefit ratio.[2] Unfortunately, this level of sophistication is very difficult to obtain in most practical analyses.

What are the difficulties? Inherent in the above method of analysis are the following principles:

1. The various impacts of a program over time can be identified.

2. The seriousness of these impacts can be judged in terms of how good and how bad they are.

3. The resource needs (costs) of the program over time can be considered in light of the availability of such resources.[3]

Given the level of maturity of most homesteading programs, their various impacts are extremely difficult to quantify. Outside of the number of units produced, how can we evaluate their effect at this point on various levels of neighborhood decline, on the economic stability of the recipient areas, and the economic benefit to the individuals involved in the program? Not able to measure these benefits, we are certainly in no position to apply standards of evaluation to them. Since these limitations prohibit us from performing the ideal program evaluation, our specific analyses of program and system structure take the following form. We simply attempt to identify those specific configurations of agency features and supportive elements which now appear to contribute most toward a smooth-running homesteading operation. Consequently, we have isolated those particular programmatic elements identified in a number of alternative programs, and examined their response to the task in question. Through interviews with the principal personnel involved in these efforts, as well as the basic information on organization structure and output—both of which enable us to evaluate the deficiencies or advantages of various organizational arrangements and program support functions—we are able to make judgments as to the utility of each of these features. We therefore evaluate the individual programs in terms of the following ten items, which constitute the main reference or evaluation framework, nine of which fall under the rubric of program elements.

THE SETTING

In any program analysis, whether or not it is possible to formally model the program and its interactions with its environment, a detailed analysis of the latter—its setting—should be undertaken. The objective of doing so is to see what non-replicable features determine the form and function of the evolving program. In appraising any program, an attempt must be made to distinguish between anecdotes—unique events peculiar to a specific point in history, a particular set of actors and a particular physical, political, and social context—and "replicables," those elements of program and environment which are substantially independent of the particular actors, unique competences, or personalities.[4] Replicables also should not be dependent on an administration's willingness to cast aside normal protective encumbrances in order to advance a specific approach, and should not be dominated by the particulars of the unique setting.[5]

The analyst must therefore attempt to sort out the "message" from the "noise." The basic question is whether a program's success or failure is generic to the general program, or is a one-of-a-kind phenomenon whose fate is intimately tied to its context.[6] These tasks are indeed laudable, and they set the standard to which we strive, however inadequately. But they also set a theme which is carried out in all the sections of the case studies and not simply the setting. In regard to the latter we try specifically to set out some of the general characteristics of the urban context which may weigh heavily on the program's formulation. For example, Baltimore is a city of masonry rowhouses whose longevity is substantial; in contrast, Newark is dominated by wood-framed, three-story, six-family residential configurations, constructed to house immigrant workers in the late 19th and early 20th centuries. Thus, the housing resources of the former are much more suited to the limitations of individualized rehabilitation efforts while the latter, given their complexity of size and more limited future life spans, may be suitable at best for large-scale organized rehabilitation. Factors such as these are highlighted for the settings of each of the case studies in their respective sections. Additionally, throughout the evaluation, attempts are made to distinguish program element *particulars* and program element *replicables. Thus the setting of each of the operational programs constitutes the initial basis of program evaluation and comparison.*

PROGRAM ELEMENTS

The successful operation of a homesteading effort also depends upon the interrelationships between a complex number of governmental regulations, state and federal support systems, and municipal programs and financial commitments. Particularly important are the many programs which in total define the entire system of homesteading. The homesteader may have accessibility to government rehabilitation funds but often only because another program's scope has been expanded to include him. Parcel acquisition comes about as a result of tax delinquency or abandonment by a previous owner; thus, the availability of a residential structure is a byproduct of an acquisition program often not initially related to homesteading. Some cities require that low income applicants receive preferential treatment knowing full well that such homesteaders may not be able to afford the high cost of rehabilitation and maintenance, or may lack the talents necessary for self-help programs. These diverse and sometimes conflicting program elements often have to be redefined and improved as the program evolves. If the goal of returning abandoned parcels into the housing supply system through homesteading is to be achieved, these elements must intermesh precisely, not work against each other.

These various programmatic aspects of homesteading can be understood by disaggregating the process into nine distinct program categories or elements:

1. *Institutional Framework.* A homesteading program requires certain commitments of statutory authority, budgetary funds, and staff allocations on the part of the sponsoring jurisdiction. The administrative positioning of a homesteading program in an existing agency or as an independent operation will have important consequences on the outcome of the program. The level of authority and powers granted to the operational agency often specifies the theoretical capacity for action. But legislation by itself will not constitute a successful program. The allocation of budgetary funds and personnel to the

administrative agency is also a firm prerequisite for a functioning program if it is really to accomplish its mandated objectives; if such support is not forthcoming, the sponsoring municipality may be employing homesteading as a publicity vehicle.

An equally important facet of a successful program is the ability of the homesteading authority to obtain cooperation from the various city agencies into whose purview aspects of a comprehensive homesteading effort fall. For example, as we will discuss below, various inspection and costing functions—evaluating the condition of the parcel and the investment required to bring it up to code enforcement levels—are often not under control of the homesteading agency yet constitute a necessary step in an operational program. If such functions are internalized within the administrative structure of the homesteading effort, a much smoother program flow will result. *Thus, the first program element of the reference framework for evaluating the case examples comprises both the capacities of the administrative agency and its positioning within the governmental hierarchy.*

2. *Parcel Acquisition: Operational Procedures.* The raw materials and basic resources of homesteading are the individual parcels which have fallen from the cities' property tax rolls. The structures currently being processed by the homesteading approach basically emanate or flow—and these latter terms may overdignify the state of the art—from two streams.[7] Abandoned and tax delinquent housing units constitute the first flow, while the second emanate from HUD foreclosures. While the supply of potential homesteads generated from these two sources appears to be quite consequential, a problem arises from the onerous difficulty, frequently unrecognized, in securing clear title to these units. The fact that a unit is abandoned does not imply the affected municipality has immediate control over it. (See Appendix A for definition.) To secure title to either abandoned or tax delinquent properties, various methods and procedures have been established under law.[8] The employment of a municipality's taxing power and police power have constituted the chief taking mechanisms to date. Since dwelling units are the basic raw material of any homesteading program, each municipality depends heavily on the aforementioned legal remedies for obtaining an adequate supply of units. However, in many jurisdictions it may take up to two, three, or four years of tax delinquency before the parcel can be secured by the municipality. Subsequently there may be up to two years in which the previous owner still maintains some claim, however tenuous, for potential repossession.

Every urban homesteading program must deal with new approaches to property transfers, each of which must be modified as experience and legal challenges dictate. In many respects, the legal and procedural remedies required by urban municipalities now are thwarted by protective prodedures instituted by previous generations. During the Depression, for example, many states created laws making tax foreclosure as difficult as possible to forestall the possible wave of defaults which then gave evidence of coming. Such protective measures, targeted principally to rural areas, now vitally constrict the avenues of action on the urban legislative scene. Thus it must be ascertained whether the taking mechanisms available to local jurisdictions are satisfactory in terms of their speed, cost, and flexibility in fulfilling the demand for a comprehensive method of obtaining title to abandoned properties.

Long transition periods between abandonment and tax delinquency, and cities' eventually taking title create serious problems: buildings which were in only minor disrepair at the time of abandonment are subject to more major deterioration due to vandalism and neglect during protracted periods of vacancy. At the same time, the city in which the abandoned property is located must wait substantial periods in order to convey the parcel, during which no taxes are being paid nor is any renovation occurring. Fast taking procedures attempt to reduce these time spans by shortening the periods before a building can be declared tax delinquent, and also shortening the redemption period between the declaration of delinquency and the eventual disvestiture of the structure through tax sale proceedings. While the above actions are taken under municipalities' taxing power, it is also possible to obtain abandoned buildings through the use of police power and nuisance law. An underlying concept is that abandoned buildings constitute nuisances and public emergencies—because they are hazardous to human life, health, and safety and have a deleterious effect on the community's living environment, and the like. Thus alternative remedies, in theory, have been advocated and in some cases implemented, and should be vitally important in securing an adequate supply of potential homesteads. Often, even if legislated, their actual operational reality falls far short of their theoretical design. The comparison, then, of the case examples' methods of parcel acquisition provides a common evaluative element.

Another central issue in the method of parcel acquisition is whether a complete inventory of the abandoned structures in a city is kept on a regular basis. Careful monitoring procedures allow communities to keep an up-to-date record of the areas of abandonment as well as act as a tracking mechanism for individual parcels. *Thus the second reference element comprises the inventorying and acquisition of the supply of homesteads.* (Appendix A presents a model housing abandonment recording system.)

3. *Evaluating the Homestead.* The detection of suitable parcels is a major element of any homesteading process. A detailed evaluation of individual structures to determine the cost of bringing the parcel into compliance with code enforcement standards is often the point of departure in a suitability assessment procedure. Additionally there should be some valid estimation of the costs to rehabilitate the structure so that the prospective homesteader has a good understanding of what to expect. Moreover, the homestead is not an isolated, independent entity, but a part of a larger neighborhood. So beyond an evaluation of the structural characteristics of the unit, an assessment of the neighborhood environment is crucial. The presence of an overwhelmingly negative milieu surrounding a new homestead, characterized by a high degree of abandonment, concentrations of crime, and other deleterious factors, dooms the homesteader to repeat the abandonment process. The suitability of a parcel for

homesteading must be determined in reference to the type of neighborhood, specifically categorized as to its level of decline or viability. The ideal typology for this task was presented in the previous chapter. Thus not only is a capable inspection and costing function an integral element of a successful program, but the capacity of the staff to evaluate the stage of neighborhood decline of the areas of homesteading implementation is a critical input factor. *Homesteading programs, then, will be examined as to their specific procedures of homestead selection.*

4. *Evaluating the Homesteader.* The person who provides the homesteading dynamic is the homesteader. The major emphasis of any program must be determining who will make the best homesteaders and pairing them with the parcels of most appropriate success potential. The first task in any selection process is the determination of the objective choice criteria so that applicants can be evaluated in terms of their ability to successfully manage the homesteading responsibilities. Once these criteria have been established a profile of minimum standards providing the desired applicant ratings on each criterion is necessary. Such variable characteristics as age, financial capacity, residency requirements, and other legal necessities must be clearly transmitted to all potential program applicants.

Beyond a formal set of requirements, a more judgmental set of criteria should be available to view individual applicants. An assessment of the skill capabilities of the applicant can provide an estimation of the tradeoffs between financial equity and sweat equity. For example, a homesteader who possessed substantial building and construction skills—abilities which would enable a large degree of rehabilitation work to be self-entertained—should be given credit for extra financial equity beyond his current financial resources since he will not be forced to contract out substantial rehabilitation work.

Criteria for matching homestead and homesteader must also be based on some evaluation of the cost of living in a particular parcel in relation to the ability of the applicant to bear those costs. Even though parcel acquisition costs—and therefore major mortgage costs—are bypassed in homesteading programs, operating costs can be substantial. In fact, the latter may have contributed to a parcel's previous abandonment and therefore may inhibit the economic viability of the structure. What we employ are sample projective techniques—*pro forma* operating statements—which are applied to the modular sample parcels in the case examples. Yearly operating costs—comprising loan repayment, property taxes, fuel and utilities, and the like—are subsequently translated into yearly income support thresholds. They also provide an easy conceptualization of the real impacts of alternative rehabilitation financing packages and of assessment and property taxing procedures.

So the selection criteria which are applied to homestead applicants provide another major dimension of comparison between the case studies. Of particular significance is the analysis of the cash flows required to successfully operate a properly homesteaded property.

5. *Financial Assistance in the Form of Mortgages and Loans.* One of the

chief obstacles to neighborhood viability in the central city is the withdrawal of financing by lending institutions. The "redlining" of neighborhoods helps create a climate of psychological abandonment by depriving owners of the essential ability to borrow on their investment. Rehabilitation efforts are then stymied since the critical parties interested in improving their properties are denied the wherewithal to do so.

Homesteading a parcel requires at least modest, and more typically, substantial outlays of capital if the homesteaders lack major construction and building skills. If the homesteader is expected to succeed where the previous owner failed, he must have available to him a financing vehicle, which is both eager to assist him and willing to lend at low interest rates. These criteria suggest that for any substantive program, local lending institutions cannot be expected to handle the financing by themselves. Present high interest rates combined with the tightness of available monies practically eliminate the necessary supply of low interest loans to the homesteader. Thus, some program capable of bridging the gap between homesteader needs and current money market requirements must be created.

It should be realized that much of the areas where homesteading is taking place have been abandoned many years ago by conventional financial mechanisms. What type of localized activity will fill this vacuum? In reference to Philadelphia, for example, the Pennsylvania Housing Financing Agency has developed lending programs for rehabilitation and homesteading.[9] In other cases it has been proposed that the local municipality become the lender. As we shall later see, this has been the case in Newark. However, Newark has been severely limited by stipulations imposed by the State of New Jersey. Newark's proposed municipal loan program is limited by New Jersey to mortgages of no more than five years. If conventional features are followed, i.e., a self-liquidating loan, the cash flow requirements must necessarily be far beyond the capacity of the market. Payback amounts for a five-year term are sure to exceed the individual homesteader's ability to pay.

The philosophy of long-term self-liquidating mortgages with or without federal or local guarantees emerged from the forms of financing developed during the 1930s when the costs of money were substantially below the present inflated rates.[10] Given the latter, the extant philosophy may well be challenged. What has been suggested in Newark are balloon-type mortgages, i.e., mortgages which are not self-liquidating but instead involve repayment of interest and little amortization during the term of the indenture. At the end of the term there is a substantial balance of the mortgage principal remaining, which is then refinanced. The Newark variation, where the city is limited to five-year mortgages, sets up the annual payback on a ten-year base lowering the amortization requirements and therefore the monthly payments; at the end of the five years, the remaining balance would again be refinanced.

The above mechanisms attempt to fill the gap left by the departure of conventional financial institutions. But some of the latter are still willing to put up a couple of conventional mortgages on a few select parcels. Often this is a gesture of good will to the immediate citizenry and to the cause of municipal bank deposits.[11] This has been one of the more visible financing mechanisms in one of our case studies, but despite its public relations value, it is no substitute for more replicable financial support mechanisms. The whole gamut of approaches is demonstrated in our four areas of observation.

Adequate financing must be made available to overcome the homesteader's difficulties in securing rehabilitation loans and to demonstrate the government's faith in what are usually considered questionable neighborhoods, thereby challenging directly one of the key elements of psychological abandonment. Lacking such, homesteading is reduced in its impact to public relations gimmicks. *The analysis of the various financial assistance packages successfully devised by the implementing homestead agencies provides another distinct index of comparison to view our study areas.*

6. *Special Tax Considerations.* To further assist the homesteader, many jurisdictions grant special tax abatements in recognition of the high costs borne during the rehabilitation phase. Typically, the improvement of any residential parcel leads to an increased assessment, thus penalizing a person who invests in his home. As has been emphasized again and again a strong negative inducement to parcel maintenance is thereby produced. An abatement on improvements softens this disincentive by minimizing assessment increases and thereby dampening the negative pressure on the owner.

The issue of tax abatement is made more complex by the generally poor financial posture of most cities. Without outside subsidies, most communities cannot afford to grant rehabilitation abatements on a wide scale, since costs are thereby shifted to other municipal residents who are presently overburdened relative to their suburban counterparts. One must question if it is fair to give just the homesteader a break on his taxes for fixing up his property, while other homeowners willing to rehabilitate their properties do not receive subsidies of this type. *The various attitudes and approaches in regard to assessment and tax abatement programs for homesteaders provide another important standard of comparison.*

7. *The Question of Title.* Most of the homestead literature to date has replicated a common format of dwelling inordinately on superficial historical analogy and public relations merchandizing. Given considerably less attention are the important "nuts and bolts" questions, each of which lacks the requisite glamour of the former, but in and of themselves determine the manifold operational realities. To understand this state of events, one must realize, as George Sternlieb has emphasized, that "ours is an age of rhetoric."[12] A program's securing attention requires a great deal of merchandizing verbiage on its potential for securing a wide range of objective results; hard sell must be relied upon. If described as exploratory and/or experimental, programs will not manifest political clout. Success stories are what now lead to funding and advanced careers of the administrators. Indeed, public relations gimmicks may be sine qua non in steering a program through the tortuous political road to funded status.[13]

Homesteading may have fallen prey to this approach; one must hope that it doesn't become "a hostage to the verbiage required to secure its passage; doomed to failure because of the gap between the practical requirements and lags in set up in the field and the promises of immediacy of delivery . . . . A program may therefore depend on the anecdote . . . . To be truly effective, however, ultimately it must yield to mass assembly if adequate throughput is to be delivered."[14]

One of the most vexing practical requirements for operational field set up is the question of holding title to the homesteaded parcel. The conventional approach requires someone to make a commitment to live in the parcel for a specified period of time, sometimes up to five years. What is the nature of parcel title during this residency requirement—can there be clear title while this commitment is being fulfilled?[15] Once again, the historical analogy is found to be shallow. In the historical context, one could live with uncertainty, since outside requirements were minimal. Today, however, financial institutions must be relied upon to provide rehabilitation capital. Who will finance or mortgage a parcel whose direct ownership title is nebulous throughout the residency requirement? In Wilmington, the answer came fast—the participating lenders wouldn't. Feet shuffled fast, the homesteading ordinance was modified, and agreements and commitments amended. *Thus a difficult shake-out process is taking place in homesteading, and the difficulties of title serve as another pivotal point of program evaluation.*

8. *Cost-Revenue Realities.* The evaluative criteria to this point have tended to focus on the impact of homesteading, and its surrounding institutional encumberances, on the homesteader. But what implications does homesteading have on the recipient municipality's fiscal and economic structure? *To evaluate this phenomenon in the case observations, an attempt is made to clarify homesteading's cost-revenue impact on the severely weak urban fiscal positions.* The formal methodology of this type of analysis is presented in Appendix B.

9. *Development of Supportive Services.* The homesteader of the 1860s dealt with virgin land whose sufficiency of natural resources provided the essential elements for his survival. The tools and procedures for coping with the homestead and the environment were elegant in their simplicity and highly suitable to the task at hand. The subsistence homesteader of the 1930s found much of the supportive elements to deal with the environment provided for him even though the individual residential structure was governmentally constructed. Today's homesteader has neither sufficient free access to the necessary raw materials nor the freedom to design his essential elements for survival as was common to the homesteader of the 1860s. Nor does the support approach the magnitude of that provided by the federally sponsored efforts of the Great Depression. Yet substantial differences exist in the social and technical milieus of both the eras and spatial areas of the principal homesteading programs. The complexity of modern urban life dictates support levels even beyond that applied to the endeavors of the 1930s. Due to our high degree of specialization a narrow scope of resources is available to a person solely for the cost of labor.

The inability to structure the tools for survival on the individual level found in the early homesteading experience is a function of the present high degree of regulation which imposes standards of performance and a standardization of product on the homesteader. This was sufficiently recognized by the Subsistence Homestead Program. In the great complexity of modern urban life it is not sufficient to set the homesteader up with a parcel and leave him to his own devices, as it was with the homesteading efforts of the 1860s.

The sponsoring jurisdiction may have to provide assistance in the form of improved city services, ownership counseling efforts, and a wide range of special assistance programming, such as the supervision of contractors who do the basic rehabilitation work to insure satisfactory performance without inflated cost charges.

A process flow encompassing all of these elements would allow a homesteading municipality to effectively combat the environmental factors which cause abandonment by dealing with them from a sophisticated approach that recognizes their complexity and interrelation. *Thus, a critical segment of homestead program evaluation should give considerable attention to the definitive provision of supportive services.*

THE TAKE-OUT MECHANISM: REALITY IGNORED

As we have emphasized in the historical chapter, homeownership and landownership are integral parts of America's heritage and national character. Given strong roots of homeownership, it was assumed that America's citizenry would give strong support to government. While the most current promulgated virtues of homeownership are its shelter function, its source of pride, its development of responsibility and its outlet for workmanship and other energies, its unheralded function, as George Sternlieb has pointed out, is its potential as an equity accumulation device, a form of forced saving.[16] For most Americans, equity in their home represents a major portion of their capital resources. It has served as an inflation-proof vehicle to maintain and build capital assets. This function of homeownership provides another standard against which urban homesteading must be measured. It is in this regard that it faces its stiffest challenge.

Urban homesteading programs which we will examine in this study require substantial investments of determination and dollars in order to effectively assume homeownership. To demand these efforts yet not explicitly incorporate equity accumulation as an integral part of the process is to deceive the participant and to entertain grave doubts about the long-term validity of the program. Much thought must be given to take-out mechanisms, the means to recoup investment and equity.[17] *None of our case programs have refined their thinking to this stage.*

What is required? First of all, as the homesteader rebuilds his parcel, as he begins to pay off the interest and amortization on any loan, his paid equity will begin to accumulate. The latter can only be made liquid through financial institutions' willingness to remortgage his parcel or to grant mortgages to subsequent buyers. The absence of such willingness means there is no capital accumulation occurring for the homesteader, and there is no mobility. "For the moment this part of the loop has not been closed, there is no assurance given to the potential homesteader that if he lives in the parcel, maintains the parcel, pays down his mortgage on the parcel—that he can ever recover in lump financial form the results of his labors. What we have then is someone who is immobilized, unable to move, unable to liquidate his holdings—except through the very abandonment process which the program was initiated to halt."[18]

Section 235 of the 1968 Housing Bill, which provided homeownership for the poor, in essence served as a take-out mechanism for white owners in core areas. A not uncommon scenario shows a real estate speculator purchasing—from a white household desiring to exit the inner city—a home for, say, $10,000. This takes the white household off the hook. The speculator, after surface rehabilitation, would then sell the structure to a welfare recipient for, say, $20,000, with the government providing a 100 percent mortgage. When the utility systems go, when the economic realities of homeownership become apparent, and when the environment begins to sag, the new homeowner has no choice but to walk away, abandoning the structure. What of the homesteader? Will he be able to liquidate his resources in the future, or will the abandonment process which the program was designed to combat be repeated. Homesteading cannot effectively exist in the long run without some workable process of providing equity insurance. "This must involve a guarantee of holding harmless the homesteader providing he does the various things which society requires of him if he proves up to his claim. Given the inflationary realities of our time it may well be that this may have to be geared not really to absolute dollars, but also to real dollars."[19] None of the case studies presented here have evolved their program formats to the extent that take-out mechanisms are even thought about.

It must be realized that any successful program must make market sense. At some stage in the near future, the homesteader should have a reasonable chance of seeing a real profit emerge from his structure even if nothing more than equity gain from loan repayment. More importantly this nest egg must be recoverable, either through resale or remortgaging.[20] This whole question boils down to market sense.[21] An underlying value of homesteading is the faith that residence ownership—as evidenced by *The Tenement Landlord*—provides bonuses of responsible maintenance, with other benefits accruing such as resident morale—getting a slice of the American pie—and attitudes toward the parcel and government.[22] But these goals should not be achieved by trapping the homesteader as a permanent caretaker in a wasting asset but rather by putting him into situations with profit potential, as was the position of his upwardly mobile precursor in post World War II Levittown. As our lack of comment within the case examples regarding take-out mechanisms shows, the homsteading bandwagons are embarking on journeys with little regard to this major dynamic force.

CONCLUSION

The above program elements or features are used to examine the various configurations of homesteading operations. Again we should emphasize that this particular mode of evaluation is second best to the ideal, the latter requiring explicit measures of program output—outputs directed toward predetermined objectives—which are subsequently used to measure the effectiveness-cost ratio of the program. The elucidation of the difficulties of this process was firmly set out in the introduction to this chapter, and it is felt that any expected pay-off of attempting to approach this ideal method of analysis would not be very high. The approach we have taken appears to be satisfactory, however, to highlight the difficulties as well as the accomplishments of the various homestead programs. As such, a contribution to operational reality may be the final result.

NOTES

1. For a general presentation of these ideal models see: Yehezkel Dror, *Public Policymaking Reexamined* (San Francisco: Chandler Publishing Company, 1968) and James W. Hughes and Lawrence D. Mann, "Systems and Planning Theory," *Journal of the American Insitute of Planners*, September 1967, Vol. XXXV, No. 5, pp. 330-333.

2. A. R. Prest and R. Turvey, "Cost Benefit Analysis: A Survey," *Economic Journal*, No. 75, 1965, pp. 683-735.

3. Donald A. Krueckeberg and Arthur L. Silvers, *Urban Planning Analysis: Methods and Models* (New York: John Wiley and Sons, Inc. 1974), p. 194.

4. The basic concept of anecdotes versus replicables is that of George Sternlieb. See: George Sternlieb, "The Myth and Potential Reality of Urban Homesteading," paper presented at Confer—In 1974, American Institute of Planners, October 14, 1974.

5. *Ibid*. p. 2.

6. *Ibid*. '

7. *Ibid*. p. 5.

8. For a summary review of the development of fast-taking procedures, see: George Sternlieb, James W. Hughes, Kenneth Bleakly and David Listokin, *Housing Abandonment in Pennsylvania*. Mimeographed (New Brunswick, New Jersey: Center for Urban Policy Research, Rutgers University, 1974).

9. *Ibid*.

10. George Sternlieb, "The Myth and the Potential Reality of Urban Homesteading," p. 6.

11. *Ibid*.

12. *Ibid*. p. 2.

13. *Ibid*.

14. *Ibid*.

15. *Ibid*. p. 5.

16. *Ibid*. p. 8.

17. Again, George Sternlieb is responsible for emphasizing this very important factor. *Ibid*.

18. *Ibid*. p. 9.

19. *Ibid*. p. 8.

20. *Ibid*.

21. George Sternlieb, "Toward an Urban Homestead Act," *Papers Submitted to Subcommittee on Housing Panels*, Committes on Banking and Currency, House of Representatives, 92nd congress, First Session, June 1971, pp. 366-371.

22. George Sternlieb, *The Tenement Landlord* (New Brunswick, New Jersey: Rutgers University Press, 1966).

Chapter 4

Baltimore:
Well Directed Pioneers

The weeks and months have gone by quickly since we were awarded our Homestead House, and, as might be expected, progress in rehabilitating the house has fallen behind our hopes and expectations. But we are finally ready in all respects to begin serious work. The contract papers have been signed; the work permits have been obtained by the contractors; and all major decisions have been made. We plan to move in by October 1, "camping-out" if necessary, and little else has held so firm as this target. [1]

Paula King's words express the mix of hope and frustration experienced by most homesteaders. Mrs. King and her family, along with 51 others in the city, are the first initiates of Baltimore's Homesteading Program. It began as part of an effort to encourage homeownership in the city in November 1973. At that time, saddled with a substantial number of abandoned parcels and enviously observing the rash of attention focused on Wilmington, Delaware, Baltimore embarked on its own program.

THE SETTING

In many respects, Baltimore is in better condition relative to the settings of our other observations. The present population barely exceeds 900,000, down from just over 939,000 in 1960. Of the 305,521 housing units in 1970, 40 percent were built after 1939, giving Baltimore the youngest housing stock of the four cities. [2] While there are 5,004 abandoned structures in the city, this accounts for only 1½ percent of the total housing stock. Yet present day Baltimore is a far cry from the city it once was.

BALTIMORE (20 alt., 804,874 pop.), proud, self-sufficient, sits beside the Patapsco River, looking nostalgically to the South but turning to the North for what it takes to make a bank account grow. Midway between North and South, a seething cauldron of dissension

*during the Civil War, it is even today a city of violent contradictions.
It is gentle and blatant, wanton and prudish, cosmopolitan and
insular. City of rarefied aristocrats and often rowdy intellectuals, of
dismal slums and spacious mansions, of the insistent odor of
fertilizer and the delicate bouquet of the Cardinal's crocuses, of
cobblestones and gas lights and monuments; gazing wistfully upon
the old, suspiciously upon the new, and benevolently upon the rest
of the country.*

*Baltimore may be an ugly city; nevertheless it is charmingly
picturesque in its ugliness. Red brick houses, row on row, with
scrubbed white steps, line the narrow streets of the old town; yellow
brick houses, miles of them, run uphill and down through the
purgatories of the twentieth century realtors; crooked alleys with
odd names meander behind old red brick fronts; lordly mansions of
the rich preen themselves in groves and parks in the smart suburbs to
the north along Charles Street Avenue Extended.*

*It is the people who live here and their lineage of
independence—those who trace their line back to the original
Maryland pilgrims and those who have no pride of ancestry nor hope
of distinguished posterity—that make Baltimore. Outwardly an old
city gone industrial, inwardly it is one of the last refuges of a way of
living and a mode of thinking long since engulfed in commercialism
almost everywhere else in the United States. Almost any idea, any
statement, is permissible in Baltimore, if it is urbanely presented . . .*

*Greeks, Italians, Scandinavians, South Americans are
here—representatives of virtually every maritime nation on the globe.
Workers on Bay and river boats are also here, though the blue-water
men feel quite superior to the green-water men . . .*

*Baltimore's compact Little Italy lies mainly south of Pratt
Street. . . . The most picturesque and self-contained of all
Baltimore's foreign sections, it consists of many small colonies, since
the Italian is homesick unless he is living among people from his
native parish . . .*

*The city has a half a dozen other districts inhabited largely by
people of European birth and their descendants. The more than
7,000 people of British and Irish birth are scattered, but the 14,000
Germans tend to live in neighborhoods where they may use their
native tongue frequently. The 17,000 people of Russian birth
counted in the census of 1930 live mostly in southeast Baltimore.
The 142,000 Negroes are scattered all over the city, but*

Pennsylvania Avenue is the Main Street of a large "black belt" in the northwest section. Here is a duplicate of the life of the white city—from bottom to top—though a few somewhat exotic touches catch the eye of foreign vision.

> Baltimore in the Late 1930's. Federal Writers Project, Maryland: A Guide to the Old Line State *(New York: Oxford University Press, 1940), pp. 196-205.*

Whether this idealized picture of a plethora of unique social neighborhoods actually depicted the reality of 1930 Baltimore, it no doubt sketches the quaint settings envisioned by many current romanticizers of "ethnicity." No matter; the world, the United States, its metropolitan areas, its cities, and their neighborhoods have long since undergone a fundamental transformation. And so has Baltimore. It has lost almost 50,000 residents over the last two decades, over 5 percent of its population. The forsaking of old neighborhoods by white family-raising households to new minority group entrants and the remnants of older ethnic concentrations is indexed by the changing demographic characteristics of the city. (Exhibit 4-1). Blacks are now the dominant racial group in the city.

But one thing hasn't changed—Baltimore's red brick row houses, with their characteristic white stoops, still line the narrow streets of its old neighborhoods. Only 17.7 percent of the housing stock is located in structures containing five or more units, a building configuration too massive and complex for individualized homesteading efforts. Thus the city's basic housing resources serve as a substantial pool of raw materials for the implementation of a strong homesteading effort. Additionally, the strong organizational set-up of Baltimore's housing and planning components make this setting as fertile as possible for a well-rooted programmatic format. If homesteading succeeds because of organization, it will probably succeed in Baltimore.

The city government had unknowingly been preparing for homesteading, having previously centralized all housing functions under a Department of Housing and Community Development. Conceptually, Baltimore had recognized the welter of interrelated phenomena which lead to abandonment; this helped significantly in designing an effective homesteading program.

This has not meant that homesteading has been implemented smoothly, however. While 136 homesteads have been awarded, only seven have been occupied with another 50 under active rehabilitation. This time lag has largely been a function of the initial unfamiliarity with the process and some procedural snags. A goal of the program is to cut the time between owner selection and settlement from the present six- to nine-month period to two months. Since the program's inception some 20 to 25 persons have dropped out, frequently citing disenchantment with the concept as well as personal reasons.[3]

EXHIBIT 4-1
BALTIMORE: A STATISTICAL PROFILE

Total Population		*1950*	*1960*	*1970*
Maryland		2,343,001	3,100,689	3,922,399
Baltimore		949,708	939,024	905,759

Black Population	
1960	323,589
1970	479,837

Median Age (Total)		*Median Age (Black)*	
1960	31.3	1960	24.7
1970	28.7	1970	22.7

Household Size (Total)		*Household Size (Black)*	
1960	2.9	1960	3.4
1970	2.8	1970	3.1

Median Family Income (Total)		*Median Family Income (Black)*	
1960	$4,676	1960	$3,354
1970	$6,796	1970	$5,590

Median Education (Total)		*Median Education (Black)*	
1960	8.9	1960	8.4
1970	10.0	1970	9.6

Median House Value (Total)		*Median House Value (Black)*	
1960	$9,000	1960	$8,200
1970	$10,000	1970	$9,400

Housing Units	
1970 Total	305,521
Built before 1939	60%
Built before 1949	75%

Units in Structure		
Structure Type	Number of Units	
1 unit	187,589	(61.4%)
2 - 4 units	63,853	(20.9%)
5 or more units	54,077	(17.7%)

Source: U.S. Bureau of the Census, *Census of Population and Housing: 1970, Census Tracts, Final Report PHC (1)-191 Baltimore, Md. SMSA.*

INSTITUTIONAL FRAMEWORK

The City of Baltimore considers urban homesteading as one important dimension of a broad-based effort to retain its present residential homeowners and to attract new ones back into the city. With the level of homeownership dropping from 54.3 percent to 44.5 percent in the last intercensal decade, the city administration recognized the need for positive affirmative action.[4] This need was particularly accentuated when it was realized that for the first time since the 1940 census, there were fewer homeowners than renters in Baltimore. The alarm over this pattern of declining homeownership led to the creation of a Homeownership Development Division to foster a healthier environment for homeowners in the city. The thrust of this effort was to secure both financing and general assistance for those persons desirous of rehabilitating city structures; operationally it attempted to reinterest the financial community in the center city area and provide homeownership counseling for both current and prospective owners.

Homesteading, evolving as one component of this program, required no special legislative mandate since the staff responsible for the homeownership development function of the Department of Housing and Community Development also had responsibility for management of city-owned properties, which had come under municipal ownership through tax delinquency, abandonment, or condemnation. The Homeownership Development Division also had the legislated task of finding new suitable owners for these parcels. Thus it already had the raw materials—the structures themselves—and the responsibility of finding a way of returning them to the housing supply system.

The city used this authority to create a homesteading program. The staff presently comprises eight people, divided among three programmatic functions: promotion-selection-postlease; construction; and work writeup-specifications, financing, and monitoring. What makes the program unique are the close ties the homesteading office has with all other city functions related to housing. All housing-oriented programs are grouped under the Department of Housing and Community Development (DHCD). This "umbrella" agency includes the planning, zoning, inspection, rehabilitation, renewal, acquisition, financing, and public housing functions. Within this comprehensive and coordinated department are many of the operating support systems necessary for a smooth-running homesteading program. While obviating the need for the homesteading staff to provide these services "in-house," such a department does not force the reliance on any overworked or hostile competing agency. For example, a detailed inspection and survey of all vacant housing in Baltimore is a principal task of the Neighborhood Development Division of the Department, relieving the homesteading staff of the responsibility of locating and initially assessing vacant structures for possible homesteads. At the same time, the survey is coordinated to the needs of the homesteading staff. The REAL program,[5] handles the evaluation and preparation of financial assistance for the homesteader, once the basic credit information is provided by the homesteading staff, further lightening the burden on the staff's time.

The Baltimore program operates without a legislatively mandated homesteading board. Deriving its authority as it does from intragovernmental policy rather than external pressure, the board is the organic response to the needs of the program. Final approval of staff actions rests with a six-man board drawn from personnel of the Home Ownership Division. It includes the Chief of City Owned Properties, Homesteading Manager, the Home Ownership Development Program Director, the Supervisor of Construction, Home Ownership Counseling Manager, and the Head of Property Sales. These individuals are intimately aware of the various facets of city life impacted by the program and as such provide an invaluable tool for coordinating the wide range of activities encompassed by homesteading. This is not a board in the traditional sense of other homestead programs, since it is an "in-house" entity. The normal function of such a body is to include the relevant external parties whose cooperation is essential to program operation and which must contribute net additional labors to the program. Since all relevant city housing functions are internalized within the umbrella agency encompassing homesteading (DHCD), a special broad-based board is not mandatory. This approach appears satisfactory if measured in terms of the community's acquiescence to the present program operations.

PARCEL ACQUISITION

The City of Baltimore is probably in the best homesteading position of the four case areas. This is primarily the result of the relative strength of its neighborhoods. Rarely is there any concentration of abandoned structures relative to the magnitudes found in Wilmington, Philadelphia, or Newark. Usually a few vacant units at most can be found on a single block, although some severely impacted blocks do exist. Thus the homesteader has an added advantage of moving into a sound neighborhood; this is a major supportive aspect of the Baltimore program. Vacant, abandoned buildings represent about 1½ percent of structures in the city. This is substantially below the ratio of abandoned to total structures found in the other case cities.

One of the strongest aspects of Baltimore's approach to abandoned housing is the Vacant Housing Monitoring System. Realizing the difficulty in operationally defining abandonment the Department of Housing and Community Development avoids the terminology completely; instead it has disaggregated unoccupied structures into two categories, unoccupied and vacant. Unoccupied units are those lacking tenants, but for all intents and purposes are still on the market. Vacant units, in contrast, are generally absent of tenants, but not always, and are either:

1. Open to casual entry, with doors open or broken

2. Have major appliances removed
3. Have their major utilities removed

The above determinations are made both by observation from the street (windshield survey) and actual entrance into the structure. Subsequent analysis of city records categorizes the status of the building into five types:

1. Private ownership
2. Private ownership to be acquired (designated as such under other programs)
3. Ownership by the Mayor-City Council
4. Demolition scheduled by the Mayor-City Council
5. Acquisition by the Housing Authority-City of Baltimore

Most likely, abandoned units would be included under the first case, but not all abandoned units would be interpreted as privately owned.[6] Appendix A includes a full description of the Baltimore monitoring and accounting system, one of the most advanced in the nation.

The Taking Mechanism

Baltimore employs several approaches for taking properties which have been or are in the process of becoming abandoned. When a parcel is abandoned the city must wait one and a half years before acting on the tax lien against the property. At the end of the waiting period, the property may be sold at a sheriff's sale, often with the property purchased by the city because of a lack of interested buyers. After the sheriff's sale, under regular procedures, there is a one-year period during which the owner may redeem his property by payment of back taxes and fees. Therefore, abandoned properties remain in a transitional state for two and a half years. Recently enacted procedures allow the period of redemption to be shortened to six months, significantly shortening the total transitional period to two years. Another procedure allows for a shorter redemption period, 60 days, when the building is declared to be in substantial violation of the city's building code or will be in violation within six months.[7] Thus the city can move to acquire an abandoned structure in a variety of methods. To date 2,200 units have been obtained through these various tax sale procedures, yielding a substantial pool of prospective homesteads. A policy has been adopted to shorten the waiting period between the time of tax delinquency and the date of the tax sale. Previous policy mandated a wait of 18 months between the date of deliquency and the tax sale. The date of the tax sale is now being moved back two months each year for five years. This will mean that in five years time the tax sale on a property will occur only 9 months after the date of delinquency. This drastic shortening of the abandonment transition period could permit a quick taking of abandoned structures before they become further deteriorated. In reality, because of delays in the judicial process, the quickest turn-around time may prove as long as 24 to 30 months.[8]

EVALUATING THE HOMESTEAD

Baltimore's approach to parcel selection employs the dual criteria of rehabilitation cost and neighborhood environmental characteristics.

The general rehabilitation cost ceiling is $17,400 under the REAL program but the ceiling can be raised, should a parcel be of particular historical value. The significance of neighborhood environment is appreciated by the program staff. Yet, to date, they do not feel they have been particularly successful in detecting areas of totally unfavorable characteristics as evidenced in the lack of interest in certain units. Judgments in this regard are based on qualitative measures rather than a quantitative classification of a neighborhood according to a neighborhood decline matrix.

The aforementioned vacant property management system gives the city an excellent monitoring device with which to gauge both the quantity and quality of its housing stock. After the abandoned parcels have been identified, the city takes title through their tax foreclosure procedure or through condemnation of properties for which no other use is contemplated. Currently 2,200 parcels are owned by the city, of which 50 to 65 percent are thought to be suitable for homesteading, as determined principally by individual unit condition. The selection of the specific parcels to be homesteaded depends both on staff evaluation and applicant interest. The staff employs the inspection department reports as the starting point of their selection process (as described in Appendix A), and then examines those units which appear to be the best suited for homesteading, obtaining rough estimates of potential rehabilitation costs and neighborhood environmental characteristics. Moreover, several parcels have been homesteaded as a result of interest on the part of prospective applicants; the staff feels this is a good indicator of the marketability of a parcel. Once the homestead is evaluated, trash and debris are cleared and the unit is sealed to prevent further decay or vandalism.

The city has recently begun a unique pilot program of handling whole neighborhoods where deterioration is occurring. Once an impact area has been designated, all vacant properties are evaluated by the Vacant House Committee and a determination, based on current condition and future worth of the parcels, is made to rehabilitate, homestead, demolish, or relinquish responsibility to the Housing Authority for management. In this process, all alternative uses for a particular parcel are explored and the interaction of all the housing functions in one area permits a more comprehensive and well coordinated approach towards neighborhood stabilization.

Another major innovation has been the homesteading of all the units of an entire block. On one block on Sterling Street, the city controlled all 42 units which were awarded to 25 homesteaders, with several working two units into one. This is the first application of the homesteading concept on a concentrated scale, and the program administrators are so enthusiastic about its results that several other sites are being readied for a similar attempt.

The unit itself whether isolated or part of a concentrated mass must either be structurally sound, or if structually deficient, the location and severity of structural problems must be noted to the prospective homesteader. The units found to be most suitable for homesteading, as expected, are the small to moderate-size rowhouses which can be rehabilitated at moderate cost. However, it is the larger, formerly elegant dwellings, which have attracted the more affluent participants, and sparked the initial press releases.

EVALUATING THE HOMESTEADER

The Baltimore homesteading effort is directed toward achieving four objectives.

1. To return to the housing supply system as many vacant buildings as possible.

2. To encourage people to move back into the city.

3. To turn tax delinquent properties into tax paying properties.

4. To increase homeownership in the city.[9]

Baltimore considers homesteading an appealing program to persons contemplating leaving, or who have already left, the city. By making the financial cost of rehabilitation extremely reasonable, the city hopes to retain present middle class residents as well as attract new residents. The program does not aim at the poor but rather at working class and middle class households, who can afford the high costs of rehabilitation and are attracted by the prospect of comparatively low cost, high quality residential accommodations in basically sound inner-city neighborhoods. In fact, one of the admitted problems with the program has been its inaccessibility to significant numbers of the poor because of the high costs involved in parcel renovation. Given such constraints, the program has geared itself to operational reality. One of the first, more visible, entrants into the realm of homesteading amplifies this philosophy.

Homestead Observation Number 8, tenanted by a professional couple both employed in the Charles Street Center is taking place in what was an abandoned domicile of the former city elite. Packed with restorable amenities—oak paneling, fireplaces, and wood in-laid floors—the substantial brick framed residence is being rehabilitated through the pyramiding of the maximum REAL financing, personal

*resources, and a private loan. While the total cost will probably
exceed $32,000, the owners liken their effort to that of the initial
pioneers of Society Hill (Philadelphia) and Brooklyn Heights (New
York). The costs incurred are not inconsequential, yet the couple
interprets the quality of residence as far superior to the more
expensive suburban alternative, while adding in the bonus of a
non-automobile journey to work. By any standards, the physical
result is stunning, and could serve as the flagship of any
homesteading program going into full sail.* [10]

One program modification which is presently being undertaken, however,
is the selection of parcels which are of a modest size and require minimal
rehabilitation, bringing the program within the reach of previously disfranchised
income groups. The initial homesteading of the more visible properties of past
glory has served its function well, providing an impetus to success stories, leading
to program expansion.

Minimum Requirements

Baltimore has established the following minimum criteria for the selection
of its homesteaders:

1. The applicant must be 18 years or older and head of a
    household.

2. The applicant must supply evidence that he or she has
    financial ability or skills required to renovate the property.

3. Work on the property must commence within 6 months.

4. The unit must meet code enforcement standards within 18
    months. [11]

Baltimore, like most other cities, requires that the major rehabilitation
work be done by licensed contractors. This includes electrical, plumbing, major
structural and roofing repairs. Beyond these items, however, the selection staff
looks for persons who have some knowledge or at least considerable interest in
attempting minor work elements themselves. No attempt is made to profile
participating households to the dominant racial characteristics of the recipient
neighborhoods. Significantly, many homesteads are located in areas of
substantial racial mix.

In a general sense, the staff is looking for persons capable of handling the
complexity of rehabilitating an old structure, viewing the participant as having
to act as a general contractor throughout the process. As an inducement to the
homesteader, the staff clearly spells out the costs involved and shows the savings

available to those willing to become their own general contractors. The program hopes to make most homesteaders confident enough to do their own general contracting work, thereby allowing a more intensive use of capital for materials rather than labor and supervision.

Selection Process

Once a set of parcels have been deemed suitable for homesteading they are publicized in the local media, along with information on specific application procedures. Coincidently some individuals request a particular site be homesteaded and, if it is both in the city's possession and is in suitable condition, it will be included. In the initial program stages, a series of open houses are held, enabling persons to walk through the parcels being offered. Recently this practice has been deemphasized and inspection of the parcels has been on an individual appointment basis. Due to the heavy increase in inspection requests, the open house policy will be resumed in the area of concentrated household sites. There has also been an effort to become more involved with neighborhood community groups, allowing them to inspect the parcel and attempting to increase neighborhood involvement in the program. One potentially important development in this regard has been the inputs of Baltimore's Neighborhood Housing Services organization which is intimately involved with local neighborhood affairs. Under an experimental program, NHS provides rehabilitation advisory services to homesteaders and acts as a local advocate for neighborhood interests. An organized informational system is evolving, linking the homesteader, the neighborhood, and the city administration. Such an arrangement develops a responsive locally based advocate to iron out problems and offer guidance in selecting contractors and merchants, a function which the city, because of its responsibility to maintain an unbiased posture, cannot assume.

In any case, the prospective homesteader applies for a particular unit but may apply for more than one. Once the submission deadline has passed, the staff begins examining all applications in regard to threshold qualifications. A credit check is run on each person and detailed financial and biographical information is gathered. On the basis of this information and the unit's physical characteristics, the selection decision is made.

The homesteading staff then forwards its recommendations including rehabilitation cost estimates to the Homesteading Board as described above, to make the final recommendation. Their findings are then sent to the Commissioner of the Department of Housing and Community Development who reserves the right to make a final decision.

Once the homesteader has been selected a detailed analysis of the cost of meeting code enforcement standards is commissioned from the National House Inspection Corporation, presenting the homesteader with an itemized list of required work elements. Estimates for noncode work desired by the homesteader are also prepared at this time, resulting in an estimate of total rehabilitation cost. The homesteader is then supplied with a list of contractors—general and sub—which were found acceptable by other program participants, providing a reliable selection guide. Receiving signed bids on the work, the homesteader makes his selection of contractors. The services of the Neighborhood Design Center are available to prepare any necessary site plans, or the participant may work directly with the contractors to develop the plans. With all this preliminary work accomplished, REAL program financing can be requested. Once financing has been arranged the homesteader can go to settlement, completing the selection process.

During the rehabilitation period the title to the property remains with the city and the homesteader is officially a leasee. At the conclusion of the mandatory residency period and when the program administrators have certified that all the responsibilities of the homesteader have been met, he receives fee-simple title to the property. This procedure is made possible by virtue of the city's role as mortgager evolving out of the REAL loan program.

Income Sufficiency

The Baltimore program has offered a wider selection of parcels in terms of size and value than is found in most homesteading programs. This results in a broader range of persons attracted to the program. Several units are being rehabilitated for as little as $6,000 while others have gone over the $40,000 level. However, for the purposes of analyzing the annual income sufficient to maintain a model homestead, a unit value of $8,000 and a rehabilitation loan of $12,000 are assumed, costs which represent the average value of each category. The annual costs of homesteading such a parcel would be $2,418.48 as determined in Exhibit 4-2. This exceeds the costs of the other case study areas, primarily because of the dollar size of the loan. Thus, financing costs are high because of the substantial increase in the amount borrowed in comparison with other cities. Twenty-five percent of after tax income is frequently cited as the most desirable ratio between household income and shelter expenses.[12] Annual costs of this magnitude necessitate an annual before taxes income for a four person household of just under $11,000,[13] demonstrating clearly the program's limited applicability to low-income Baltimoreans. The staff's records of the typical homesteader so far bear out this conclusion, with most of the homesteader's incomes falling in the $10-$15,000 category.[14]

SPECIAL TAX CONSIDERATIONS

Baltimore does not have a direct abatement program at present but two significant, if indirect, forms of tax relief do exist. When a homesteader moves into the parcel he is a leasee rather than an owner. The city, to avoid the problems inherent in the marketability of encumbered titles in the State of Maryland, decided to hold title until the two-year waiting period has expired, preferring to "lease" the parcel to the homesteader during that period. Since the

EXHIBIT 4-2

TYPICAL ANNUAL COSTS INCURRED BY BALTIMORE HOMESTEADERS

Expense	Cost
Taxes[1]	$ 292.32
Loan Payment[2]	1,046.16
Utilities & Fuel[3]	640.00
Insurance[3]	40.00
Miscellaneous[3]	400.00
TOTAL	$2,418.48

1. This is an average for the first 5 years based on an $8,000.00 assessment at a city tax rate of $6.09/$100 of assessed valuation including the first 2 years in which $0 per year are paid under the special reassessment deferment. (See Special Tax Considerations section in text.)

2. This is the annual cost of a $12,000 loan at 6 percent for 20 years, the average loan issued through early 1975. The annual cost was determined as follows:

$$R = P\frac{i(1+i)^n}{(1+i)^n - 1} = \$12,000 \frac{.06(1+.06)^{20}}{(1+.06)^{20} - 1} = \$12,000(.08718)$$

R = $1,046.16

where i represents an interest rate per interest period
n represents a number of interest periods
P represents a present sum of money (total mortgage)
R represents the end-of-period payment in a uniform series continuing for the coming n periods

See: Eugene L. Grant and W. Grant Ireson, *Principles of Engineering Economy* (New York: The Ronald Press Company, 1964), p. 43 and p. 550.

3. Average estimate based on rehabilitated units in the Northeast. See George Sternlieb, James W. Hughes, and Lawrence Burrows, *Housing in Newark* (New Brunswick, New Jersey: Center for Urban Policy Research, Rutgers University, 1974), and Robert W. Burchell, James W. Hughes and George Sternlieb, *Housing Costs and Housing Restraints: The Realities of Inner City Housing Costs* (New York: Life Insurance Association of America, 1970).
Other estimates of occupancy costs are presented in George Sternlieb, *The Urban Housing Dilemma: The Dynamics of New York City's Rent Controlled Housing* (New York: Housing and Development Administration, 1972), George Sternlieb, *The Tenement Landlord* (New Brunswick, New Jersey: Rutgers University Press, 1969), and David Listokin, *The Dynamics of Housing Rehabilitation: Macro and Micro Analyses* (New Brunswick, New Jersey: Center for Urban Policy Research, 1973).

city obviously does not pay property taxes to itself, the homesteader is absolved from his first two years of taxation on the structure, reducing initial costs significantly. The impact of this is considerable in relation to other abatement programs. (See Exhibit 8-2, Chapter 8.) Baltimore's indirect abatement policy allows the owner to recover $975 of his loan monies when compared with the full assessment figure for the parcel analyzed in Exhibit 4-2. This is almost $400 less than the Philadelphia program.

The second form of tax consideration arises in the operational procedures of tax reassessment. Improved properties have been reassessed in relation to the value of the surrounding properties rather than on the straight determination on the value of the improvements. This means in practice, that a unit assessed at $4,000 which has $16,000 of improvements in a neighborhood comprising homes assessed at $6-$8,000 would be reassessed closer to the $6-$8,000 average rather than the supposed $20,000 new value of the unit if reassessment were to be based solely on the value of improvements. This seems to be an equitable method of approaching this difficult problem and may well be a fair indicator of resale value. The increase in value must be reflected in the assessment if the property tax is to have any basis in reality—this method achieves this objective. It is also necessary to insure that an increase in assessment is not so severe that it serves as a deterrent to other neighborhood property owners who want to improve their structures but fear drastically higher taxes—this objective is also served, striking a balanced policy which is a combination of two seemingly contradictory political necessities.

SPECIAL FINANCIAL ASSISTANCE

Baltimore has a well defined and smooth functioning system for supplying the necessary financial backing to the homesteader. Under the provisions of the aforementioned Residential Environmental Assistance Loan Program (REAL), established in 1972 to provide loans to persons rehabilitating parcels ineligible for "312" financing, the homesteaders have access to a substantial pool of low cost capital. From an initial $2,000,000 bond issue, since increased to $3,000,000, a sizeable loan fund has been established with a mandate to grant loans at 6 percent for 20 years in amounts up to $17,400. After a homesteader has been selected, a detailed breakdown of costs provided, and bids received, negotiations commence with the loan officers for financing.

The typical loan to date has ranged between $10,000 and $12,000, with substantial spread around those figures occasioned by the degree of property deterioration and homesteader aspiration. Similar to Philadelphia and Wilmington procedures, an escrow account is established for each homesteader, with all bills for completed work presented to the account officer for evaluation before payment. The REAL officer inspects the parcel to see both if the work meets necessary code standards and is in agreement with the bill presented. Based upon an affirmative finding in both instances, the contractor is paid. For needed start-up monies, the loan program usually authorizes a draw in cash to the homesteader. This can cover the cost of "do-it-yourself" materials and preliminary work done before the hiring of contractors is necessary.

The impact of the REAL loan program on the costs incurred by the homesteader is very significant. By allowing a homesteader to borrow, say, $12,000 at 6 percent for twenty years, the annual payments are $1,046.16. This is approximately $2,300 less for annual payments for the first five years when compared to a conventional home improvement loan of 12 percent for five years (See Exhibit 4-3). Baltimore was fortunate in having this program already established when homesteading was begun. It has allowed the city to effectively lower the burden of the first few years of homesteading substantially, serving as a demonstration of the commitment Baltimore is making toward rehabilitation and revitalization of the inner city—a psychological "shot-in-the-arm" of no little import.

Exhibit 4-3 also provides another way of conceptualizing the difference between the REAL Loan Program and conventional financing. Given the different interest rates and particularly the difference between the lengths of the payback period (five versus twenty years), direct comparisons of annual costs may not be sufficient in themselves. The problem becomes sticky since the current value of future disbursements over time becomes less, given an inflation rate. For example, if we have a rate of inflation of 5 percent, $105 one year from now is equivalent to only $100 today. Given this fact of life, we must convert total future annual payments to present value or worth in order to make a *direct* comparison of the full cost implications of each program. Such total cost differences in current dollars are presented in Exhibit 4-3.

Assuming an inflation rate of 8 percent, the present value of five years of $3,298.92 annual payments amounts to *$13,292.38*. What this means is that $13,292.38 at an interest rate of 8 percent per annum will be sufficient to support five future annual disbusements of $3,328.92, leaving nothing remaining. In contrast, the REAL Loan Program requires a present amount of *$10,271.20* at 8 percent per annum to support 20 years of $1,046.16 annual payments. In the long term, then, the special financing produces a saving of *$3,000* if defined in terms of present worth.

COST-REVENUE REALITIES

Baltimore finds itself heavily subsidizing the homesteader during the first five years in terms of the relationship between services received and revenues collected. The cost-revenue calculation detailed in Exhibit 4-4 shows that during the first five years Baltimore can expect an average deficit of $1148.59 per unit. (See Appendix B for cost-revenue methodology.) The magnitude of this single unit deficit will mushroom if a significant number of units are so homesteaded. A change in this picture could come during the second five year period if the buildings are assessed closer to their worth in terms of improvements and general condition. If their assessments double, cost-revenue parity would still not be

EXHIBIT 4-3
COST SAVINGS OCCASIONED BY REAL LOAN PROGRAM

Conventional Financing

$12,000 @ 12% - 5 years

$$R = P \frac{i(1+i)^n}{(1+i)-1} = \$12,000 \frac{.12(1+.12)^5}{(1+.12)^5 - 1} = \$12,000(.27741)$$

R = $3,328.92 for five annual payments

REAL Loan Program

$12,000 @ 6% - 20 years

$$R = P \frac{i(1+i)^n}{(1+i)^n - 1} = \$12,000 \frac{.06(1+.06)^{20}}{(1+.06)^{20} - 1} = \$12,000(.08718)$$

R = $1,046.16 for twenty annual payments

Program Differences

$3,328.92 - $1,046.16 = $2,282.76 annually, for first five years

Total Cost Differences in Current Dollars (Assuming an Inflation Rate of 8%)
Conventional Financing

$$P = R \frac{(1+i)^n - 1}{i(1+i)^n} = \$3,328.92 \frac{(1+.08)^5 - 1}{.08(1+.08)^5} = \$3,328.92(3.993) = \$13,292.38$$

REAL Loan Program

$$P = R \frac{(1+i)^n - 1}{i(1+i)^n} = \$1,046.16 \frac{(1+.08)^{20} - 1}{.08(1+.08)^{20}} = \$1,046.16(9.818) = \$10,271.20$$

Note: This last calculation deflates future annual payments to present value assuming an inflation rate of 8 percent. By employing a present worth factor (above formula), we are estimating the present value of total future annual disbursements. The reason for REAL's low present value is due to the interest rate being significantly lower than the inflation rate. In other words, given $10,271 today at 8 percent, 20 years of $1,046 annual payments can be made.

See Eugene L. Grant and W. Grant Ireson, *Principles of Engineering Economy* (New York: The Ronald Press, 1964) for details of computational formulas. In the above, R = annual payment, P = present sum of money, i = interest rate, and n = the number of annual interest periods. See also Exhibit 4-2.

achieved. Yet, at what cost? With the income sufficiency level close to $11,000 already, it seems illogical to raise it further by increasing tax assessments. Yet other city residents pay their full share of costs. A dilemma emerges which will not go away given the inadequate status of the municipal fiscal base.

SPECIAL SERVICES

Baltimore has a variety of services available to the homesteader both inside and outside of the formal program.

To assist him in unit rehabilitation, a list of contractors is available as well as instructions detailing the steps involved in an effective reconstruction process. The Division of Planning has prepared a pamphlet entitled *Design Guide: Exterior Residential Rehabilitation* to aid the homesteader in refurbishing the exterior structure in a manner faithful to the buildings' design and neighborhood aesthetics.[15]

The City of Baltimore has already undertaken a massive upgrading of essential city services in the neighborhoods undergoing intense rehabilitation. These areas encompass many of the homestead sites.

The above programs aim primarily at the unit and its environs. The homesteading office, through the Homeownership Division, also offers a homeownership counseling service targeted to assist the participating household. With their reasonably moderate incomes, most homesteaders have not required a substantial amount of assistance after they have obtained their parcel. This situation would change if the program began to take in lower income persons unfamiliar with the requirements of homeownership.

SUMMARY

Baltimore may well turn out to be the success story of urban homesteading. A unique institutional configuration—whereby the program is formally linked to other indispensible functions related to housing; an advanced indicator system guaging the flows from the abandonment pipeline; innovative fast-take procedures; an established $2,000,000 housing loan fund—which has since been increased to $3,000,000—financed through the sale of city tax-supported bond issues; an initial success pattern which has led Baltimore to implement the first "wholesale homesteading" of an entire block, attempting through sheer critical mass to revitalize a whole neighborhood; and substantial tax abatement procedures and special services, all appear to optimize the state of the art. Additionally, the internalization of the loan program minimizes the problems with title encumberances which would occur with outside private financing. Close scrutiny of this effort in the future may very well reveal the ultimate workability of the homestead concept in urban America.

EXHIBIT 4-4

COST–REVENUE IMPACT OF HOMESTEADING IN BALTIMORE
(See Appendix B for Cost-Revenue Methodology)

General Parameters

Total Assessed Valuation	$3,034,500,000
Total Population	864,610
Total School Enrollment	182,911
Tax Rate Per $100 Assessed Valuation	
City	2.59
School	3.50
Total	6.09
Assessed Valuation/Pupil	$16,590.04
School Property Tax Levied/Pupil	$580.65[1]
Assessed Valuation/Person	$3,509.67
Municipal Property Tax Levied/Person	$90.90

Property Tax Revenues

Assessed Valuation of Homestead	$5,000.00
Assessed Value of Improvements[2]	3,000.00
Total Assessed Valuation of Rehabilitated Unit	$8,000.00

Property Tax Revenue = Assessed Valuation/Dwelling x Assessed
Property Tax Rate

Revenue = $8,000(.0609) = ($487.20) or $292.32[3]

Property Tax Costs

Educational Costs = Public School Children/Dwelling Unit x School
Property Taxes Levied/Pupil
= (1.871) ($580.65) = $1,086.40[4]

Municipal Costs = Persons/Dwelling Unit x Municipal Property Tax
Levied/Capita
= (3.90) ($90.90) = $354.51[4]

Total Costs = $1,440.91

Revenue Deficit Per Unit: $1,148.59

---

1. This represents 37 percent of the total expenditure per pupil, the remainder
of which is raised through other forms of taxation as well as state and federal
aid.

EXHIBIT 4-4 (Cont'd.)

COST-REVENUE IMPACT OF HOMESTEADING IN BALTIMORE
(See Appendix B for Cost-Revenue Methodology)

2. The assessed value of the improvements is substantially less than their market value because reassessments have been made relative to surrounding property values. (See sub-section on special assessments.)

3. This second figure ($292.32) is the average payment over the first five years including the approximately $ 0 assessment which occurs while the city holds title to the parcel during the first two years and only the land is assessed.

4. We are assuming a three bedroom unit, using the parameters presented in Appendix B.

NOTES

1. *The Settler*, monthly publication by the Department of Housing and Community Development Home Ownership Development Division, Baltimore, Maryland, July/August 1974, p. 6.

2. U.S. Bureau of the Census, *Census of Population and Housing: 1970 Census Tracts, Final Report PHC (1)-191 Baltimore, Md. SMSA.*

3. Interview with Program Official, Home Ownership Development Division, Baltimore, Maryland, March 6, 1975.

4. *Ibid.*

5. The REAL Program—Residential Environmental Assistance Loans—enables a home owner to borrow up to $17,400 per dwelling unit from the city at 6 percent interest over 20 years for the purpose of improving his residence. The city provides a detailed rehabilitation estimate and seeks bids from three contractors, awarding the work to the lowest bidder. Factors taken into account in establishing loan priorities include vacancy status, future owner or rental occupancy, the financial capacity of the occupant, and its location relative to federally assisted areas, such as urban renewal and code enforcement areas.

6. Interview with Program Official, Vacancy Monitoring Division, Department of Housing and Community Development, Baltimore, Maryland, August 1, 1974.

7. Maryland Statutes, Article 81 § 100.

8. Interview with Program Official, Home Ownership Development Program, March 6, 1975.

9. *Ibid.*

10. In each of the case studies used in this volume, informal surveys of the sites in progress were made or compiled by the Center for Urban Policy Research. These open-ended interviews were undertaken to obtain a better feeling of operational realities and to substantiate the opinions of the program administrators. For reasons of confidentiality they have been given a numerical code.

11. Paul C. Bropky, *Urban Homesteading: Prospects for the Pittsburgh Area* (Pittsburgh: ACTION-Housing, Inc. 1974), p. 10.

12. Jerome G. Rose, *The Legal Advisor of Home Ownership* (Boston: Little, Brown and Company, 1964), p. 8.

13. U.S. Internal Revenue Service Form 1040. (Washington, D.C., 1975).

14. "Urban Homesteading Awardees Socio-Economic Data," mimeograph (Baltimore, Maryland: Home Ownership Development Program, November 1, 1974).

15. The Home Ownership Development Division has also prepared a guide, entitled *Home Rehabilitation: How to Start It, How to Finish It, How to Manage It,* which outlines the pitfalls of the process.

EXHIBIT 4-5

CAPSULATED DESCRIPTION
BALTIMORE HOMESTEAD PROGRAM

THE CONTEXT: Baltimore's 1970 population of just over 900,000 is approximately 5 percent below its 1960 level. There are 5,004 abandoned structures in the city representing less than 1 percent of the total housing stock. Since its peak in the 1950s, the city has undergone a decline in center city activity, a development generally afflicting this nation's urban centers. Home-ownership in Baltimore declined from 54.3 percent to 44.5 percent in the last intercensal decade. The city government has adopted many innovative programs trying to abate extant trends; some, like homesteading, are more successful than others.

PROGRAM
INITIATION: An outgrowth of the previously established Home-ownership Development Division, which was devised to secure financing and provide general assistance for persons desirous of rehabilitating city residences. This program had the legislated task of finding suitable owners for city owned properties for which it bears full responsibility. The homestead program was initiated under this agency's purview.

PROGRAM
OBJECTIVES: 1. To return to the housing supply system as many vacant buildings as possible.
2. To encourage people to move back into the city.
3. To turn tax delinquent properties into tax paying properties.
4. To increase homeownership in the city.

ADMINISTRATIVE
FRAMEWORK: An umbrella agency, the Department of Housing and Community Development, comprises all city functions related to housing. Homesteading is an activity of the Homeownership Development Division, one of the main sub-agencies of the DHCD. There is no formal policy board, perhaps a consequence of the close ties the homesteading office has with all other housing functions and their support systems. The operational staff comprises eight people, divided among three programmatic functions: (1) promotion,

EXHIBIT 4-5

CAPSULATED DESCRIPTION
BALTIMORE HOMESTEAD PROGRAM (Cont'd.)

---

selection, post-lease; (2) construction; and (3) work writups—specifications, financing, and progress monitoring.

OTHER PROGRAM
PARTICIPANTS:
All program participants are located within the Department of Housing and Community Development.

PROGRAM
STRUCTURE:

Parcel Acquisition:

1. Surplus properties (Nonutilized City Condemnations originally acquired for other construction purposes).

2. Fast-take procedures of abandoned units identified through Vacant Housing Monitoring System.

3. HUD foreclosures.

Homestead Evaluation:

The vacant property management system is the basic monitoring device to isolate suitable units and to evaluate neighborhood conditions. The selection of specific parcels to be homesteaded depends on staff evaluation of management system reports and applicant interest. Field evaluations of the best of these units provides detailed cost estimates and a current environmental evaluation.

Homesteader
Evaluation:

Fixed minimum criteria. (See text.)

EXHIBIT 4-5

CAPSULATED DESCRIPTION
BALTIMORE HOMESTEAD PROGRAM (Cont'd.)

PROGRAM *STRUCTURE:* *(Cont'd.)*	*Financial* *Assistance:*	Residential Environmental Assistance Loan Program (REAL), fueled by a $3,000,000 city bond issue, provides a substantial pool of rehabilitation capital. This housing loan fund provides loans at 6 percent for 20 years in amounts up to $17,400.
	Special Tax *Considerations:*	With the city providing financing, the homesteader is a leasee rather than owner the first two years in order to avoid the problem of encumbered titles. Thus no property tax payments are made during this period. Upon granting of title, the property is reassessed to value of surrounding parcels rather than on improvement value.
	Special Services:	Rehabilitation counseling to educate the homesteader to the role of general contractor. Homeownership counseling and general improvement of adjacent city services are strongly emphasized.
COST REVENUE *IMPACT:*		A modular homestead, assessed at $8,000, will generate a cost revenue deficit exceeding $1,100.
PROGRAM OUTPUT:		136 units homesteaded to date.

Chapter 5

Wilmington: The Original Homesteaders

I *don't think many people applied for this house. But me, I liked it. It's just the right size for my grandson and me. It's a very small house—but that makes it very easy to fix up so beautiful, as you can see.*[1]

Annie May Barksdale is proud of her home. The City of Wilmington, Delaware, is proud of her home and of Annie Mae Barksdale. The reason for this mutual admiration is that Ms. Barksdale is Wilmington's first urban homesteader.

From this drab little industrial town has come the first operational example of the homesteading of vacant abandoned housing. Though long overshadowed by Philadelphia, Wilmington does not lack its fair share of the problems which plague the major urban centers of America. Unabated suburbanization of people and jobs, a declining central business district, increased crime and the subsequent deterioration of all aspects of city life have struck hard in Wilmington. Never a great metropolis, its former image had declined markedly in the middle third of the 20th century.

THE SETTING

WILMINGTON *(alt. 225; pop. 110,356), only town of more than 7,000 population in Delaware, contains within the immediate suburban area more than half the State's 318,085 inhabitants. It is situated on the west bank of the Delaware River, and occupies a series of low, rolling hills overlooking the river at its broadest point, and a strip of low land, much of it formerly marshes, a mile to two miles in width between the river and the hills. From "The Rocks," landing place of the Swedes, first permanent settlers, the city extends fanlike between two streams—the Christina River and Brandywine Creek—and beyond these streams north into wooded highlands and south into undulating lowlands. From the lowlands, the slopes of the main central area of the city rise terrace-like to a crest crowned by several high office buildings observable for miles in all directions.*

The main city crowds densely about tiny, open Rodney Square near the tall buildings that mark its business center. A few blocks away at Brandywine Creek Bridge is the entrance to the one parkway that penetrates the solidly built-up central city. Other parked open spaces are at long distances from the center and the large area of parks lies chiefly on or beyond the city boundaries.

Motor traffic converging through all sections of the city into the narrow streets of the business section intensifies the effect of congestion created by the solidly built-up blocks, though vistas through the straight streets, to the river, the creeks, and the hills, serve somewhat as relief to pedestrian and driver as they await their turns at the crossings.

The people of Wilmington are still chiefly native Delawareans of an admixture of the early Swedish, Finnish, and Dutch strains and of the earliest Quaker and non-Quaker English, with a goodly infusion of French, Irish, and Scotch, especially since the middle of the eighteenth century. But native Americans from other States form a large and rapidly increasing part of the population. Italians and Poles are substantial groups having their own communities since the days of industrial growth following the Civil War. Ukrainians, also, though a much smaller group, have kept together in a neighborhood where they maintain their Old World culture. Germans, Russian and German Jews, Scandinavians, Greeks, and a few Asiatics form minority groups.

The Negroes, present from the earliest settlement, form slightly more than 15 percent of the population and are employed in industry and in service occupations and to a limited extent have entered the professions. They live in communities of generally bad housing at high rents, with a few better sections, and suffer from the lack of parks, playgrounds, and other recreation facilities. Despite disadvantages the Negroes in Wilmington play their part in the local life with interest and good humor.

> *Wilmington in the Late 1930's. Federal Writers Project,* Delaware: A Guide to the First State *(New York: Hastings House, 1938) pp. 259-263.*

With   the   obvious   advantage   of   "20-20   hindsight   vision,"   the prognostication of Wilmington's eventual demise should not have been difficult from the city's 1930s description. Heavy suburbanization, white ethnics poised to leave the city, growing concentrations of blacks, and intense traffic congestion all have taken their toll.

Yet, Wilmington still is the home of the chemical giants, as it has been since E.I. duPont settled on the banks of Brandywine Creek over 170 years ago. Dupont, Hercules Inc. and International Chemical Industries have kept their headquarters within Wilmington, heartened by an improved downtown, complete with a new mall and widened streets. However, rarely do the headquarters personnel reside in the city; their daily trek to and from the suburbs mirrors the dominant lifestyle of suburban America. At the same time, the outlook of the graying neighborhoods surrounding the downtown area continues to pale.

The suburban flight has lowered the population from 110,000 in 1950, to just over 80,000 in 1970, a decline of almost 30 percent. At the same time, the increase in Wilmington's black population brings it to the verge of becoming a majority (Exhibit 5-1). Perhaps more significantly, at least 85 percent of the city's public school children are black, a realistic portent of Wilmington's future racial mix.

Of the city's basic housing resources—29,959 units—72 percent were built prior to 1939.[2] Forty-five percent of the privately owned housing stock is below code level. Two thousand homes in the city are abandoned.[3] Yet the city's small scale—predominantly small residential structures—sets the stage for an individualistic approach for combatting abandonment.

Enter Mayor Thomas Maloney. During his mayoralty campaign he proposed that Wilmington become the first city in the nation to implement a homesteading program and from that concept gained considerable support. Soon after his election the necessary administrative machinery to operationalize the concept was established and on August 24, 1973 the first ten homesteads were designated. Since then another 18 have been awarded.

INSTITUTIONAL FRAMEWORK

The first homesteading program in the nation got its official start on May 18, 1973. On that date Mayor Thomas Maloney signed ordinance 73-047, obtaining the basic statutory authority to establish the organizational framework for carrying out the concept.

Under that ordinance, the chief responsibility for administering the homesteading program rests with a Homesteading Board.[4] No specifics are given in the ordinance as to who should sit on the board or what their terms of office should be.[5] In practice the board has been manned entirely by city officials. Presently its members are: Director of Planning, Commissioner of Licenses and Inspections, Deputy Commissioner of Public Works, Assistant City Solicitor, and the Mayor's Public Policy Adviser.[6] Each board member is assigned several of the homesteaders and acts in a "big brother" capacity overviewing the entire

EXHIBIT 5-1
WILMINGTON: A STATISTICAL PROFILE

Total Population		*1950*	*1960*	*1970*
Delaware		318,085	446,292	548,104
Wilmington		110,356	95,827	80,386

Black Population
1960	25,075
1970	35,072

Median Age (Total)		*Median Age (Black)*	
1960	34.0	1960	26.2
1970	32.3	1970	21.4

Household Size (Total)		*Household Size (Black)*	
1960	2.6	1960	3.0
1970	2.6	1970	3.5

Median Family Income (Total)		*Median Family Income (Black)*	
1960	$4,442	1960	$6,103
1970	$3,072	1970	$4,903

Median Education (Total)		*Median Education (Black)*	
1960	10.2	1960	8.9
1970	10.9	1970	10.2

Median House Value (Total)		*Median House Value (Black)*	
1960	$10,400	1960	$7,900
1970	$11,000	1970	$10,100

Housing Units
1970 Total	29,959
Built before 1939	71%
Built before 1949	82%

Units in Structure
Structure Type	Number of Units	
1 unit	20,120	(68%)
2 - 4 units	5,021	(16%)
5 or more units	4,818	(16%)

Source: U.S. Bureau of the Census, *Census of Population and Housing: 1970, Census Tracts, Final Report PHC (1)-234 Wilmington, Del.–N.J. – MD. SMSA.*

process and insuring quick accessibility to top city officials.[7] This approach also keeps the city policy-makers intimately aware of the promises and the problems of homesteading.

The board, acting as the chief policy-making body for the program, is responsible for making the final homesteader selection after evaluating the informational base provided by its staff.

The latter, working under the aegis of the city's Urban Renewal Office, handles much of the day-to-day work of the program. Its chief administrative officer is the Homesteading Program Director who directs a staff of two, a rehabilitation specialist and a financial officer. Because of the relatively small size of the city and its homesteading program, the staff splits its time between homesteading and various urban renewal responsibilities.

Because of the program's small scale, the city can hypothetically develop and administer it on a less structurally rigid basis than larger communities. This permits a more personal program, but it also does not allow the depth of supportive services found in larger cities.

PARCEL ACQUISITION

Of a total of 2,000 abandoned units only 150 are controlled by the city. Title to these units was obtained primarily through tax sale proceedings which allow the city to obtain title through foreclosure on parcels delinquent in taxes. The average transitional period from the time of delinquency until the unit is obtained by the city under tax sale proceedings is 13 months. This has been shortened in some cases to six months and on abandoned or deteriorated properties the period can be as short as 60 days.[8] Another important source of potential homesteads is the U.S. Department of Housing and Urban Development which holds title to 322 abandoned units in the city obtained through mortgage foreclosures.[9] Under the provision of the New Communities Act of 1974, the Department of Housing and Urban Development has awarded the city 47 of the homes in its possession for the purposes of homesteading.

Of the remaining 1,500 abandoned units, a careful appraisal of their worth would show many are unsuitable for homesteading. Many are so badly deteriorated that rehabilitation is probably as expensive as replacement. Others are located in areas of such widespread abandonment that their use as homesteads would not appear feasible.

EVALUATING THE HOMESTEAD

The task of wisely selecting suitable units for homesteading is a formidable one. Of the 150 units controlled by the city only 50 exceed marginal potential. This determination rests on two key criteria:

1. *The units are evaluated in terms of the adequacy of their structural characteristics.* A member of the Department of Licenses and Inspections surveys the property in terms of code violations and structural soundness,

drawing up a detailed list of all deficiencies. In conjunction with the homesteading rehabilitation specialist, cost estimates are prepared for the work necessary to bring the unit up to code. The homesteading staff then evaluates the results to see if they come within the pre-set guidelines, normally not to exceed $10,000. Homestead rehabilitation estimates have exceeded this ceiling on several occasions, but if the staff believes the homesteader's financial capacity is sufficient, precedents for exceptions have been established.

   2. *If the unit is deemed suitable it is then evaluated in terms of its neighborhood environment.* If it is in the vicinity of a large number of abandoned buildings, the level of neighborhood decline is gauged to see if isolated homestead units would be able to stand on their own. Thus suitable buildings are not homesteaded in severely deteriorated neighborhoods.

   The application of this evaluative framework carefully avoids putting homesteaders into parcels which are undesirable from either a structural or environmental perspective. Early homestead selections were not evaluated within this framework and the present program administration feels many of the early homesteads would not have been chosen because of severe neighborhood deterioration.[10]

EVALUATING THE HOMESTEADER

   In outlining the selection process for homesteaders, it is first necessary to examine the program's objectives since the selection criteria are predicated on their fulfillment. Wilmington's stated homestead objectives are:

1.   To turn abandoned and untaxable properties into maintained and taxable properties.

2.   To provide for increased homeownership.

3.   To retard urban decay by giving responsible people a stake in their neighborhood.[11]

4.   To foster migration back to the city from the suburbs.

   Mayor Maloney summed up the attitude of the city most succinctly when he said: "We are not trying to provide housing for people. We are trying to provide people for housing."[12]

   Experience has shown that homesteading does not widely serve low-income residents. Of the 28 homesteads awarded, only 22 are active today. Those dropping out of the program have cited the increased burdens of homeownership and the massive work load involved in bringing the unit up to building code standards as the rationale for their unwillingness to continue with the program.[13] The present high costs of homeownership, increasing as a result of spiraling fuel and utility costs, is another factor preventing many families with marginal incomes from becoming successful homesteaders. One widely disseminated success story in Wilmington bears out the economic strictures.

> *Homestead Observation Number 11 is a young E. I. Dupont Lawyer. Exasperated with a daily round trip commute of 70 miles, the lawyer and his wife, a teacher, began homesteading in late 1973. $17,000 and a lot of sweat converted a boarded up eyesore into a spacious residence only four blocks from his office. The utility system work was contracted out to professionals, but demolition, refinishing, and redecorating were handled enthusiastically by the couple. Households with this level of financial wherewithal, knowledgeability about rehabilitation, and resourcefulness, all in one package are not in abundant supply.*

Additionally, the attitudes of the dropouts are illuminating.

> *Homesteader Observation Number 12, a mid-fifties homestead recipient, gave his house back to the city. The strain of borrowing $7,000 to make the parcel habitable, induced by fear of never getting his money back due to declining neighborhood conditions, was too much. Add in the hesitancy that heavy work would lead to health problems, and if unable to make bank payments, the house would be lost anyway. So the experiment was terminated.*

These realities have set the program on a particular course which affects the selection criteria used for finding suitable homesteaders.

Minimum Requirements

An applicant must be 18 years of age and a family head; a United States citizen; have proven financial resources; the ability to rehabilitate a dwelling; willingness to bring the parcel up to code standards in 18 months after the date of the closing; and willingness to live in it for three years.[14]

The ideal homesteader has been described as one who meets income flow requirements, is a good risk for financial institutions, and/or has substantial craftsman ability. While few applicants rate highly on all three criteria, many satisfy at least two.[15]

The city has compiled a statistical profile of current homesteaders. The average rehabilitation costs total $6,900, while the average participant income approaches $9,300, with an average of four persons per household. Of the initial homesteading families fifteen have been black, five white, and one Hispanic.[16] The city gained considerable publicity mileage out of one of the latter entires into the homestead sweepstakes.

> *Homestead Observation 17 is a black refugee from New York, a*

*college graduate, and a successful stock broker who is homesteading
a parcel in the Harlem Park section of Wilmington. "The benefits of
city living are significant; it offers a variety of contacts, I get up later
in the morning, and I take advantage of downtown activities with
my family."*

No effort is made to place homesteaders according to the racial profile of
the recipient area; however applicants from the immediate neighborhood would
be given preference if they wanted a homestead in their area.

Overall, the first group of homesteaders was as diverse as their early
western counterparts.

Selection Process

Periodically as the supply of homesteads builds up, advertisements are
placed in the Wilmington newspapers. Persons interested in a particular parcel
are instructed to contact the Department of Urban Renewal, under whose roof
the homesteading program operates, for an application form. The applicant
returns the completed form to the homesteading office. Either before or after
the applicant completes the form, an inspection of the parcel is arranged by the
homesteading staff, providing the applicant with a realistic evaluation of the
property. Upon receipt of the completed application, the applicant is granted a
formal interview.

After all applications submitted before the deadline have been received,
they are evaluated by the Homesteading Board, which makes the final
homestead allocations. If more than one applicant is qualified for a particular
parcel, the homesteader is chosen by lot in a public drawing. Since such a
process would necessarily penalize equally qualified applicants, applications of
those not receiving homesteads are filed and actively urged to reapply should
any other property interest them.

Income Sufficiency

Perhaps the prime criterion in selecting a homesteader centers on the
question of who can afford to live in the parcels. Wilmington does not have a
"hard" minimum income threshold. Yet, it is obvious that some guidelines are
applied to determine whether a person could afford a homestead. These
approximations are based on the staff's past experience with public
rehabilitation efforts. Little empirical work has been done in estimating how
much a prospective homestead would cost per year and, from these estimates,
the income necessary to support such annual required disbursements.

To evaluate housing cash flow requirements, an approach for ascertaining
minimum income thresholds necessary to maintain a parcel can be illustrated.
This methodology has been applied to the Baltimore case study previously
examined and provides a rigorous basis for determining income sufficiency

utilizing standard income-cost ratios.

Examining Wilmington's first homesteaders, the average annual expenses facing the homesteader were estimated. (See Exhibit 5-2.) These figures reflect both the present housing stock in Wilmington, which is largely composed of small two- and three-bedroom rowhouses of modest value, and previous experiences in the northeastern United States. It should be noted that the units sampled required only minimal rehabilitation ($6,000-$10,000) with higher reconstruction costs obviously increasing the financial burden to the homesteader, further raising the minimum base income.

Recently rehabilitation costs have been running as high as $17,000.[17] As a result, homesteaders are putting money into the units far in excess of their assessed valuation, making a sufficient return on their investment very doubtful. This problem poses a potential danger to the homesteaders who see their homes as an investment in a growing financial asset.

Based on the analysis presented in Exhibit 5-2, the total annual operating costs approach $1,966. Using the "25 percent of income rule" as a guide to income sufficiency,[18] the minimum after tax income necessary to financially carry the homestead would be $7,818. Based on Internal Revenue Tax Tables, assuming a standard deduction and four exemptions, before tax income would be approximately $8,400.[19] This final income figure is particularly low since Wilmington's prolonged low assessment period lowers property taxes from $451.71 to $60.00 annually. (Other programs in other cities have a substantially higher tax burden because of their less generous assessment policies. See Exhibit 8-2.) By applying the technique emphasized in Exhibit 5-2 to other individual units, a clear measurement of the income sufficiency for that parcel can be derived. Such an approach should assist in matching homesteader to homestead by correlating operating costs to the distinct ability to pay.

SPECIAL FINANCIAL ASSISTANCE

One of the most important efforts any city can make to ease the transition into the new homestead, especially for persons who are lacking a history of homeownership, is the provision of some special financial assistance. While it has been suggested that provision of a free dwelling unit should be sufficient incentive to attract homesteaders, this argument fails to appreciate the critical role financing plays in the success or failure of the overall endeavor. More importantly such an attitude fails to grasp the fact that the lack of sufficient financing may have precipitated the initial abandonment of the parcel.

Several approaches are available for dealing with this problem. Wilmington has had to work within severe constraints. The fact that its early homesteaders found difficulty in securing adequate financing at low cost on their own led to the development of a new mechanism to provide the needed capital without employing city funds directly. The latter, in fact, was forbidden under Delaware constitutional strictures; public funds cannot be used by municipalities to improve private property.[20]

EXHIBIT 5-2

TYPICAL ANNUAL COSTS INCURRED BY WILMINGTON HOMESTEADERS

Expense	Cost
Taxes[1]	$ 60.00
Loan Payment[2]	907.00
Utilities & Fuel[3]	540.00
Insurance[3]	40.00
Miscellaneous[3]	419.00
TOTAL	$1,966.00

1. This is the tax paid on an initial assessment of $12,120 from which 150% of the total cost of rehabilitation, assumed at $7,000, is subtracted. Thus property taxes = .03727 ($12,120 - 10,500) = $60.00.

2. This is the annual cost of a $7,000 loan at 9.75 percent for 15 years, the average loan issued through early 1975. The annual cost was determined as follows:

$$R = p\,\frac{i(1+1)^n}{(1+i)^n - 1} = \$7,000\,\frac{.0975(1+.0975)^{15}}{(1+.0975)^{15} - 1} = \$7,000(.12964)$$

$$R = \$907.00$$

where i represents an interest rate per interest period

n represents a number of interest periods

P represents a present sum of money (total mortgage)

R represents the end-of-period payment in a uniform series continuing for the coming n periods

See: Eugene L. Grant and W. Grant Ireson, *Principles of Engineering Economy* (New York: The Ronald Press Company, 1964), p. 43 and p. 553.

3. Average estimate based on rehabilitated units in the Northeast. See: George Sternlieb, James W. Hughes, and Lawrence Burrows, *Housing in Newark*, mimeograph (New Brunswick, New Jersey: Center for Urban Policy Research, Rutgers University, 1974) and Robert W. Burchell, James W. Hughes and George Sternlieb, *Housing Costs and Housing Restraints: The Realities of Inner City Housing Costs* (New York: Life Insurance Association of America, 1970).

Other estimates of occupancy costs are presented in George Sternlieb, *The Urban Housing Dilemma: The Dynamics of New York City's Rent Controlled Housing* (New York: Housing and Development Administration, 1972), George Sternlieb, *The Tenement Landlord* (New Brunswick, New Jersey: Rutgers University Press, 1969), and David Listokin, *The Dynamics of Housing Rehabilitation: Macro and Micro Analyses* (New Brunswick. New Jersey: Center for Urban Policy Research, 1973).

The city established a special agreement with a consortium of eight local financial institutions which allows a moderate reduction in homestead loan interest rate and assures the availability of a limited amount of capital to the homesteaders.[21] Under this program each participating institution agreed to carry up to three mortage loans per year with the loan assignments to occur on a rotating basis.

Each year one financial institution serves as the central agency, taking responsibility for the loan administration for that year. When a homesteader has been accepted by the homestead board, a loan application is submitted to this agency and is then reviewed by all eight participants, six of which must approve it. Having been approved, the loan is assigned to one institution which handles all remaining contact between the lending agency and the homesteader. The current agreement calls for each participant to accept no more than three loans annually and to limit each loan to no more than $10,000. However, these amounts are negotiable in any transaction if the particulars of the situation so merit.[22]

While the general attitude of the city's lending institutions was skepticism toward the homesteading program, vigorous lobbying by the city administration was able to secure their commitment. Since that time they have become increasingly supportive of the program as the positive results accruing from it have been evident.

Two chief problems arose in enacting this special loan system. Initially the lenders were unwilling to commit themselves without some form of guarantee. Should there be a loan default on properties of negligible value, the participating insitution insisted on a guarantee from the city. This requirement was satisfied by the city's pledge to cover 40 percent of any loan which went into default. Initially the money necessary to cover this loan percentage was received in the form of a grant from the Sachem Fund (a philanthropic institution) and from other city sources.[23] As the homesteader begins loan payback, the amount guaranteed by the city declines in direct proportion. So, once 40 percent of the loan has been paid back, the city no longer must commit any funds to cover potential default, thereby freeing money for other loans. This feature prevents the city from tying up vast sums of money in loan guarantees. Because of the close scrutiny given the early applicants a spokesman for one of the participating lenders expressed the belief that the default reserve could be lowered dramatically on the basis of experience to date.

Another problem arose since the financial lenders could not secure a first lien on the property should the homesteader default. The cause of this problem was the conditional deed arrangement, in which the title to the property remains in city hands. This deficiency was corrected by one of the homesteaders, an attorney with the Du Pont Corporation, who drafted a proposal subsequently adopted by the Wilmington City Council on May 5, 1974.[24] This granted the title to the homesteader at the time of the closing, permitting the lender to obtain a first lien position upon granting a homestead loan.

Also under current arrangements, the participating lending institutions have agreed to lower their interest rates on loans from about 12 percent to 9.75 percent, saving the homesteader more than two percentage points. The term of the loans is negotiable, but it can run as long as ten to fifteen years.

The lowered interest rate and longer repayment period has some beneficial impact on the cost incurred by the homesteader. (Exhibit 5-3.) Before adoption of this agreement the homesteader could expect an interest rate of 12 percent with a five- to seven-year term.[25] A $7,000 loan on these terms would result in an annual cost to the homesteader of $1,703 for a six-year term. With the introduction of the special loan program the interest rate dropped to 9.75 percent, and the term for mortgages over $6,500 was lengthened to 15 years reducing the annual payment on $7,000 to $907, but for 15 years. This has a considerable impact on total operating costs. Instead of the total annual costs equalling $2,743, they are lowered to $1,953. This also greatly affects the income level necessary to afford a homestead. Instead of after-tax income of $10,972 necessary (assuming housing costs are 25 percent of after-tax income) if higher financing were required, the lower interest rate and longer term have reduced the income sufficiency level to $7,818. However, if we convert the loans of various terms to net present worth, as was detailed in the Baltimore case example, we find little long-term savings occasioned by the 9 3/4 percent loan (Exhibit 5-3).

The complete dependence upon conventional lenders appears to place a straight jacket on the scope of Wilmington's homesteading efforts. The overall financial picture, when compared to Baltimore's, is, at best, less than triumphant. Not only are there a limited number of commitments, with interest rates approaching the extant conventional levels, but the ceiling on each may be unrealistic to the task at hand. The experience of one homesteader stresses the inadequacies.

> *Homestead Observation Number 3 was able to borrow $7,500 at 10.5 percent interest from one of the participating lenders. This enabled the engagement of two contractors to reconstruct the plumbing and heating systems, but that's all. The gloomy prospects for further financial assistance led the homesteader, a painter and contractor by trade, to devote full time to rehabiliate the balance of the structure, recently completing the replacement of all electrical wiring. In the interim, his wife, a secretary, has assumed the role of breadwinner. Substantial repairs are still in progress, which will consume considerable amounts of time and money.*

This example also reflects the dilemma engendered by the program's eligibility criteria. Even with substantial construction skills, outside contractors must be depended upon to rehabilitate the major utility systems. How much credit can thus be given to "sweat equity?" At the same time, those with substantial construction skills must fully employ them, due to the inadequacy of the scope of available financing. But to adequately utilize these skills, they may

EXHIBIT 5-3
COST SAVINGS OCCASIONED BY
WILMINGTON'S SPECIAL LOAN PROGRAM

Conventional Financing

$7,000 @ 12% - 6 years

$$R = P \frac{i(1+i)^n}{(1+i)^n - 1} = \$7,000 \frac{.12(1+.12)^6}{(1+.12)^6 - 1} = \$7,000 \,(.24323)$$

R = $1,703 for six annual payments

Special Loan Program

$7,000 @ 9 3/4% - 15 years

$$R = P \frac{i(1+i)^n}{(1+i)^n - 1} = \$7,000 \frac{.0975(1+.0975)^{15}}{(1+.0975)^{15} - 1} = \$7,000 \,(.12964)$$

R = $907 for 15 annual payments

Program Differences

$1,703 - $907 = $796 annually, for first five years

Total Cost Differences in Current Dollars (Assuming an Inflation Rate of 8%)

Conventional Financing

$$P = R \frac{(1+i)^n - 1}{i(1+i)^n} = \$1,703 \frac{(1+.08)^6 - 1}{.08(1+.08)^6} = \$1,703 \,(4.623) = \$7,873$$

Special Loan Program

$$P = R \frac{(1+i)^n - 1}{i(1+i)^n} = \$907 \frac{(1+.08)^{15} - 1}{.08(1+.08)^{15}} = \$907 \,(8.559) = \$7,763$$

Notes: This last calculation deflates future annual payments to present value assuming an inflation rate of 8 percent. By emphasizing a present worth factor (above formula) we are estimating the present value of total future annual dispersements. Using conventional financing, $7,873 today at 8 percent is sufficient to support six annual payments of $1,703. Employing the Special Loan Program, $7,763 today at 8 percent will support 15 annual payments of $907.

See Eugene L. Grant and W. Grant Ireson, *Principles of Engineering Economy* (New York: The Ronald Press, 1964) for details of computational formulas. In the above, R = annual payment, P = present sum of money, i = interest rate, and n = number of annual interest periods. See also Exhibit 5-2.

EXHIBIT 5-4

COST-REVENUE IMPACT OF HOMESTEADING IN WILMINGTON
(See Appendix B for Cost-Revenue Methodology)

General Parameters

Total Assessed Valuation	$397,875,820
Total Population	80,336
Total School Enrollment	14,688
Tax Rate Per $100 Assessed Valuation	
City	1.134
School	2.593
Total	3.727
Assessed Valuation/Pupil	$27,088.49
School Property Tax Levied/Pupil	$702.40[1]
Assessed Valuation/Person	$4,952.40
Municipal Property Tax Levied/Person	$56.16

Property Tax Revenues

Initial Assessed Valuation of Homestead	$12,120.00
Special Tax Abatement on Improvements	$10,500.00[2]
Total Assessed Valuation of Rehabilitated Unit	$1,620.00

Property Tax Revenue = Assessed Valuation/Dwelling x Assessed
            Tax Rate
        Revenue = $1,620 (.03727) = $60.38

Property Tax Costs

Educational Costs = Public School Children/Dwelling Unit x School
            Property Taxes Levied/Pupil
          = (1.871) ($702.78) = $1,314.90[3]

Municipal Costs = Persons/Dwelling Unit x Municipal
          Property Taxes Levied / Capita
          (3.90) ($56.16) = $219.02[3]

Total Costs   = $1,533.92

Revenue Deficit Per Unit: $1,473.54

---

1. The total expenditure per pupil is more than doubled by a grant of an
   additional $717.12 per pupil from the state under a complex aid program,
   bringing the educational expenditure per pupil to $1,424.52.

EXHIBIT 5-4

COST-REVENUE IMPACT OF HOMESTEADING IN WILMINGTON(Cont'd.)
(See Appendix B for Cost-Revenue Methodology)

2. Wilmington's special tax procedures allow the owner making residential improvements to deduct 1.5 times the improvements' value from his previous assessment. We are hypothesizing an improvement loan of $7,000.

3. We are assuming a three bedroom unit using the parameters presented in Appendix B.

have to exercise them full time, thereby interrupting the normal income flow. Other observations have revealed unique employment cycles occurring with the homesteader, after accumulating some minimal level of capital, quitting his job and investing the accrued resources into the parcel, devoting his time entirely to the renovation labors. When the money runs out, back to work he goes, starting the cycle again. And the approach appears to be working, adding credence to the claim of flexible eligibility criteria to insure such hearty individuals are not excluded. So a web of interrelated factors surrounds the seemingly straight-forward procedure of rehabilitation financing.

SPECIAL TAX CONSIDERATION

The City of Wilmington has adopted a procedure whereby persons making improvements in their homes actually have their assessments lowered.[26] (See Exhibit 8-2 for program comparisons.) This goes to the heart of the negative rehabilitation pressures inherent in most jurisdictions' taxing procedures.

This procedure operates by allowing the owner, for the first five years after an improvement is made, to deduct 150% of the value of that improvement from his previous assessment, thus lowering his original assessment and thereby, automatically, his taxes.[27] (See Exhibit 5-4 for an example of how this would affect the taxes on a homestead.) Thus owners are rewarded in the form of lower taxes for improving their property, rather than being punished as is the common practice in most cities. At the end of the five-year period the property is reassessed at its new market value, only then increasing the tax burden to the homesteader. In essence the homeowner is allowed to recoup the cost of a rehabilitation loan through a property tax deduction. In terms of the unit used in Exhibit 5-4 this would mean a savings of $2,000 in property taxes over the five year period.

COST REVENUE REALITIES

The earlier subsections have tended to focus on the impact of homesteading on the homesteader. But, what of the impact homesteading will have on the city's fiscal structure? Utilizing the same sample unit which appeared in the preceding subsection, a cost revenue analysis will be undertaken to estimate the economic impact of homesteading on Wilmington. (See Exhibit 5-4.) By obtaining basic population and tax program data from easily accessible public sources, the methodology and parameters developed by the Center for Urban Policy Research, Rutgers University for evaluation of the fiscal impact of development can be used. (See Appendix B for a description of these procedures.)

An average unit assessed value of $12,120 was used for the analysis in Exhibit 5-4. By subtracting 1.5 times the value of the improvements ($7,000) to the homestead as allowed under Wilmington's special assessment practices, the value of the parcel for property tax purposes declines to $1,620. The present property tax rate of $3.737 per $100 assessed valuation would provide an annual property tax income of $60 from the unit. Using referenced estimates of household size and public school pupils and current average service costs, the total property tax costs occassioned by the unit approach $1,534. By comparing this with the $60 property tax revenue, it is clear that the city will face a deficit of $1,474 from the property annually for five years. If this is repeated in a large enough number of units, it could become a substantial drain on the already limited financial capabilities of the city. After the five-year special assessment period elapses, revenue from the property will rise to $712 if the property is reassessed to the $19,120 level. This will ease the deficit somewhat, yet the homesteaded unit will remain a burden on the economic resources of the community. This is true of all low valuation residential units, with school aged children, in Wilmington.

SPECIAL SERVICES

Despite the recognition of the hardships which can be anticipated by the homesteader in settling into his new life style, the city has established relatively few special services. However, countervailing this apparent lack of new programmatic initiatives, a widespread concern for the homesteaders was expressed by all levels of the administrative framework. Beyond mere sympathy there was a genuine desire to help and participate. The aforementioned "buddy" system provides the homesteaders with quick, direct access to city leaders, department heads, etc., and it also serves as a monitoring device for those same leaders to gauge the workings of the program.

Because of the small scale of the program and the relative compactness of the city, formalized channels of authority for dealing with homesteaders' special needs are not well defined. We cannot help but be impressed, however, with the obvious commitment being made to the program by the city and civic leaders.

This is not to say that present efforts are wholly sufficient. Because of frequent personnel changes the rapport so valued by the program administrators between the homesteaders and the program staff has suffered. There has also been a slackening of activity in the past several months resulting in a dulling of the driving impact of the program.

Present servicing efforts have tended to focus on the homestead rather than on the homesteader. This is unfortunate since the overall homestead effort was geared toward persons with low and modest incomes, unfamiliar with homeownership. Because of the rising income of the typical homesteader—as a result of a cautious effort on the part of the Homesteading Board to select those households best able to financially carry the rapidly increasing cost of homeownership—this emphasis on the unit may not prove harmful. This is due to the greater familiarity higher income groups are likely to have with homeownership, its problems and responsibilities.

SUMMARY

Wilmington's pioneering homestead program is beset with a number of limitations. The alleged small-scale, intimate approach appears as a euphimistic explanation of weak administrative structure. Part-time staff cannot be rescued by board members acting the role of big brothers. The financial picture is considerably less bright than in Baltimore; limited by the Delaware constitution, private lenders had to be depended upon. The latter's high visibility does not truly reflect their exposure (degree of risk), and many homesteaders cannot obtain nor afford needed improvement funds. The special assessment procedures applied to rehabilitation improvements, though, are very well thought out, but their effect is probably cancelled by the interest rates applied by the financial institutions' loan provisions. Moreover, Wilmington's neighborhood parcels may just not have the structural quality—much of the housing stock was built for workers—that is extant in some of the other homesteading settings. While the city is trying, the difficulties of finding truly salvageable areas and the complexities of getting loans have forced the realities of homesteading to fall far short of its early expectations.

NOTES

1. Quoted in Art Spikol, "On the House," *Philadelphia Magazine,* March 1974, p. 88.

2. U.S. Bureau of the Census, *Census of Population and Housing: 1970 Census Tracts, Final Report PHC (1)-234 Wilmington, Del–N.J.–Md. SMSA.*

3. Interview, Housing Coordinator, Wilmington, Delaware, September 1, 1974.

4. Wilmington, Delaware, City Ordinance 73-047 § 7.

5. "From Plows to Pliers—Urban Homesteading in America," *Fordham Urban Law Journal,* Vol. 2, Winter 1974, p. 277.

6. Interview, Housing Coordinator, Wilmington, Delaware, September 1, 1974.

7. Interview, Director of Urban Renewal, Wilmington, Delaware, March 2, 1975.

8. Wilmington City Code § 3-49.

9. Art Spikol, "On the House," p. 76.

10. Interview, Director of Urban Renewal, Wilmington, Delaware, March 2, 1975.

11. *Ibid.*

12. Urban Coalition, *Urban Homesteading: Process and Potential* (Washington, D.C.: Urban Coalition, 1974), p. 41.

13. Interview, Urban Renewal Director, Wilmington, Delaware, March 2, 1975.

14. Wilmington, Delaware City Ordinance 73-047 § 4.

15. Interview, Urban Renewal Director, Wilmington, Delaware, March 2, 1975.

16. Interview, Public Information Officer, Wilmington, Delaware, March 2, 1975.

17. Nick Tatro, "Homesteading Continues with Mixed Success," *Sunday Times-Advertiser* (Trenton, N.J.), March 23, 1975.

18. "The total of amortization, interest, taxes, and insurance should not exceed 25 percent of your annual income after taxes," Jerome G. Rose, *The Legal Advisor on Home Ownership* (Boston: Little, Brown & Co., 1964), pp. 8-9.

19. U.S. Internal Revenue Service, Form 1040 (Washington, D.C., 1975).

20. *Philadelphia Inquirer*, March 24, 1975.

21. Wilmington Special Agreement, April 24, 1974.

22. Interview, Bank Officer, Delaware Trust, Wilmington, Delaware, March 2, 1975.

23. *Ibid*.

24. Wilmington, Delaware, City Ordinance 74-001.

25. Interview, Branch Officer, Delaware Trust, Wilmington, Delaware, March 2, 1975.

26. Wilmington, Delaware, City Ordinance 72-081.

27. "Homesteading as an Option," unpublished (Wilmington, Del.: Urban Homesteading Board, 1973), p. 3.

EXHIBIT 5-5

CAPSULATED DESCRIPTION
WILMINGTON HOMESTEAD PROGRAM

THE CONTEXT:	Wilmington, Delaware is faced with major housing abandonments; over 2,000 residential units, 6.7 percent of the city's housing resources, are abandoned. The population of Wilmington declined from 110,000 in 1950 to 80,000 in 1970, a result of long-standing suburbanization trends. The decline is so entrenched that whole blocks are now being converted from formerly sound neighborhoods to functionless areas of vacant homes.
PROGRAM INITIATION:	During his recent mayoralty campaign, Mayor Thomas Maloney emphasized the deteriorated condition of much of the city's housing stock and pledged to halt decline by instituting an urban homesteading program. On May 18, 1973, ordinance 73-047, the Urban Homesteading Act, was signed by the Mayor; the act was amended on May 5, 1974, providing lenders with first lien positions.
PROGRAM OBJECTIVES:	1. To turn abandoned and untaxable properties into maintained and taxable properties. 2. To provide increased homeownership. 3. To retard urban decay by giving responsible people a stake in their neighborhood. 4. To foster migration back to the city from the suburbs.
ADMINISTRATIVE FRAMEWORK:	Homesteading Board, the major policy body which also oversees program administration, comprises six city agency heads. Its staff numbers three: a Homesteading Program Director, a rehabilitation specialist, and a financial officer. The staff, responsible for day-to-day operations, is part-time, focusing also on urban renewal. The city justifies this less than rigid structure in terms of small city size.
OTHER PROGRAM PARTICIPANTS:	*City of Wilmington* — Insures 40 percent of any loan default; offers partial tax abatement for a five-year period.

EXHIBIT 5-5

CAPSULATED DESCRIPTION
WILMINGTON HOMESTEAD PROGRAM (Cont'd.)

OTHER PROGRAM PARTICIPANTS: (Cont'd.)	*Consortium of Local Banks:*	Provides special financing to the homesteaders. One bank official is an ex-officio member of the board.
	Department of Licenses and Inspection:	Identifies vacant parcels and evaluates those thought suitable for the program in terms of code violations. Monitors rehabilitation work to insure its compliance with extant codes.
PROGRAM STRUCTURE:	*Parcel Acquisition*	1. Fast taking procedures applied to abandoned structures. 2. HUD foreclosures.
	Homestead Evaluation:	Properties surveyed by Department of Licenses and Inspections. Staff evaluates inspection results in terms of neighborhood context and provides more detailed cost estimates.
	Homesteader Evaluation:	Fixed selection criteria.
	Financial Assistance:	Technical assistance provided to the homesteader in closing on his parcel; a special rehabilitation program with 8 cooperating local banks; funds are made available to the homesteader at a 9¾ percent interest rate for a

EXHIBIT 5-5

CAPSULATED DESCRIPTION
WILMINGTON HOMESTEAD PROGRAM (Cont'd.)

PROGRAM STRUCTURE: (Cont'd.)	*Financial Assistance (Cont'd.)*	term of 10 to 15 years. Commitments on the city's part consist of an agreement to cover 40 percent of any loan which goes into default.
	Special Tax Considerations:	For the 5 year period following parcel improvement, 1.5 times the value of the improvement is deducted from the previous assessment.
	Special Services:	"Buddy System" assigns a set group of homesteaders to each board member.
COST REVENUE IMPACT:	On the modular unit, with an initial assessment of $12,120 and $7,000 worth of improvements, the cost-revenue deficit exceeds $1,470.	
PROGRAM OUTPUT:	28 units homesteaded; only 22 still active.	

Chapter 6

Philadelphia: Colonists In The Nation's Birthplace

Carolyn Hayes stepped around the paint cans on the floor, moved past the unpainted door leaning against the middle-room wall and joined her husband Glenn, who was talking to two workmen.

It was Saturday morning and the Hayes were overseeing work that was being done on their two-bedroom row house in the West Oak Lane section of Philadelphia.

The house was special. It was the first that the Hayes were to own. And it was special because it was one of the 20 houses awarded in the City of Philadelphia's Urban Homestead program.[1]

Atop Philadelphia's City Hall stands a statue of William Penn, the city's founder. Since he assumed his perch many years ago, great changes have occurred in the fabric of Philadelphia's urban life, not all for the better. The central area has been the scene of frantic high rise development while the territory most familiar to Penn—Society Hill—has been restored. More significant and demonstrably less pleasant than these bright spots of civic achievement has been the vast deterioration of many of the city's neighborhoods. The sweeping urban decay has so determinedly been eating away at once viable neighborhoods that now sections of the city are veritable "no man's" lands of vacant buildings. The standard ameliorative programs used in most cities have been tried in Philadelphia as well, usually with the same unsatisfactory results. Changes gauged even from the 1930s are marked.

THE SETTING

PHILADELPHIA (110 alt., 1,950,961 pop.), third largest of American cities, the Nation's birthplace and its first citadel of high finance, is today a sprawling industrial giant that William Penn would never recognize as his "greene countrie towne." Conterminous with Philadelphia County, the Quaker City lies along the west bank of the Delaware River and on both sides of the Schuylkill, on terrain rather more typical of the low flatlands of New Jersey and Delaware than of the mountainous remainder of Pennsylvania. Within its 130 square miles of territory the City of Brotherly Love embraces, as do all our large cities, a number of smaller communities, many of which were formerly independent and still possess their own shopping centers, business enterprises, and distinctive characteristics . . . .

Jews, of whom there are approximately 270,000, have contributed much to Philadelphia's commercial growth; their desire for knowledge has manifested itself in their rise to leadership in many of the professions, notably law and medicine. The Italian group, centering about 9th and Christian Streets, has done much to counteract the gravity of the early Quaker and German settlers. The Italian-born, numbering more than 68,000, are inclined to settle in sharply defined districts. The foreign-born Germans number about 38,000; after a generation or more, many of them preserve the customs brought over from the Fatherland. When the breweries were concentrated in northwest Philadelphia, a large settlement of Germans existed in the "Brewerytown" section of Master and Thompson Streets, between 29th and 31st Streets. Philadelphia's Irish-born population, some 52,000, living in almost all sections of the city, has played a leading part in many phases of municipal life, especially in the field of politics. The Russian-born population of 90,000 living with other Slavic peoples in the neighborhood of Fourth and Brown Streets, is inclined to hold aloof from other national groups.

From the handful of slaves who arrived with the Dutch and Swedish settlers, in the days of Johan Printz, the Negro population, concentrated in South Philadelphia and in the north central section, has grown to approximately 220,000, more than 11 percent of the total population. There are about 2;500 Negroes employed in the government of the city and county. An act of legislature in 1780, providing for the gradual abolition of slavery, bore its first fruits in the early 1800s. Negroes, who had been restricted to domestic and manual service, found employment as mechanics, seamen, carpenters, and skilled workers in the industries. They became home-owners, supporters of their own schools and welfare societies, and financiers of their own business enterprises. The catering business in Philadelphia was, for a time, monopolized by Negroes through the guild of caterers . . . .

> *Philadelphia in the 1930s. Federal Writers Project,*
> Pennsylvania: A Guide to the Keystone State *(New York:*
> *Oxford University Press, 1940), pp. 256-258.*

The mosaic of social worlds that was pictured in the 1930s—most appealingly—has given way to the forces of suburbanization, assimilation, and racial and ethnic invasions and confrontations. The city's present population, 1,948,609, is 200,000 persons shy of what it was in 1950, and slightly below the 1930 level. The black population now exceeds 653,000, one-third of Philadelphia's total[2] (Exhibit 6-1). Median age and household size indices gauge the replacement of middle-age white families with young family-raising blacks and substantial residuals of elderly white ethnic households.

Of the city's 673,524 dwelling units, 69 percent were constructed before 1939.[3] Philadelphia is primarily a city of row houses and small structures, mostly of masonry construction; only 16 percent of its residential housing is concentrated in structures containing 5 or more units. This is a fortuitous distribution of configurations for homesteading purposes—single-family attached masonry housing has high rehabilitation potential. With severe abandonment over wide areas of the city, 24,000 residential units serve as homesteading's raw materials. This represents 3.6 percent of the city's existing housing stock.

The momentum to change this dismal picture through a localized innovative approach dates back to 1968. It was in that year that Councilman Joseph E. Coleman first suggested, in tentative fashion, that the city develop a homesteading program, granting homes to persons willing to revitalize and reside in them.[4] This was before the HUD moratorium and before the end of the War on Poverty, when most urban leaders were still looking to Washington for answers. Thus, little heed was paid to Coleman's suggestion. By 1973, the War on Poverty was defeated and HUD was embroiled in scandals and hobbled by a lack of faith from the White House. Suddenly local governments realized they were going to have to "go it alone" if any progress was to be made in solving their housing problems. The homesteading concept suddenly looked viable.

Philadelphia formally adopted a homesteading ordinance in July 1973, but not before Wilmington had gotten a head start. On June 27, 1974 the first homesteads were awarded; a second group of parcels were distributed in March 1975.

Internal Dilemmas

Philadelphia's homesteading design serves to partially illuminate a major facet of its urban soul, offering a brief glimpse of its nontraditional attitude toward its role as centerpiece of a modern metropolis. Philadelphia is the City of William Penn, painstakingly laid out during the earliest portions of this nation's history, oriented toward horse carriages and pedestrians. The current administrations have firmly believed, and insisted, that this is the way it should remain. If any one large American city has rejected the bulldozer brand of urban

EXHIBIT 6-1
PHILADELPHIA: A STATISTICAL PROFILE

Total Population	1950	1960	1970
Pennsylvania	10,498,012	11,319,366	11,793,909
Philadelphia	2,071,605	2,002,512	1,948,609

Black Population	
1960	535,033
1970	653,791

Median Age (Total)		Median Age (Black)	
1960	33.4	1960	27.4
1970	30.9	1970	25.0

Household Size (Total)		Household Size (Black)	
1960	2.8	1960	3.0
1970	2.9	1970	2.8

Median Family Income (Total)		Median Family Income (Black)	
1960	$4,789	1960	$3,399
1970	$7,206	1970	$5,644

Median Education (Total)		Median Education (Black)	
1960	9.6	1960	9.0
1970	12.4	1970	10.4

Median House Value (Total)		Median House Value (Black)	
1960	$8,700	1960	$7,000
1970	$10,600	1970	$8,500

Housing Units	
1970 Total	673,356
Built before 1939	69%
Built before 1949	79%

Units in Structure

Structure Type	Number of Units	
1 unit	448,564	(66.8%)
2 - 4 units	115,047	(17.0%)
5 or more units	109,745	(16.2%)

Source: U.S. Bureau of the Census, Census of Population and Housing: 1970, Census Tracts, Final Report PHC (1)-159 Philadelphia, Penna.–N.J. SMSA.

renewal, it has been Philadelphia. Attesting to this fact is Society Hill, a large scale historic rehabilitation district whose birth was two decades ago and today stands as the example *par excellence* of the lost opportunities of other major urban centers. Moreover, Philadelphia did not follow other cities' leads into adapting its character and structure to accommodate the on-rushing automobile age, nor did it succumb to the lure of federal dollars, which induced its counterparts to adjust to the demands of car-oriented life. Thus the circumferential freeways enveloping the built-up environs of most American cities, which spurred rampant development on the cities' perimeters while draining the urban centers, did not materialize in Philadelphia. Many civic leaders and planners believe this fortuitous decision to bypass such transportation arrangements has helped maintain the economic viability of Philadelphia's downtown areas.

Acting in seemingly contradictory fashion, the city does not allow any downtown structure to grow beyond the 537 foot height of the William Penn statue perched atop Philadelphia's City Hall, the geometric apex of the city. This is a startling decision, given the fact that a centralized urban configuration not oriented to freeways demands concentrations of great magnitude at the convergence point of mass transportation. It is all the more so since there is substantial demand for downtown office space and the exhorbitant cost of inner city land shows little sign of abatement. Such dilemmas are encountered in most of Philadelphia's civic life.

And so it is with homesteading. The City Council originally approved $1.5 million for mortgage guarantees as the homesteading bandwagon gained momentum. Yet despite such actions, and the continued promulgation of homesteading's virtues, the money has yet to be released. While private foundation grants have helped the program weather the stormy interim, the full-scale implementation has continually faced contradictory obstacles since its approval, when the homesteading bill was loudly cheered on the floor of the City Council.[5]

INSTITUTIONAL FRAMEWORK

Ordinance 543, approved by Mayor Rizzo in July of 1973, created the Philadelphia homesteading program. Under its provisions, an Urban Homesteading Board was established, comprising eleven members, one from each of the following groups: architects, contractors, the Building Trades Council, clergymen, representatives of savings and loan institutions, the general public, and two City Council members. The Deputy Managing Director of Housing, the Executive Director of the Redevelopment Authority, and the Executive Director of the Philadelphia City Planning Commission serve on the Board as ex officio members.[6] The selection process requires the City Council to submit three names for each position from which the Mayor will appoint the board and the chairman.[7] The term of office for members is three years with the exception of the first term members, who serve for staggered terms of one, two, and three years to allow for program continuity and policy regardless of city administration turnover.

The Philadelphia Ordinance is quite specific in granting powers to the Homesteading Board. It mandates assistance from other agencies and obtains vacant properties by recommending the institution of foreclosure proceedings against usable abandoned structures by the City Law Department. Demolition of sufficiently deteriorated or blighted buildings by the Department of Licenses and Inspections through nuisance proceedings can also be urged.[8] The board is empowered to aid the homesteader in securing adequate financing and obtaining parcel reassessment to its present worth before conveying title. In recognition of the strong block council tradition in Philadelphia, the Homesteading Board is empowered to create local councils to facilitate interaction between these groups and, "to promote, assist, and advise the Board on homesteading programs in their respective areas."[9] The ordinance also provides the board with a technical staff. To date, twelve positions have been funded with the present staff numbering eight.

In contrast to Baltimore and Wilmington, Philadelphia's homesteading program did not receive priority treatment from City Hall. In the former, the mayors assumed activist roles in the concepts' implementation, were politically identified with it, and stubbornly maintained support when the initial growing pains caused discomfort. In Philadelphia, however, the mayor's office has been accused of obstructionism and of employing numerous tactics to thwart the program, one of these being the delaying of funds to fill legislatively mandated staff allocations. Homesteading's status as political football may have been a result of its sponsor, Councilman Coleman, being a political foe of Mayor Rizzo. Philadelphia thus provides a clear example of the substantial gap which exists between ordinance specification and field operationalization.

Currently, in charge of the daily operations of the program is an Executive Director; assisting him in the general administration of the program currently are two Assistant Program Directors. A Community Resources Coordinator acts as a liason between the homesteading office and community groups as well as the contact person for the homesteaders. Completing the staff are a Housing Rehabilitation Specialist and two Housing Rehabilitation Technicians—who evaluate potential homesteads and prepare rehabilitation cost estimates—and a Researcher-Investigator.[10]

The considerable increase in staff relative to Wilmington's approach generates a greater degree of internalization of program operations. No estimates of the administrative cost per homestead are available due to the short operating history of the program.

PARCEL ACQUISITION

The capability to monitor abandoned units in the city has recently undergone a major upgrading. In 1970 the Long Term Vacancy Monitoring System was established at the urging of the City Planning Commission, Housing

Director, City Finance Director, and Department of Licenses and Inspections. Its chief objective was to overcome the previously erratic methods of inventorying abandoned units. By using the Water Company's semi-annual inspection of all water meters in the city as its initial canvasing vehicle, with followup investigations by the housing inspection staff, the Division of Management Information Services of the Department of Finance processed the status of every structure in the city on a periodic basis. But comparison tests between the efficiency of the meter readers and daily checks by the Department of Licenses and Inspections' housing inspectors, as well as demand inspections keyed to resident complaints, resulted in the discontinuance of the water meter observations as an integral part of the accounting system. This decision was based on the comparatively long periods between meter observations relative to the quick detection generated by neighbor complaints and daily inspections of the canvasing vehicle.[11]

When an abandoned parcel is detected, it is evaluated by the Department of Licenses and Inspections in terms of the City Housing Code. The structure is then computer coded, classifying its residential, commercial, or industrial usage and its abandonment status. (See Appendix A for a comparative analysis of abandonment accounting systems.) An abandoned structure can either be defined as:

locked vacant—a permissable building status based on the city's criteria for being secured.

unsealed—a parcel is either left open or in need of being resealed due to vandalism or other causes.

certified public nuisance—this is a legally defined category which allows the city to take the property through nuisance proceedings should it meet established criteria:

1. Be a place where vagrants congregate in an otherwise sound neighborhood.

2. Be continuously reopened by vandals after it has been sealed.

3. Have suffered extensive fire damage.

4. Have been the scene of numerous small fires.

5. Be the only severely deteriorated home in an otherwise "sound and useful" neighborhood.[12]

The use of this legal definition has allowed the city to quickly take parcels and dispose of them. (Under a related demolition program, an annual goal of

2,500 demolitions of abandoned structures has been set, with 1,800 being removed in the last two years.)

By classifying parcels in this manner, not only are aggregate abandonment figures available but the subsequent parcel dispositions may be observed. By using this system, along with demolition statistics of the Department of Licenses and Inspections, it is estimated that the number of current abandoned residential units in Philadelphia now totals 24,000, somewhat lower than the 33,000 tally previously thought to be accurate. Periodic updating of the computer-stored data records changes in the status of abandoned units, principally their demolition or their economic reuse. Thus, Philadelphia possesses an operational procedure for monitoring abandoned properties and their disposition.

The large number of abandonments seems to offer an almost endless supply of potential homesteads. Yet, of the 24,000 abandoned units, only 250 are controlled by the city. This is a result of a deliberate effort of not foreclosing on tax delinquent properties, hoping at some point there will be a resuscitation of owner interest in the parcel. This policy is based also on the city's unwillingness to be the legal owner of worthless parcels, which it has neither the will nor the financial capacity to improve. Moreover, the homesteading staff estimates that of the 250 properties owned by the city, only 7 or 8 are suitable for homesteading. Due to the prolonged transition period spanning the time of abandonment until the city finally takes control, most units have become so deteriorated as to be worthless from any perspective. This problem was recently addressed by the Pennsylvania State Legislature when it passed a special fast-take procedure, enabling the city of Philadelphia to take title to deteriorating and blighted properties in six months.[13] In practice, however, even this method has found to take from nine months to a year or more.[14]

The homesteading staff does feel an adequate supply of suitable parcels is available from sources other than tax delinquent city properties. Presently the Department of Housing and Urban Development owns 3,261 units obtained through mortgage foreclosure.[15] The staff believes these are the best source of potential homesteads especially those which were recently foreclosed since many of them have experienced only slight deterioration. Their importance is evidenced by the first 20 units homesteaded. Fourteen were HUD-owned and one was a gift, while only five were previously city-owned properties.[16] The second group of homesteads was taken exclusively from a list of recent foreclosures available from HUD and were purchased directly by the program with an average cost of $500.

In response to a federal mandate to assist local homesteading jurisdictions, HUD is establishing a Local Property Option Program which would turn over long foreclosed properties to local homesteading programs. Even before this effort has gotten under way, criticism has been voiced over the fact that these properties are generally the worst in the HUD inventory and most probably would be unsuitable for homesteading because of their severe deterioration.[17]

Another potentially significant vehicle for obtaining usable homesteads is a "gift" procedure recently established by the city. Under the provisions of

Ordinance 909A the owner is allowed to give notice that he intends to give his parcel to the city. The city then appraises the property both in terms of its structural characteristics and neighborhood environment, determining if it wants the parcel. Should both interests coincide, the owner may transfer title and receive absolution from all back taxes. Thus the legal formalities inherent in tax sale proceedings can be circumvented, thereby speeding up the parcel acquisition process.

A complication with vesture of title has arisen in that only certain city agencies may hold title to public property. Since the Homesteading Office is not one of those agencies, this necessitated the location of an appropriate agency to hold title to the parcels. Because of a recent court ruling the Philadelphia Housing Development Agency has been designated as the only group in the city which can hold title to properties being treated for removal of lead-based paints. This fact combined with the inability of the Homestead Office to hold title has lead to an arrangement whereby the PHDC holds title to all homesteading properties until the transfer to the homesteader, during which time each of the units has all lead-based paint removed.[18]

EVALUATING THE HOMESTEAD

The Philadelphia approach to parcel evaluation parallels many of the procedures used in Baltimore and Wilmington. There is a serious effort to evaluate the parcel both in terms of its structural condition and its neighborhood environment.

The criteria used by the city are twofold.

1. The unit must have a moderate rehabilitation cost so as to be marketable in relation to surrounding parcels.

2. The neighborhood quality must be rated satisfactory in terms of vacancy rates and maintenance levels.

The first criterion is assessed by the city's Department of Licenses and Inspections' housing and building inspection team. Units are evaluated in terms of code violations; the inspector's report is transmitted to the Homesteading Office, where rehabilitation specialists undertake a careful parcel evaluation. Structural soundness, deterioration levels and rehabilitation costs are all determined. A work sheet is prepared breaking the rehabilitation costs into such components as major systems, structural repairs, and other useful categories. These individual costs are then aggregated to find if the total rehabilitation package does not exceed the $5,200-$6,000 price range, the general feasibility threshold to economically bring the parcel within code standards.[19] (There have been units homesteaded which cost both considerably more and considerably less to reconstruct, but the general costing framework desired by the staff would be in this $5,200-$6,000 range.)

Once the unit's structural systems have been evaluated, an analysis of the surrounding neighborhood environment is undertaken. Owners must occupy at least 65 percent of the houses in the neighborhood. Vacancy levels in the immediate area are allowed to vary, since it is felt that the nature of the vacancies is more important than their absolute number; for example, if in the last year five homes have been vacated, rapid decline in the neighborhood may be underway and the chances are this area will be avoided.[20] Visual determinants of neighborhood decline include: the presence of large amounts of trash and garbage in streets, in yards, and vacant lots; derelict automobiles and other forms of major street rubbish; low levels of exterior parcel maintenance; a high visibility of vacant properties, and a lack of an effective neighborhood organization. These neighborhood decline determinants are evaluated by the Community Resources Coordinator, cataloging them in terms of possible ameliorative actions by the city on a short-term basis. Should the neighborhood problem be a relatively minor item, such as several abandoned automobiles, the city agency responsible for their removal is contacted and prodded into action. Should the neighborhood's decline be deemed irreversible, units within its boundaries will not be homesteaded.

An important contextual element of Philadelphia's program, which sets it apart from other homesteading efforts, is the presence of strong block associations, which give many areas a functioning mini-government. The city's heritage since colonial times has been its focus on tightly integrated groups of neighborhoods rather than one large urban community;[21] the homesteading program has wisely sought to capitalize on this tradition. By working closely with local block associations and developing their potential for leadership in neighborhood improvement efforts, the staff has approved homesteads in neighborhoods which in other settings would have been deemed too risky.[22] The use of these de facto governmental structures as aids to homesteading is a unique element of the Philadelphia program; close ties with the grass roots attitudes of the city's residents are thereby fostered.

Once the parcel has been selected for homesteading, the city provides several services to the homesteading program to upgrade the parcel. Accumulated trash is removed, and if it is rodent-infested, control measures are implemented. There is also a service to remove lead paint from each of the homesteads before occupation, which is paid for by the program and carried out by the Health Department. These preparatory measures eliminate some of the initial rehabilitation costs which normally befall the homesteader.

EVALUATING THE HOMESTEADER

The basic objectives of the Philadelphia Homesteading Program are:

1.   The return of vacant properties to the tax rolls.

2. The placement in homes of people who want to be homeowners but are not able to do so in the normal market structure.

3. The use of homesteading as a first effort to begin devising more sophisticated processes for dealing with abandoned housing.[23]

Though a long-term commitment has been made to bring homeownership to those heretofore excluded, the main program thrust is to find people for housing across a broad socioeconomic strata. One of the most encouraging developments in the Philadelphia program is its realization of the potential homesteading holds as a first step in the development of more sophisticated processes for dealing with abandonment and the extant resources the parcels may hold.

Minimum Requirements

To qualify for a homestead, a person must:

1. Be twenty-one years of age or a head of a family.

2. Be a citizen of the United States or declare an intention to become such.

3. Have proven financial ability and/or building trade skills to rehabilitate a parcel to building and housing code standards.

4. Begin rehabilitation no later than 60 days after title has been acquired (and completed in two years).

5. Agree to live in the structure for no less than five years.[24]

Beyond these formal requirements the program looks for individuals with proven construction skills or access to someone with those skills, ranging from electrical or plumbing capabilities to more simple painting and other finishing know-how. In the rapidly developing jargon which seems to come with new programs, these skills are dubbed as "sweat equity," with financial requirements lowered to reflect the amount of reconstruction which can be undertaken by the homesteader. Also, some estimation is attempted of the willingness of the person to actually devote the many hours required to return a unit to habitability standards, a quality which may be correlated with employment records and family stability. Another selection criteria centers on the consistency of financial resources available to the applicant. The ability to hold a steady job and have a constant flow of year-round income is an important determinant of the fitness for homesteading.

Selection Process

When a group of homesteads have been selected they are advertised in the local media. Persons interested are instructed to contact the Homesteading Office for an application. The applicant is requested to put down first, second, and third choices regarding the available units. However, because of the high ratio of applicants received to applicants accepted (50:1), only the first choice has any real chance.[25] It is left up to the applicant to inspect the parcel, but since they are sealed, only a strictly exterior evaluation is possible. The Homesteading Office does supply the applicants with the number of bedrooms and other unit characteristics, however. The staff then evaluates all applications in terms of the aforementioned criteria and the parcel parameters, selecting households exhibiting the best survival abilities. Those from the immediate neighborhoods are given preference should all other criteria be equal. Final approval of all homesteaders rests with the City Council, which acts on the recommendation of the board.[26]

Income Sufficiency

Small rowhouses with two, three, and four bedrooms constitute the bulk of Philadelphia's housing resources. Not surprisingly, such units make up the majority of those homesteaded. The homesteading staff, in general, estimates it will cost between $5,200 and $6,000 to render them suitably habitable. Thus, a homesteader must be able to carry a substantial debt payment annually if he is to be successful in sustaining himself in the homestead. While it is possible for some hard-working households to amass such resources, we will calculate income sufficiency assuming financing of improvements. Exhibit 6-2 estimates the basic cost thresholds and the annual income necessary to bear the emerging expense.

Assuming a $6,000 loan at 3.25 percent for a period of 15 years, an annual yearly payment of $520.98 is required. Add in utilities and fuel, property taxes, insurance, and miscellaneous expenses, and a total yearly expense budget of $1,739.58 results. If the "25 percent of after tax income" devoted to housing standards is applied to this example, a family of four not itemizing deductions should have a gross income in the vicinity of $7,450.[27] Since the average income of the first 20 homesteaders has ranged between $6,000 to $10,000, it would appear that most participants so far have met the threshold income level developed in Exhibit 6-2.

SPECIAL FINANCIAL ASSISTANCE

To overcome the problem of scarcity of rehabilitation financing in the city, the Homesteading Board has established a two-step procedure designed to secure the necessary financing for the homesteader. This approach must be viewed as an interim measure, since $1.5 million in loan and mortgage guarantees approved by the City Council have been impounded by the executive office. The

EXHIBIT 6-2

TYPICAL ANNUAL COSTS INCURRED BY PHILADELPHIA HOMESTEADERS

Expense	Cost
Taxes[1]	$ 238.60
Loan Payment[2]	520.98
Utilities & Fuel[3]	540.00
Insurance[3]	40.00
Miscellaneous[3]	400.00
TOTAL	$1,739.58

1. This is the average amount of taxes paid over the first five years of ownership under the special assessment procedure equal to a value of $5,000.00. (See Exhibit 6-4 for explanation of the increasing special assessment procedure.) Thus property taxes = .04775 ($5,000) = $238.60.
2. This is the annual cost of a $6,000 loan at 3.25 percent for 15 years, the average loan issued through early 1975. The annual cost was determined as follows:

$$R = P \frac{i(1+i)^n}{(1+i)^n - 1} = \$6,000 \frac{.0325\,(1+.0325)^{15}}{(1+.0325)^{15} - 1} = \$6,000(.08683) = \$520.98$$

> where   i represents an interest rate per interest period
> n represents a number of interest periods
> P represents a present sum of money (total mortgage)
> R represents the end-of-period payment in a uniform
> series continuing for the coming n periods.

See: Eugene L. Grant and W. Grant Ireson, *Principles of Engineering Economy* (New York: The Ronald Press Company, 1964), p. 43 and p. 545.

3. Average estimate based on rehabilitated units in the Northeast. See: George Sternlieb, James W. Hughes, and Lawrence Burrows, *Housing in Newark*, mimeograph (New Brunswick, New Jersey: Center for Urban Policy Research, Rutgers University, 1974) and Robert W. Burchell, James W. Hughes and George Sternlieb, *Housing Costs and Housing Restraints: The Realities of Inner City Housing Costs* (New York: Life Insurance Association of America, 1970).

Other estimates of occupancy and operating costs are presented in George Sternlieb, *The Urban Housing Dilemma: The Dynamics of New York City's Rent Controlled Housing* (New York: Housing and Development Administration, 1972), George Sternlieb, *The Tenement Landlord* (New Brunswick, New Jersey: Rutgers University Press, 1969), and David Listokin, *The Dynamics of Housing Rehabilitation: Macro and Micro Analyses* (New Brunswick, New Jersey: Center for Urban Policy Research, 1973).

Director of the Philadelphia Homestead Office, after repeated failures to obtain the release of the money, turned to private foundations for help. Yet, the alternative format which has resulted appears to be an effective way of administering homestead rehabilitation financing.

Once a homesteader has been selected and matched with a parcel, an estimate of necessary rehabilitation costs is submitted to the Urban Homesteading Finance Corporation for the approval of initial financing. The latter organization is a consortium of interested churches, volunteers, and financiers who have independently established a $300,000 loan fund to be used as an underlying resources for rehabilitation financing. The loan is very similar to a conventional construction loan in that it quickly grants start-up monies to qualified homesteaders to begin reconstruction and thereby begin to establish equity in their parcels. The loan usually lasts for six months at 6 percent interest. To facilitate rehabilitation, the homesteader is supplied with a list of recommended contractors which he may or may not use. Once the contractor is selected, major cost estimates (typically around $6,000)[28] are submitted to the Urban Homesteading Finance Corporation and, after an evaluation to determine their veracity, the loan is granted.

The second phase of the financing process involves the securing of long-term financing on the parcel from the Pennsylvania Housing Finance Agency. The PHFA has established a $250,000 loan pool to provide long-term mortgages to homesteaders.[29] Interest rates vary from 3 percent to 7 percent with terms ranging from five to fifteen years, with specific levels set by a "20-25 percent of income" analysis of the homesteaders' ability to pay. This means a loan of $6,000 at 3.5 percent interest rate for a 15-year term (figures most typically cited by the Homesteading office and PHFA) will cost the homeowner $520.98 annually. The savings to the homesteader in relation to conventional financing are examined in Exhibit 6-3. A conventional home loan—12 percent interest over five years—requires an annual payback of $1,664.46, almost $1,150 more than the PHFA program for the first five years. Even if we convert all future annual disbursements to present worth (Exhibit 6-3), the savings to the homesteader still appear great. The Housing Finance Agency is able to offer such lucrative terms to the homesteader—which exceed those available under its conventional program—by using its profit as the capital for the loans rather than using bond financing, which requires that a higher interest rate be charged. By utilizing this special pool, the homesteader can have a significant saving both in terms of conventional loans and in relation to the financing available under most programs.

The financial vehicle used in the Philadelphia homesteading program satisfies three significant needs. First, it provides seed money (as construction loans) to stimulate initial rehabilitation and creates equity in the property. Second, through the special long-term financial arrangement with the Housing Finance Agency, loans are provided at low cost. Third, it limits the risk to the long-term lender through the use of the two-stage process by obviating the need for any early commitment until some equity has been established through property rehabilitation.

EXHIBIT 6-3
COST SAVINGS OCCASIONED BY PENNSYLVANIA HOUSING
FINANCE AGENCY (PHFA) SPECIAL LOAN PROGRAM

Conventional Financing

$6,000 @ 12% - 5 years

$$R = P \frac{i(1+i)^n}{(1+i)^n - 1} = \$6,000 \frac{.12(1+.12)^5}{(1+.12)^5 - 1} = \$6,000 \,(.27741)$$

R = $1,664.46 for five annual payments

PHFA Financing

$6,000 @ 3½% - 15 years

$$R = P \frac{i(1+i)^n}{(1+i)^n - 1} = \$6,000 \frac{.0375(1+.0375)^{15}}{(1+.0375)^{15} - 1} = \$6,000 \,(.08683)$$

R = $520.98 for fifteen annual payments

Program Differences

$1,664.46 - $520.98 = $1,143.48 annually, for first five years

Total Cost Differences in Current Dollars (Assuming an Inflation Rate of 8%)

Conventional Financing

$$P = R \frac{(1+i)^n - 1}{i(1+i)^n} = \$1,664.46 \frac{(1+.08)^5 - 1}{.08(1+.08)^5} = \$1,664.46 \,(3.993) = \$6,646.19$$

PHFA Financing

$$P = R \frac{(1+i)^n - 1}{i(1+i)^n} = \$520.98 \frac{(1+.08)^{15} - 1}{.08(1+.08)^{15}} = \$520.98 \,(8.559) = \$4,459.07$$

Note: This last calculation deflates future annual payments to present value assuming an inflation rate of 8 percent. By employing a present worth factor (above formula), we are estimating the present value of total future annual disbursements. The reason for PHFA's low present value is due to the interest rate being significantly lower than the inflation rate. In other words, given $4,459.07 today at 8 percent, 15 years of $520.98 annual payments can be made.

See Eugene L. Grant and W. Grant Ireson, *Principles of Engineering Economy* (New York: The Ronald Press, 1964) for details of computational formulas. In the above, R = annual payment, P = present sum of money, i = interest rate, and n = the number of annual interest periods. See also Exhibit 6-2.

EXHIBIT 6-4

COST-REVENUE IMPACT OF HOMESTEADING IN PHILADELPHIA
(See Appendix B for Cost-Revenue Methodology)

General Parameters

Total Assessed Valuation	$5,575,000,000
Total Population	1,937,900
Total School Enrollment	272,000
Tax Rate Per $100 Assessed Valuation	
City	1.975
School	2.800
Total	4.775
Assessed Valuation/Pupil	$20,496.32
School Property Tax Levied/Pupil	$573.90[1]
Assessed Valuation/Person	$2,876.83
Municipal Property Tax Levied/Person	$56.81

Property Tax Revenues

Initial Assessed Valuation of Homestead	$3,500
Assessed Valuation of Improvement	$3,000
Total Assessed Valuation of Rehabilitated Unit	$6,500
Average Assessment over 5 Year Period	$5,000[2]

Property Tax Revenue = Assessed Valuation/Dwelling x Assessed
Property Tax Rate
Revenue = $5,000 (.04775) = $238.60[2]

Property Tax Costs

Educational Costs = Public School Children/Dwelling Unit x
School Property Taxes Levied/Pupil
= (1.871) ($573.90) = $1,073.77[3]

Municipal Costs = Persons/Dwelling Unit x Municipal Property
Taxes Levied/Capita
= (3.90) ($56.81) = $221.56[3]

Total Costs = $1,295.33

Revenue Deficit Per Unit: $1,056.73

EXHIBIT 6-4 (Cont'd.)

COST-REVENUE IMPACT OF HOMESTEADING IN PHILADELPHIA
(See Appendix B for Cost-Revenue Methodology)

1. This represents 33 percent of the total educational cost per pupil. The majority of the school budget is obtained through various special tax programs and aid from the state and federal governments.

2. This represents the average annual tax assessment and payment over the five year special assessment period:

Year	Assessment
0	$3,500 + $0 = $3,500
1	3,500 + 600 = $4,100
2	3,500 + 1,200 = $4,700
3	3,500 + 1,800 = $5,300
4	3,500 + 2,400 = $5,900
5	3,500 + 3,000 = $6,500

3. We are assuming a three bedroom unit, using the parameters presented in Appendix B.

SPECIAL TAX CONSIDERATIONS

Under the provisions of Pennsylvania Statutes Title 72§§4711-4714, special assessments may be granted to persons rehabilitating their homes. The method utilized is a step-gradation over a five-year period, with the improvement assessed at zero percent the first year to full assessment the sixth year, with 20 percent increments in between. This results in a property's slowly increasing in value rather than experiencing a sharp jump during the year the improvement takes place. (See Exhibit 6-4). Another form of tax relief occurs when the Homesteading Board takes control of a property. At that time it is reassessed down to between $3,000 and $4,000 in value. This provides a double break for the homesteader in terms of initial tax burdens. While the Philadelphia program is by no means as generous to the homesteader as Wilmington's, it does offer some relief in terms of the normal immediate assessment upgrading under standard taxing procedures. In terms of the unit in Exhibit 6-4 this would mean about a $400 savings on taxes for the first 5 years, not taking into account the savings engendered by the initial reassessment down to $3,500.

COST-REVENUE REALITIES

The methodology presented in Appendix B for calculating homestead cost-revenue impacts was applied to a representative Philadelphia homestead. (See Exhibit 6-4.) The average annual loss to the city during the first five years of the homestead's life comes close to $1,056.73. This is a substantial amount, but considerably less than the $1,473.54 deficit occurring in Wilmington and is about the same magnitude as Baltimore's. This difference can be attributed to the substantially higher assessments the Philadelphia homesteader must bear relative to Wilmington's more generous special abatement procedures. Another important factor contributing to this difference is the lower percentage of school revenues raised through the property tax in Philadelphia in comparison with Wilmington. Education costs constitute the largest element of the property tax burden; since Philadelphia must raise only 33 percent of its public school expenditures via the property tax, as compared with 50 percent in Wilmington, Philadelphia's cost-revenue gap is substantially less.

When the special assessment period ends, the amount of taxes collected on the parcel will rise to $310.38 annually. While this will serve to further lessen the deficit caused by homesteading, it is startlingly clear that severe fiscal burdens are associated with housing family-raising households which are not affluent.

SPECIAL SERVICES

Philadelphia's most significant special services attempt to treat deteriorating neighborhoods and subareas comprehensively. All of the vacant houses in an area are evaluated in terms of their use as homesteads and their need for centralized rehabilitation programs or demolition. In many cases, vacant lots are reemployed according to neighborhood desires and needs. Block improvement projects have also been organized ranging from paint-up and fix-up efforts to removal of derelict autos to a neighborhood parks program. The homesteading effort is also coordinated with a neighborhood program to insure maximum impact on target neighborhoods. The Community Resources Coordinator is largely responsible for seeing the relationship between the homesteader and neighborhood develop, as well as monitoring any needed and achievable improvements in the surrounding socioeconomic environment.

Programs aimed specifically at the parcel include the aforementioned removal of lead-based paint and erradication of rat infestation before the resident moves in. Tentative plans call for a creation of a "tool bank" which would lend expensive equipment to homesteaders unable to afford their purchase.

In terms of resident-oriented services, the staff feels the homesteaders can handle themselves well enough without the provision of homeownership counseling and other programs aimed at assisting the new homeowner adjust to the responsibility of his new life style.

SUMMARY

Philadelphia has implanted its own individualistic mark on urban homesteading. The conventional program evolution, as evidenced in Baltimore and Wilmington, saw homesteading as the apple of their respective mayors' eyes. Not so in Philadelphia. If policy is measured by executive actions, not verbiage, then considerably less than enthusiastic backing by the mayor's office has been evident. Homesteading has been caught in the realm of ever-present political maneuvering. Consequently, the program has had to adapt itself to this limiting context.

With $1.5 million in city loan and mortgage guarantees held in abeyance, financing has been achieved only with the participation of private foundations and the Pennsylvania Housing Finance Agency. And the going has not been easy. The administrative posturing of the programming has made it dependent on a number of external parties, considerably slowing its potential throughput.[30] Strong elements, however, do exist—special assessment procedures serve as a substantial incentive, and potential local leadership may be developing on the basis of historically strong block associations. But these positive program aspects have yet to counter the lack of full administrative backing.

NOTES

1. Housing Association of Delaware Valley, *A Consumer's Guide to Urban Homesteading* (Philadelphia: Housing Association of Delaware Valley, 1975), p. 7.

2. U.S. Bureau of Census, *Census of Population and Housing: 1970 Census Tracts, Final Report PHC(1)-159.*

3. *Ibid.*

4. Art Spikol, "On the House," *Philadelphia Magazine*, March, 1974.

5. *Philadelphia Inquirer*, March 10, 1975.

6. Philadelphia, Pennsylvania, City Ordinance 73-543 §2.

7. *Ibid.*, §1.

8. *Ibid.* §6.

9. *Ibid.* §6(k.).

10. Interview, Program Director, Philadelphia Urban Homesteading Office, August 7, 1974.

11. Interview, Program Officer, Vacant Property Monitoring System, August 12, 1974.

12. *Ibid.*

13. Pennsylvania Statutes §7293.

14. Interview, Program Director, Philadelphia Urban Homesteading Office, August 7, 1974.

15. *U.S. Congressional Record*, 20145 (daily ed., November 9, 1973).

16. Interview, Program Official, Philadelphia Urban Homesteading Office, November 8, 1974.

17. *Ibid.*

18. Interview, Program Official, Philadelphia Urban Homesteading Office, April 6, 1975.

19. Interview, Program Director, Philadelphia Urban Homesteading Office, August 7, 1974.

20. *Ibid.*

21. *Ibid.*

22. *Ibid.*

23. Interview, Program Officer, Philadelphia Urban Homesteading Program, August 12, 1974.

24. Philadelphia, Pennsylvania, City Ordinance 73-543 §6(3).

25. Interview, Program Official, Philadelphia Urban Homesteading Office, November 8, 1974.

26. Philadelphia, Pennsylvania, City Ordinance 73-543 §24.

27. U.S. Internal Revenue Service, Form 1040 (Washington, D.C., 1975).

28. "Profile of Philadelphia's first 20 Homesteaders" mimeograph (Philadelphia: Urban Homesteading Office, 1974).

29. Interview, Program Official, Pennsylvania Housing Finance Agency, August 14, 1974.

30. For a detailed review of the Philadelphia Urban Homesteading Ordinance, see Shelly Scott Friedman, "Philadelphia's Urban Homesteading Ordinance: A Poor Beginning Toward Reoccupying the Urban Ghost Town," *Buffalo Law Review*, Vol. 3, No. 3, Spring 1974, pp. 273-304.

EXHIBIT 6-5

CAPSULATED DESCRIPTION
PHILADELPHIA HOMESTEAD PROGRAM

THE CONTEXT: Philadelphia, Pennsylvania is the scene of over 24,000
                          abandoned residential units, more than 3.6 percent of
                          the city's 673,524 dwelling units. At the same time, a
                          net outmigration of 200,000 persons since 1950
                          leaves Philadelphia with 1,948,609 residents. The
                          conventional renewal and rehabilitation programs
                          used in other settings have been tried in Philadelphia
                          as well, usually with the same unsatisfactory results.

PROGRAM   Philadelphia formally adopted a homesteading ordi-
INITIATION: nance on June 20, 1973, when Mayor Rizzo signed
                          Ordinance 543, creating the Philadelphia Home-
                          steading Program. An original impetus was the urging
                          of Councilman Joseph E. Coleman, who in 1968
                          suggested a program of granting homes to persons
                          willing to revitalize and reside in them.

PROGRAM   1. The return of vacant properties to the tax rolls.
OBJECTIVES: 2. The placement in homes of people who want to be
                             homeowners but are not able to do so in the
                             normal market structure.
                          3. The use of homesteading as a first effort to begin
                             devising more sophisticated processes for dealing
                             with abandoned housing.

ADMINISTRATIVE   Homesteading Board, the major administrative and
FRAMEWORK: policy body comprises eleven members of groups and
                          agencies whose cooperation is necessary to a success-
                          ful program. The homesteading ordinance mandates
                          assistance from these agencies. The technical staff,
                          responsible for program operations, has twelve posi-
                          tions, covering administration, liason and publicity,
                          rehabilitation estimation, research, and investigation.
                          Each of the staff members are full-time members of
                          the program.

OTHER PROGRAM   *Board Members:*   Includes   non-government
PARTICIPANTS: representatives from each
                                                    of the following groups—

EXHIBIT 6-5

CAPSULATED DESCRIPTION
PHILADELPHIA HOMESTEAD PROGRAM (Cont'd.)

OTHER PROGRAM PARTICIPANTS: (Cont'd.)	Board Members: (Cont'd.)	architects, contractors, clergymen, and representatives of the Building Trades Council, savings and loan institutions, and the general public.
	Block Associations:	Develop the potential for leadership in neighborhood improvement efforts.
	Division of Management Information Services of the Department of Finance:	Carries out the computer processing of the long term vacancy monitoring system along with Department of Licenses and Inspections.
	Department of Licenses and Inspections:	Carries out abandonment inspections and identifies suitable parcels.
	Health Department:	Rodent control and lead paint removal.
	Urban Homesteading Finance Corporation:	A consortium of interested organizations which provide seed money and construction loans.
	Pennsylvania Housing Finance Agency:	Provides special financing to homesteaders.
PROGRAM STRUCTURE:	Parcel Acquisition:	1. HUD foreclosures constitute the principal source of homesteads. 2. Tax foreclosure and gift procedures.

EXHIBIT 6-5

CAPSULATED DESCRIPTION
PHILADELPHIA HOMESTEAD PROGRAM (Cont'd.)

PROGRAM *STRUCTURE:* *(Cont'd.)*	*Homestead Evaluation:*	Detailed cost estimates an internal program function; block associations provide an input in neighborhood evaluation.
	Homesteader *Evaluation:*	Fixed minimum selection criteria.
	Financial Assistance:	Urban Homesteading Finance Corporation has established a $300,000 revolving loan fund to provide seed and construction financing (equity build-up). Pennsylvania Housing Financing Agency has established a $250,000 loan pool to provide long term financing with interest rates varying between 3 to 7 percent (according to household income) with terms of 5 to 15 years.
	Special Tax *Considerations:*	Special rehabilitation assessment procedure—step gradations over five years with the improvement assessed at zero the first year, increasing by 20 percent increments annually.
	Special Services:	Block improvement projects, community resources coordination, "tool banks," but no homeownership counseling services.

EXHIBIT 6-5

CAPSULATED DESCRIPTION
PHILADELPHIA HOMESTEAD PROGRAM (Cont'd.)

COST REVENUE   On the modular unit with an average assessment of
IMPACT: $5,000 over 5 years, the cost revenue deficit exceeds
                        $1,050.

PROGRAM OUTPUT: 20 units homesteaded; some units turned over to
                        second homesteaders.

Chapter 7

Newark: Rugged Settlers
In A Hostile Environment

Vlado Filev experiences both a common bond and a distinct difference between himself and homesteaders in other cities. While he must reside in and rehabilitate his property over a set period of time—an endemic homesteading feature—he and his fellow Newark settlers are unique in that they have had to bid for their homes at public auction. This is just one of the major differences between Newark's program and our other case experiences. This unconventional approach is directly attributable to the perceptions of one man, Steve Rother. As Tax Collector of Newark, Mr. Rother had been concerned with the deterioration of the city in general and the increase in abandoned properties in particular. He saw in homesteading a way to combat the ravages of abandonment and begin the revitalization of Newark, though his method of program operation deviated from the procedures found in most cities.

THE SETTING

No one can deny Newark's need for revitalization. Rocketed to national exposure by race riots in the sixties and the then-novel indictment and conviction of its mayor, Newark has replaced Philadelphia as the repository of all the platitudes about the maladies of urban life.

The city's population in 1970 was 376,752, down from 396,562 in 1960. Of its 127,000 residential units, approximately 87,172 were built before 1939.[1] Over 5,000 units or 3.9 percent of the housing stock, are abandoned. Newark has come a long way since its heyday in the 1930s.

NEWARK (33 alt., 442,337 pop.) is the metropolis of New Jersey, and the focus of the vast complex of industrial and suburban cities that modern machinery and transport has made of the northeastern corner of the State. From the days of sail and stagecoach, most of the great transportation routes from the south and west have concentrated here. Successively, steam, automotive, and air transportation have followed the same trend for the same natural causes. The grouping of giant modern industries in this area is a logical consequence; so that today, this two-century-old city presents a picture of a huge industrial beehive built over the staid old seaport and local market center that was once Newark. Since 1890 the city's population has doubled, and the variety of national admixtures that are always a part of this sort of expansion in America has given Newark a genuinely cosmopolitan tone.

The straight, spacious reach of Broad Street from Lincoln Park to Military Park where it bends to parallel the Passaic River ranks among the attractive commercial thoroughfares of the country. On this mile of exceptionally wide street, with its landscaped restful parks at each end, are the city hall, many churches, banks and the city's skyscrapers, housing insurance companies, banks and administrative offices of the area's industries. Broad Street serves as a promenade for the office worker and the shopper. Its sidewalks are thronged all day, and when the big insurance companies and banks and offices dismiss their employees even its spaciousness becomes crowded to a degree unsurpassed in other metropolitan areas.

> *Newark in the late 1930's. Federal Writers Project, New Jersey: A Guide to its Present and Past (New York: The Viking Press, 1939), p. 313.*

Newark today is but a mere shadow of its former self. Located in a state with a relatively high growth rate—New Jersey's population increased from 4.8 million in 1950 to 7.2 million in 1970—Newark has experienced a long-term economic and population decline. (See Exhibit 7-1.) Buffeted by successive waves of ethnic and racial groups, the city saw its black population become dominant sometime between 1960 and 1970. Other demographic changes have rapidly been taking place. The median age level in the city, both white and Negro, has dropped sharply as has household size. Moreover, rates of murder and non-negligent manslaughter, forcible rape, robbery, and other measures of the quality of life such as infant mortality rates, the ratio of people to medical practitioners, percentage of families below poverty level income, percentage of housing units owned by occupants, percentage of housing units with 1.01 or more persons per room, percentage of housing units lacking some or all plumbing facilities, percentage of college graduates, park and recreational acreage, and places of amusement and recreation all rate nationally among the five worst cities in America, according to a national study. The study, a compendium of social indicators, arrived at a somewhat expected conclusion that Newark stands without serious challenge as the worst city in America.[2]

As was discussed in Chapter 2, one interpretation of neighborhood decline and housing abandonment saw the lack of new immigration from abroad into

EXHIBIT 7-1
NEWARK: A STATISTICAL PROFILE

Total Population	1950	1960	1970
New Jersey	4,835,329	6,066,782	7,168,164
Newark	417,172	405,220	382,417

Black Population

1960	136,372
1970	207,458

Median Age (Total)		Median Age (Black)	
1960	31.6	1960	25.3
1970	25.9	1970	21.1

Household Size (Total)		Household Size (Black)	
1960	3.1	1960	3.2
1970	2.7	1970	3.0

Median Family Income (Total)		Median Family Income (Black)	
1960	$4,619	1960	$3,710
1970	$7,735	1970	$5,634

Median Education (Total)		Median Education (Black)	
1960	8.9	1960	8.8
1970	10.0	1970	10.4

Median House Value (Total)		Median House Value (Black)	
1960	$13,500	1960	$13,000
1970	$17,300	1970	$17,100

Housing Units

1970 Total	127,375
Built before 1939	68%
Built before 1949	81%

Units in Structure

Structure Type	Number of Units	
1 unit detached	10,110	(7.9%)
2 unit attached	1,752	(1.3%)
2 - 4 units	54,908	(43.1%)
5 or more units	60,574	(47.6%)

Source: U.S. Bureau of the Census, *Census of Population and Housing: 1970, Census Tracts, Final Report PHC (1)-147 Newark, N.J. SMSA.*

core cities as *one* major dynamic in the creation of nonviable neighborhoods and structures. The magnitudes of population decline in all of our case settings may attest to the possibility of the irrelevance of these cities' oldest and least serviceable neighborhoods due simply to the lack of effective market demand. But while new outmigration represents a flow of substantial consequence, it does not mean that immigration is but a trickle. Certainly, while the vast stream of immigrants into this country and its cities from 1880 through 1920 may never again be replicated—it should also be remembered that the extant housing supplies in cities such as Newark were a response to these population masses—the liberalized immigration law adopted in 1965 has occasioned a very significant flow of immigrants to the United States.[3] The cities and neighborhoods receiving these new populations, among them Newark, demonstrate that immigration is not a historical artifact but an ever present reality. While not so naive about America's shortcomings as their forebearers, the newcomers are quick to take advantage of opportunities not readily available in their home countries. One of these advantages may be that of homeownership offered through urban homesteading. A pool of such ready applicants, although difficult to isolate through the basic census tabulations, may be quite consequential for any homesteading program.

Also critical for homesteading are the basic housing resources of the city. Newark's characteristic residences are wood-framed, three-story, six-unit configurations, a type designed to house the wave of immigrant laborers arriving in the city in the early parts of the 20th century. Over 47 percent of Newark's housing stock—60,574 units—comprise structures with more than five units. Another 43 percent, 54,908 units, are located in structures with two to four units. So 90 percent of the city's units must be regarded as obsolete housing geared to another time, another age. Only 12,000 units are one-family detached or attached structures. This does not bode well for individual homesteading efforts in comparison with the other case studies, whose settings are dominated by rowhouses, generally masonry framed, which can be described as single-family attached units. Given these basic resources, and the disastrous levels of its social indicators, Newark evolved a homesteading program which, after long evaluation, may be best suited for its context.

So far, 77 properties have been auctioned off as homesteads with interest in the program constantly mounting. But what is as important as the number of homesteads is Newark's questioning of homesteading's underlying principles, so readily accepted by other cities, yielding a program which is often different and sometimes antithetical to the current homesteading dogma.

Newark employs a "bare bones" procedure, attempting to maximize the number of units resettled while minimizing every possible cost to the city. Instead of elaborate parcel evaluations, deriving detailed specifications of housing rehabilitation needs, the homesteads are simply sold at an auction held in each of the city's six wards on a rotating bimonthly basis.

INSTITUTIONAL FRAMEWORK

It is important to note at the outset just how different Newark's homesteading effort is from that of other jurisdictions. Typically, a special ordinance is passed by the city legislative body, creating a separate agency, staffed, budgeted, and mandated to operate the homesteading program. This is not the case in Newark. Homesteading is seen as an adjunct element of an upgraded public sale procedure instituted by the city in 1974 to dispose of a large number of city-owned properties taken under *in rem* tax foreclosure proceedings.[4] The staff of the Tax Collector's office provides much of the research on which properties should be sold, while clearing away any encumbrances which might cloud the title before sale. To make the selection and pricing of suitable parcels equitable, a Real Estate Commission was established. It comprises an Executive Director, the Tax Collector, a City Councilman, Planning Officer, the Tax Assessor, and a representative of the Newark Economic Development Corporation.[5] The Real Estate Commission has a staff of two—a real estate officer and the secretary of the Commission. It is the task of this staff to help prepare for the bimonthly sale of property by assisting in parcel selection, auction location, advertising, and overall coordination.

PARCEL ACQUISITION

Of the approximately 5,000 abandoned buildings in Newark, 3,500 are controlled by the city.[6] The ratio of city-owned to total abandoned parcels is the highest of any city examined in this study, a result of a concerted effort by the city to obtain title as quickly as possible to all abandoned structures and immediately to turn them into useful revenue-producing properties. This is a radical departure from Philadelphia which purposely avoids taking title to large numbers of tax-delinquent units desiring to avoid the responsibility for their welfare. Abandoned properties are monitored by the Newark Fire Department which has assumed this function as part of its program of fire hazard accounting within the city. Information is catalogued manually and updated on a regular basis. This system affords an accurate record of the number and condition of its abandoned parcels.

Properties are obtained via two procedures: tax foreclosure and gifts. By utilizing *in rem* tax foreclosure proceedings, the average time between abandonment and city takeover is three and a half years. The first one and a half years of that time is the required waiting period before a lien may go into effect. The remaining two years are the redemption period during which the original owner may redeem his property for payment of past taxes with interest.[7] New Jersey law recently reduced the waiting period to six months on all delinquent properties.[8] Also contained in this measure was a provision for an even shorter redemption period for buildings deemed a health hazard. In such cases the city may obtain clear title in 60 days through a court proceeding. Additionally, under New Jersey law a property owner may deed his premises in lieu of foreclosure to the municipality. This sudden generosity on the part of the owner is usually induced by a fear of liability suits or charges for housing violations. Newark acquires approximately 100 homes this way each year.[9]

Newark, unlike other homesteading cities, prefers to homestead occupied parcels. The reasons cited for this are twofold. First, the city believes that parcels continually occupied have a substantially higher level of maintenance than those long vacant. Second, most of the city-owned, but occupied, parcels have not been receiving a satisfactory level of maintenance, so their return to private hands may prevent even further deterioration. The parcel acquisition stage of this homesteading effort forecloses on tax-delinquent occupied properties as quickly as possible and does so in a very large volume.

EVALUATING THE HOMESTEAD

Very little detailed evaluation of the parcel occurs, nor are its surrounding environmental characteristics scrutinized explicitly. Interest centers on location for identification purposes, and on a determination of the abandoned structure's size and use for suitability as a homestead.

Parcels zoned either industrial or commercial are not homesteaded, nor are residential structures consisting of six units or more. A structural evaluation, however, is undertaken, establishing the auction price. Should a sound unit require only modest rehabilitation work, the cost will be set fairly high, usually between $7,000 and $10,000. If the same unit required major rehabilitation, the price would be drastically lowered to the $100 to $500 range; yet, the unit would still be auctioned.[10] The city also proposes to do major structural work on extremely poor units raising their level of suitability and passing the cost along in a higher sale price.

This major program feature departs from the norm of most homesteading programs. Newark estimates that if a unit is of such poor physical condition that it is not fit for rehabilitation, then no one will buy it. Their faith in the operational logic of the free enterprise system is strong. Newark, unlike other cities, does not give the parcels away—it seems reasonable to the program administrator that no one will be willing to commit resources to purchase or restore a parcel which is totally worthless.

It should be noted that little detailed parcel inspection for structural soundness or other code-related characteristics is done by the auction staff beyond that undertaken to establish auction price. Nor are any rehabilitation cost estimates prepared for the homesteader.

EVALUATING THE HOMESTEADER

Newark has one basic objective for its homesteading program—to bring tax-delinquent parcels back onto the rolls of tax-paying properties.[11] Little interest is manifested in doing anything more with the program. Poor people are considered as desirable as middle and upper class homesteaders provided they can pay for the unit with hard cash. No effort is made to tailor the program to the needs of particular neighborhoods. This is a straightforward, no-frills attempt to find persons willing to pay taxes on a parcel that was abandoned by other owners. As Steve Rother has said, "The goal of homesteading shouldn't be to sell dilapidated buildings for one dollar each, but rather to assure the occupancy and upgrading of abandoned buildings."[12] And interestingly enough, the initial participants tend to justify this approach. Despite Newark's plethora of urban ills, many long term residents are wholly committed to the city.

> *Purchaser Number 4 owns several private businesses located within the geographical boundaries of Newark including a tavern. Bidding almost $18,000 for a long neglected but imposing three-story brick Georgian structure, the recently unsuccessful local politician exclaimed: "I have lived in the city all of my life and I am not afraid of it."*

This surprising show of local concern has manifested itself in the pattern of sales, with much of the buying done by persons residing in close proximity to the parcel they purchased. Purchaser Number 2 exhibits similar sentiments:

> *"I was born and raised in this city; Newark is my home, and that is why I bought this house." The latter, a three-story frame house had its price bid up to $900 from the minimum opening offering of $25, advertised in the pre-auction hoopla as "the bargain's bargain."*

Minimum Requirements

The homestead auctions are open to anyone who can legally sign the necessary documents and can present payment at the required intervals, the latter detailed in the next section. There are no stipulations about marital status, former residence, income level, or satisfactory credit rating.

The only requirements the homeowner must meet are bringing the parcel up to code standard in eleven months and residing in it for five years.[13]

Selection Process

The vehicle used for distributing homesteads is an upgraded auction procedure. The major change in city policy over time has been the increased stimulation of interest in the auctions through a heavy media campaign emphasizing the low cost and substantial stock of housing which will be available. This process has been highly successful in boosting the previously poor attendance at auctions. A recent sale held in the central ward, considered Newark's worst neighborhood, drew 500 persons who purchased $200,000 worth of properties.[14]

Bimonthly auctions are held in one of the city's six wards on a rotating basis. The staff designs a promotional theme to assist in creating a festive atmosphere surrounding the proceedings. The themes selected so far have been associated with the season in which the sale occurs—a Sweetheart Sale for one occurring in February—or the sale's location—Westward Ho for the auction held in the city's West Ward. The sales are held at the most popular public gathering places nearby the predominant number of properties offered for auction, adding further to the auction's sense of community.

All the eligible parcels are evaluated and prices are set at levels that are intended to encourage bidding. To induce interest in homestead properties, the minimum bid price is lowered below the assessed values of non-homestead properties. This is necessary because a homestead designation adds requirements to a property—the correction of code violations and residence for a fixed period of time—which could be avoided by purchasing a non-homesteaded parcel, if the two were competitively priced. The units up for bid are then described in a comprehensive directory, which is distributed publicly some time before the sale. The interested parties may then locate those parcels of interest, with inspection allowed with a member of the Real Estate Commission staff. When auction day arrives, the parcel is placed open for bids.

It should be noted that homesteading occupies only a small segment of an upgraded auction process utilized by Newark to dispose of tax-delinquent properties. Of 800 potential properties eligible for sale only 200 were placed on the block at a recent bimonthly auction. A large number of the remaining 600 were taken by the Newark Housing Authority and various city agencies, with other properties zoned commercial or industrial and therefore unsuitable for homesteading. Of the 200 auctioned units many were vacant lots or multifamily structures, further lowering the number actually homesteaded.

The bidding has often been intense with some properties having their price inflated far over their true market value. The average sale price for a sample group of recent offerings was $3,277.[15] At the time of sale the bidder must put down 10 percent of bid price as security and within 72 hours an additional 15 percent. Full payment is due at the time of closing,[16] which must occur within 30 days from the auction date. Thus, anyone considering homesteading in Newark must have access to substantial financial resources; this separates the Newark program from other homesteading efforts simply by the level of funding necessary to successfully obtain a parcel. Several of the recent purchasers were recent immigrants who managed to accumulate the required capital within a relatively short period of time.

> *Homestead Purchaser Number 6 arrived from Portugal three years ago with his seven-member household. With all eligible family members employed to some degree, enough money was saved to purchase a two-family, two-story frame dwelling, for which they bid $2,200, and began rehabilitating it. Work currently proceeds with the household head working full time on the house while the remainder of the household serves as breadwinner, as well as*

participating in the reconstruction. The homesteader considers this an opportunity not available in his home country, and is putting forth yeoman efforts to realize the chance put before him. Moreover, he will rent the first floor unit to newly arrived relatives.

After the completion of the closing, the only remaining restraint on a homesteader in residence is an evaluation of the rehabilitation effort by city building inspectors to insure that it complies with the code requirements.

Income Sufficiency

As evidenced by the auction procedure, the city is only interested in the homesteaders' financial capacity to the extent that they can meet the payment schedule. Newark takes little interest in the income flow backing up their ability to both pay for the parcel and successfully survive in the unit. This is a direct outgrowth from its efforts to maximize sales while minimizing all roadblocks, legitimate or otherwise, to that objective. Applying Newark's cost parameters to the income estimation procedure yields a total annual cost of $3,277.94 to maintain the sample unit. (See Exhibit 7-2.) This is significantly higher than the Wilmington and Philadelphia cases, which required annual payments of $1,966.00 and $1,739.58, respectively. The chief areas of increased cost are the higher financial charges and greatly increased tax payments. At this level of expense, in the case of a family of four not itemizing deductions, it would require an income of about $15,000 before taxes to successfully reside in the new unit. This represents at least an 80 percent increase over the annual cost for the units in either Philadelphia or Wilmington.

Yet a mitigating presence in Newark may moderate the severity of these cost estimates. As exemplified by the Portuguese homesteader (Purchaser Number 6), several of the multi-family parcels are being rehabilitated not only to house the homesteader, but also to serve as an income producing property. While our observations are obviously too few to indicate the strength of this phenomenon, a pattern is appearing that replicates past ethnic experiences. Many Northeastern cities such as Newark comprise numerous blocks of two- and three-family wood frame dwellings. Before World War II, these served both as a vehicle for capital accumulation and a source of income for upwardly mobile first and second generation ethnics. Obviously a very sensible way to "make it," such living arrangements fell out of fashion in the great post-war suburbanization and the unrelenting drive for single-family homeownership. This scenario may well be reemerging with the entrance of new immigrants into Newark, who recognize the economic benefits of owning and residing in a small multi-family structure and are not seduced by the media-fashioned image of the good life in America. There appears to be a clear recognition of the long hard road that must be traveled before that dream—a single-family suburban home—is obtained, and they are prepared to trek the well worn route of their earlier predecessors. If the serious environmental decay of Newark does not abort the efforts of those such

EXHIBIT 7-2

TYPICAL ANNUAL COSTS INCURRED BY NEWARK HOMESTEADERS

Expense	*Cost*
Taxes[1]	$ 697.48
Loan Payment[2]	1,664.46
Utilities & Fuel[3]	476.00
Insurance[3]	40.00
Miscellaneous[3]	400.00
TOTAL	$3,277.94

1. This is the tax paid on an initial assessment of $10,536. Thus property taxes = .0662 ($10,536) = $697.48.
2. This is the annual cost of a $6,000 loan at 12 percent for 5 years, the hypothesized rehabilitation cost. The annual cost was determined as follows:

$$R = P \frac{i(1+i)^n}{(1+i)^n - 1} = \$6,000 \ \frac{.12(1+.12)^5}{(1+.12)^5 - 1} = \$6,000 \ (.27741)$$

$$R = \$1,664.46$$

where   i represents an interest rate per interest period
n represents a number of interest periods
P represents a present sum of money (total mortagage)
R represents the end-of-period payment in a uniform series continuing for the coming n periods.

See: Eugene L. Grant and W. Grant Ireson, *Principles of Engineering Economy* (New York: The Ronald Press Company, 1964), p. 43 and p. 553.

3. Average estimates based on rehabilitated units in the Northeast. See: George Sternlieb, James W. Hughes, and Lawrence Burrows, *Housing in Newark*, mimeograph (New Brunswick, New Jersey: Center for Urban Policy Research, Rutgers University, 1974) and Robert W. Burchell, James W. Hughes and George Sternlieb, *Housing Costs and Housing Restraints: The Realities of Inner City Housing Costs* (New York: Life Insurance Association of America, 1970).

Other estimates of occupancy and operating costs are presented in George Sternlieb, *The Urban Housing Dilemma: The Dynamics of New York City's Rent Controlled Housing* (New York: Housing and Development Administration, 1972), and George Sternlieb, *The Tenement Landlord* (New Brunswick, New Jersey: Rutgers University Press, 1969) and David Listokin, *The Dynamics of Housing Rehabilitation: Macro and Micro Analyses* (New Brunswick, New Jersey: Center for Urban Policy Research, 1973).

as Purchaser Number 6, we may well have to modify our original statement regarding the Newark housing supply—mostly multifamily frame dwellings—as a limiting constraint on the possibilities of homesteading in this setting.

FINANCIAL ASSISTANCE

One of the most valuable homestead services has been the provision of special financing, characterized by below-market interest rates and long payback periods. At present, Newark has been the only case not establishing any financial assistance. Yet, two proposed programs are currently being considered by the city. Given the serious financial straits of Newark, these programs do not involve the simple subsidies evident in Philadelphia, Wilmington, and Baltimore; their financial complexity may be a function of the exhaustion of conventional remedies within the city. While these are just proposals, for illustrative purposes we will compare them to the costs of conventional financing.

Exhibit 7-3 presents the annual payments associated with each of the programs. Employing $6,000 as our modular loan amount, conventional financing—12 percent at five years—requires an annual payment of $1,664.46. These are the magnitudes current homesteaders must face. However, before homesteading came into being, Newark had already established the Housing Development and Rehabilitation Corporation, for the purpose of supplying needed rehabilitation capital. While not designed for homesteading, the corporation offers an established financial vehicle which could be adapted to it. To be eligible, the corporation requires that the participant be a resident of Newark and reside in the parcel to be rehabilitated. Working with local financial institutions, the HDRC, in effect, subsidizes the conventional loan between the bank and borrower. After the financial institution is contacted as to its willingness to negotiate a loan, a determination is made of the required principal and interest payment, and the length of the term.

The subsidy arises in the following manner. (See Exhibit 7-3.) Assume again a modular loan of $6,000 with an interest rate of 12 percent and a term of five years. The applicant is required only to make annual payments of $1,200. Given the interest rate and term, this would support a present loan of $4,326, somewhat short of the desired $6,000. The corporation then provides a grant bridging this shortfall, in this case $1,674.00. Thus, the homesteader would receive a $4,326.00 loan from the bank, and a $1,674 grant from HDRC, giving him the necessary $6,000 rehabilitation money. His annual loan payment, therefore, is only $1,200 a year. This is approximately $464 less than that required by conventional financing.

The above programmatic format is applicable to homesteaders paying less than 65 percent of their income on housing. If they spend more than 65 percent of their current annual income on housing, the corporation may give a grant of up to $5,000 to cover the cost of the reconstruction work. In both cases, in return for this subsidy, the homesteader allows the Housing Development and Rehabilitation Corporation's technical specialists to manage the reconstruction,

EXHIBIT 7-3
COST SAVINGS OCCASIONED BY
PROPOSED LOAN PROGRAMS IN NEWARK

Conventional Financing

$6,000 @ 12% - 5 years

$$R = P \ \frac{i(1+i)^n}{(1+i)^n - 1} = \$6,000 \ \frac{.12(1+.12)^5}{(1+.12)^5 - 1} = \$6,000 \ (.27741)$$

R = $1,664.46 for five annual payments

Housing Development and Rehabilitation Corporation

R = $1,200 required annual payment

$$P = R \ \frac{(i+i)^n - 1}{i(1+i)^n} = \$1,200 \ \frac{(1+.12)^5 - 1}{.12(1+.12)^5} = \$1,200 \ (3.605)$$

P = $4,326.00 value of loan
    Grant = $6,000.00 - $4,326 = $1,674.00

Municipal Mortgage Program (Balloon Mortgage)

$6,000 @ 8% - 5 years computed on a 10 year payback schedule

$$R = P \ \frac{i(1+i)^n}{(1+i)^n - 1} = \$6,000 \ \frac{.08(1+.08)^{10}}{(1+.08)^{10} - 1} = \$6,000 \ (.14903)$$

R = $894.18 Average 10-year payment paid only for first five years

Total Mortgage Cost = 10 years ($894.18) = $8,941.80

After 5 years: $4,470.90 paid back
                 $4,470.90 remaining in balance
Refinance $4,470.90 @ 8% - 5 years

$$R = P \ \frac{i(1+i)^n}{(1+i)^n - 1} = \$4,470.90 \ \frac{.08(1+.08)^5}{(1+.08)^5 - 1} = \$4,470.90 \ (.25046)$$

R = $1,119.78 for five annual payments beginning sixth year

Program Differences: Annual Costs

Conventional (five years)	$1,646.46
Housing Development and Rehabilitation Corporation (five years)	$1,200.00
Municipal Mortgage Program (10 year average)	$1,006.98

Note: See Eugene L. Grant and W. Grant Ireson, *Principles of Engineering Economy* (New York: The Ronald Press, 1964) for details of computational formulas. In the above, R = annual payment, P = present sum of money, i = interest rate, and n = the number of annual interest periods.

approve of contracts, and co-sign all checks. The HDRC sends out bids to interested contractors, who within seven days must examine the parcel and tender a bid. The lowest bidder receives the contract, with all subsequent work supervised by the HDRC.

Thus, this organization can assume much of the responsibility for the parcel evaluation and rehabilitation monitoring usually found within the homesteading operations of other cities. The main program difficulty has been the reluctance of banks to lend on any terms to homeowners in Newark, thereby limiting the number of subsidies the corporation can give. It is an unfortunate measure of Newark's desperate condition that financial institutions have all but deserted the city, essentially "redlining" for investment purposes most of its neighborhoods.

A second problem centers on the maximum loan ceiling of $7,500, which does not permit the HDRC to assist homesteaders needing more than that amount to adequately rehabilitate their structures. The program, therefore, has limited ability to assist homesteaders during the crucial first five years of ownership. As a result, it has yet to be utilized by any homesteaders.

A source at the HDRC has expressed skepticism about the ability of the homesteaders to survive. "They are being lured by the apparent low cost of homeownership into spending most or all of their savings on the purchase of a parcel which they then cannot afford to adequately rehabilitate and maintain. In a sense, the city is trapping many of these people into a worthless and hopeless investment."[17]

The third program is not yet a reality, but we have entitled it the Municipal Mortgage Program. Under New Jersey law, municipalities are permitted to provide mortgage financing bearing the interest rate provided for in Title 31, the Usury Statute, or bearing the interest rate last paid by the municipality pursuant to the local bond law, whichever of the two is greater.[18] Title 31 permits a maximum interest rate of 8 percent, which is higher than the present rate of return on municipal bonds.

While at first glance this program appears reminiscent of Baltimore's, its detailed operationalization again reflects Newark's sad fiscal plight. Given the fact that Title 31 fixes loan periods at five years, the yearly payments thus required may be out of reach of most potential homesteaders. As a result, it has been proposed that the annual payments be calculated on the basis of a ten-year term, with a "balloon payment" at the end of the first five years of the mortgage. At the end of the five-year period, if the owner has been successful in meeting the annual cost obligations, the unpaid balance would be refinanced for a period of five years. To get a better grasp of this approach, the analysis in Exhibit 7-3 is provided. Again we use our modular $6,000 loan hypothesizing an interest rate of 8 percent. If we compute the annual payments required, assuming a ten-year payback schedule, the yearly annual cost approaches $894. The total mortgage cost can then be determined by multiplying the number of periods—ten—times the annual payment of $894. Thus, the total mortgage cost of a $6,000 loan is $8,941.80. After five years of the aforementioned annual payments, $4,470.90

will have been paid back, leaving a remaining balance of equivalent amount. If this remaining balance of $4,470.90 is refinanced at 8 percent for a period of five years, the new annual payments for the last five years amount to $1,119.78. The use of this procedure keeps annual payments to minimum levels, yet during the last five years, the participant would actually be paying interest on an amount of money which also includes interest. But in any case the average annual payment over the ten-year period under the Municipal Mortgage Program would be $1,006.98, substantially less than the other two programs. Whatever the case though, this procedure has only been proposed by the Real Estate Commission and has not yet received approval from the City Council in Newark.

Each of the alternative programs have different interest rates and different payback periods. How can we obtain a single measure to compare the total cost? Exhibit 7-4 calculates the equivalent present worth of the annual payments attached to each of these loan programs. In this analysis, a determination is made of the present amount of money, assuming it is invested at 8 percent, that will be sufficient to pay the future annual costs of each of the programs leaving nothing left of this present sum of money after the last annual payment is made. Viewed in this fashion, the present worth of future annual disbursements of the Housing Development and Rehabilitation Corporation program is only $4,791.60. This is about $2,000 less than either the proposed Municipal Mortgage Program or conventional financing. It is interesting to note that despite lower annual payments for a longer period of time, the Municipal Mortgage Program is probably just as costly as conventional financing, with both requiring about $6,600 at present to cover future annual disbursements. Thus, the balloon mortgage concept does not provide a substantial subsidy to those using it, but simply lowers the average annual cost through a lengthening of the mortgage term and through refinancing.

It has been the understanding of the Real Estate Commission that most homesteaders have done a great deal of the rehabilitation work themselves, thereby lowering the costs associated with the task. A significant development has also been their willingness to draw from their savings to pay for the work. This has made the Newark effort the most independent in terms of receiving outside financing.

SPECIAL TAX CONSIDERATIONS

No special tax consideration is given to the Newark homesteader. With the sole program purpose of returning properties to the tax rolls, the administrators feel it would be absurd to then turn around and absolve the new owner from his tax burden; if the new owner is unwilling or unable to carry the financial burden of a home from the outset, he simply should not be in the program. This perspective has particular validity in this context; since little in the way of assistance is provided the homesteader, it is all the more necessary he be able to "go it alone." While no direct assistance is available, an indirect method could be an assessment reduction of properties to their auction sale value after the new

EXHIBIT 7-4
EQUIVALENT PRESENT WORTH OF ANNUAL PAYMENTS
ALTERNATE LOAN PROGRAMS

Present Worth Determination

Conventional Financing

$$P = R \; \frac{(1+i)^n - 1}{i(1+i)^n} \; = \$1,664.46 \; \frac{(1+.12^5 - 1}{.12(1+.12)^5} = \$1,664.46 \,(3.993)$$

$P = \$6,646.19$

Housing Development and Rehabilitation Corporation

$$P = R \; \frac{(1+i)^n - 1}{i(1+i)^n} \; = \$1,200 \; \frac{(1+.12)^5 - 1}{.12(1+.12)^5} = \$1,200 \,(3.993)$$

$P = \$4,791.60$

Municipal Mortgage Program

Present Worth: First Five Payments (Assumes 8% inflation rate)

$$P = R \; \frac{(1+i)^n - 1}{i(1+i)^n} \; = \$894.18 \; \frac{(1+.08)^5 - 1}{.08(1+.08)^5} = \$894.18 \,(3.993)$$

$P = \$3,570.46$

Worth Five Years From Now: Payments Six Through Ten

$$P_5 = R \; \frac{(1+i)^n - 1}{i(1+i)^n} \; = \$1,119.78 \; \frac{(1+.08)^5 - 1}{.08(1+.08)^5} = \$1,119.78 \,(3.993)$$

$P_5 = \$4,470.90$

Worth Today of P_5 (\$4,470.90)

$$P = S \; \frac{1}{(1+i)^n} = \$4,470.90 \; \frac{1}{(1+.08)^5} = \$4,470.90 \,(.6806)$$

$P = \$3,042.89$

Total Present Worth of Balloon Mortgage Payments

$\$3,570.46 + \$3,042.89 = \underline{\$6,613.35}$

Notes: The last calculation deflates future annual payments to present value assuming an inflation rate of 8 percent. By emphasizing a present worth factor (above formula) we are estimating the present value of total future annual disbursements. In other words, we are determining that present amount of money, invested at 8 percent, that will be sufficient to pay future annual costs, leaving nothing after last payment is made.

See Eugene L. Grant and W. Grant Ireson, *Principles of Engineering Economy* (New York: The Ronald Press, 1964) for details of computational formulas. In the above, R = annual payment, P = present sum of money, S = future sum of money, i = interest rate, and n = the number of annual interest periods.

owner takes title. This reform is also repugnant to the program administrators. Using the Newark sample grouping, the average sale price for the units was $3,277, while the average assessed value for those units was $10,536. This means a homesteader could make $6,000 worth of improvements in his parcel and still not have a unit with a market worth equal to the assessed valuation. Under the practices of the city's assessment policies, the span between reassessments has been as long as 10 years. To receive a more logical assessment on his homestead, the new owner can make an appeal to the tax adjustment board and receive a hearing, but under the provision of the auction procedures he may not use the auction price as a measurement of the market value of his property.

Taxes then become doubly burdensome for homesteaders in Newark—they not only do not receive a special tax break for improvements, but their assessed valuation remains unrealistically high. In addition, Newark's tax rate has often been described as confiscatory.

THE COST-REVENUE REALITIES

The approach Newark takes towards homesteading has a definite impact on the cost-revenue relationship in the homesteaded parcels (Exhibit 7-5). Because the primary thrust of the program is a maximization of unit turn-over while avoiding special services, the revenue picture is somewhat brighter for the city, but still not beneficial. Unlike the communities which subsidize the homesteader in terms of tax assessment, Newark permits unrealistically high assessments to continue. This means that for our sample three-bedroom unit which has consistently shown cost-revenue deficits between $1,000 and $1,500 in earlier case examples, an $800 deficit results. This shift from earlier patterns is directly attributable to the high assessment the Newark homesteader must face.

The issue facing the city seems to be the equity inherent in lowering taxes for a special group such as the homesteaders while everyone else in the city is bearing the burden of an extremely high tax rate and an equally unrealistic property valuation. It may be that because the tax burden is so severe in Newark, it is all the more unlikely any inequities can be permitted in the system.

SPECIAL SERVICES

As should be obvious, the concept of a major special services program to assist the homesteader is alien to the orientation and objectives of the Newark effort. As a result, very little after-sale assistance is provided by the Real Estate Commission. What programs do exist are largely the result of involvement by outside agencies. The Architect's Community Design Center has offered to assist homesteaders desiring architectural assistance in preparing homestead alterations. To date this service has been underutilized, but better communication with the homesteaders should alter this.

These, then, constitute the programs presently operating to provide special services to the homesteader. With severe fiscal constraints binding the city and

EXHIBIT 7-5

COST-REVENUE IMPACT OF HOMESTEADING IN NEWARK
(See Appendix B for Cost-Revenue Methodology)

General Parameters

Total Assessed Valuation	$1,200,804,900
Total Population	382,000
Total School Enrollment	77,300
Tax Rate Per $100 Assessed Valuation	
City	2.52
School	4.10
Total	6.62
Assessed Valuation/Pupil	$15,534.35
School Property Tax Levied/Pupil	$636.90[1]
Assessed Valuation/Person	$3,143.46
Municipal Property Tax Levied/Person	$79.21

Property Tax Revenues

Valuation of Homestead $10,536.00[2]

Property Tax Revenue = Assessed Valuation/Dwelling x Assessed Tax Rate

Revenue = $10,536.00 (.0662) = $697.48

Property Tax Costs

Educational Costs = Public School Children/Dwelling Unit x School Property Taxes Levied/Pupil
= (1.871) ($636.90) = $1,191.64[3]

Municipal Costs = Persons/Dwelling Unit x Municipal Property Taxes Levied/Capital
= (3.90) ($79.21) = $308.92[3]

Total Costs = $1,500.56

Revenue Deficit Per Unit: $803.08

1. Total expenditure per pupil almost tripled by state grants of over $1,100 per pupil.

2. We are assuming non-reassessment after improvements, the current practice in Newark in regard to homestead properties.

3. We are assuming a three bedroom unit, using the parameters presented in Appendix B.

the aforementioned necessity to maintain as equitable a tax system as possible, Newark's prerogatives are extremely limited in trying any of the innovative special service approaches of other cities.

SUMMARY

Name an urban malady and Newark has experienced it. Create an urban program and Newark has tried it. Examine shattered optimisms and failures, and Newark will serve as a case example. Given such reality, it is not difficult to see Newark's apparent skepticism of elaborate homesteading endeavors. It has tailored its program to maximize action with a minimum of bureaucratic preemption. There may well be truth to the belief that if the homesteader by himself cannot grapple with current conditions, support services will only serve to forestall eventual reabandonment. The city is probably facing up to reality; its bitter experiences prevent it from seeing in this latest in a long line of urban panaceas a program with long-term success potential.

But out of this milieu has come a demonstration of the possible validity of another historical approach to housing in America—the small multifamily owner-occupied dwelling. In the earlier years of this century, the more enterprising immigrants employed this residential configuration to gain an economic foothold in urban settings. Not so large and complex as a full-scale apartment building, it made it possible for the resident owner to perform most maintenance chores without substantial difficulties and keep close scrutiny over the behavior of his one or two tenants. An income flow was obtained, often enabling the owner to live rent free, while providing decent housing to other city households. As a vehicle for economic advancement, as well as satisfying its housing function, it served its job well.

Accompanying the relentless drive to suburbia in the post World War II era was the new image of the way Americans were supposed to live. Partly fashioned by the mass media, the detached single-family dwelling situated on a half acre plot became the nation's dream and ideal. In the process, the two- or three-family house lost favor, even though it still offered the economic means for less affluent households to accumulate the resources to eventually realize the ideal. While we may be overestimating the scale of the phenomenon, the homesteading program in Newark is providing the starting point for new arrivals to the city to replicate the patterns of their forebearers. Not imbued by the promulgated standard of what the good life is for middle-class Americans, they are using the small multifamily homestead not only as a vehicle to obtain homeownership, but to gain economic leverage and supplement their income. This may well be an approach to homesteading which should be given much closer scrutiny—in fact, it could evolve into its most salient mode.

NOTES

1. U.S. Bureau of the Census, *Census of Population and Housing 1970, Census Tracts, Final Report PHC(1)-146 Newark, N.J. SMSA.*

2. Arthur M. Lewis, "The Worst American City," *Harpers*, January 1974, p. 67-71.

3. *New York Times*, September 14, 1974, p. 33.

4. Interview, Tax Collector, City of Newark, October 14, 1974.

5. "Newark Westward Ho!" catalog of auction properties (Newark, N.J.: Newark Real Estate Commission, March 1974), p. 2.

6. Interview, Tax Collector, City of Newark, October 14, 1974.

7. *Ibid.*

8. New Jersey Statutes Title 54 § §54: 5-54, 54: 5-77.

9. Steve Rother, "Urban Homesteading: It May Be a Way to Reclaim Abandoned City Dwellings," *New Jersey Municipalities*, January 1974, p. 14.

10. Interview, Tax Collector, City of Newark, October 14, 1974.

11. *Ibid.*

12. Steve Rother, "Urban Homesteading," p. 17.

13. "Westward Ho!" p. 6.

14. *New York Times*, September 14, 1974.

15. Survey of 12 parcels chosen from the records of Newark's Tax Collector.

16. "Westward Ho!" pp. 4-6.

17. Interview, Program Official, Housing Development and Rehabilitation Corporation, Newark, New Jersey, August 21, 1974.

18. Steve Rother, "Urban Homesteading," pp. 16-17.

EXHIBIT 7-6

CAPSULATED DESCRIPTION
NEWARK HOMESTEADING PROGRAM

THE CONTEXT:

The City of Newark is the major respository of all the negative platitudes voiced about urban America. During the last 20 years (1950-1970), it has lost 35,000 residents; the 1970 population stands at 382,000. Over 5,000 units, or 3.9 percent, of the housing stock, are abandoned and contribute significantly to a drastically shrinking tax base. The property tax rate has been described as confiscatory. Little hope at stemming the city's degenerative spiral appears on the horizon.

PROGRAM INITIATION:

The transfer of title of abandoned housing to the city, following tax sale procedures, has meant that Newark assumed the role of receiver in bankruptcy over parcels for which it had neither immediate use nor the manpower to oversee. As such it developed a land and building auction program; homesteading developed as an adjunct element of an upgraded public sale procedure, instituted to reduce nonresident homeownership.

PROGRAM OBJECTIVES:

1. To bring tax delinquent parcels back onto the rolls of tax-paying properties.
2. Reduce non-resident homeownership which had been associated with the auction program.

ADMINISTRATIVE FRAMEWORK:

A Real Estate Commission, comprising an Executive Director, the Tax Collector, a City Councilman, Planning Officer, the Tax Assessor, and a representative of the Newark Economic Development Corporation. This Commission, the main policy-making body, has an operational staff of two—a real estate officer and the Secretary of the Commission. The staff prepares for the bimonthly sale of property by assisting in parcel selection, auction location, advertising, and overall coordination.

EXHIBIT 7-6

CAPSULATED DESCRIPTION
NEWARK HOMESTEADING PROGRAM (Cont'd.)

OTHER PROGRAM PARTICIPANTS:	*Fire Department:*	Abandoned parcel monitoring.
	Tax Collection Office:	Provides much of the research on what properties should be sold while clearing away any encumbrances which might cloud the title before sale.
PROGRAM STRUCTURE:	*Parcel Acquisition:*	1. *In rem* tax foreclosure proceedings on abandoned parcels identified by the Newark Fire Department 2. Owners deeding property in lieu of foreclosure by the municipality.
	Homestead Evaluation:	Very little detailed parcel evaluation; interest centers on location for identification purposes and a determination of the abandoned structure's size and use for suitability as a homestead.
	Homesteader Evaluation:	Anyone who can legally sign the necessary documents and can present payment at the required intervals. No other fixed minimum criteria.
	Basic Process:	The vehicle used for distributing homesteads is an upgraded auction procedure. An extensive pub-

EXHIBIT 7-6

CAPSULATED DESCRIPTION
NEWARK HOMESTEADING PROGRAM (Cont'd.)

PROGRAM STRUCTURE: (Cont'd.)	Basic Process: (Cont'd.)	lic relations and advertising campaign accompanies the property transfer process. The latter follows an auctioning format as the tax delinquent properties are sold to the highest bidders. The auction itself is held bimonthly in one of the city's wards on a rotating basis. At the time of the sale the bidder must put down 10 percent of bid price as security and within 72 hours an additional 15 percent. Full payment is due at the time of closing, which must occur within 30 days from the auction date. With the completion of the closing, the only remaining restraint on the homesteader is an evaluation of the rehabilitation effort insuring it complies with the code requirements.
	Financial Assistance:	None operational but several proposals, including a balloon mortgage, currently are being considered.
	Special Tax Considerations:	None
	Special Services:	None

EXHIBIT 7-6

CAPSULATED DESCRIPTION
NEWARK HOMESTEADING PROGRAM (Cont'd.)

COST REVENUE
IMPACT:
A modular homestead, assessed at $10,536, will generate a cost revenue deficit of over $800.

PROGRAM OUTPUT: 77 units homesteaded to date.

Section III

Program Synthesis And Evaluation

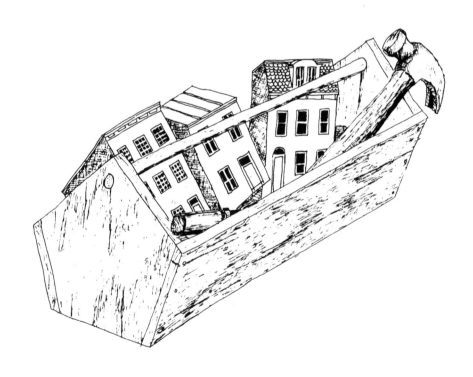

Chapter 8

Program Synthesis
And Evaluation

INTRODUCTION

Before searching out and appraising our case observations in depth, we suggested that the ideal analysis could not be performed since substantive output quantities were not yet available. Accordingly the model analytical paradigm—whose potency is revered in academic realms—was not implementable in its prescribed format. Such a process would have involved the following tasks:

1. The evaluation of goal statements and measurable program objectives.

2. The analysis of the overall system or structure, probing the problem, the environment, and the program, attempting to model the entire system.

3. The employment of this model to examine net program outputs in relation to stated goals and to determine the critical factors leading to these results.[1]

Since program impacts and outputs are not yet measureable or are of limited magnitude, the relevance of this analytical framework, at present, was found to be restricted. It cannot be overemphasized that we are evaluating evolving programs whose final configurations remain to be seen. Moreover, we should not underestimate the quantities of time required by a program to become fully operational. Unfortunately, this fact has become obscured, especially with the high degree of fanfare which accompanied the launching of these pioneering ventures. Their slow evolution has caused them to fall victim to the common American attitude of excessive expectations and instant cynicism.[2] But the length of time between implementation of the programs and the initial publicity put forth securing their legislative passage is substantial. And given the fact that these were actually *ad hoc* efforts rather than full scale programs makes it even more difficult to attempt their evaluation in terms hinging on output quantities. It was with this reality in mind that the case studies were undertaken.

The purpose of this chapter is to weave the many configurations and procedures examined in the previous four chapters into a more coherent fabric. This "state of the art" analysis also tries to emphasize the substantial potential which homesteading offers, despite the many strictures and limitations advanced in the case studies. Each of these programs asks many things of the homesteader, and a successful program has considerable reward to our society as a whole. But what our studies ultimately reveal is that the typical modest homesteader on his own has inordinate difficulties pressing down on him from the start. The basic problem revolves around society's willingness to pay for the support elements attendant to meaningful homesteading.

The following evaluations are structured on the basis of the analytical partitions employed in each of the case studies. The commentary also takes the form of recommended approaches to each of the elements under scrutiny. After a discussion of the settings of the case studies, we review the administrative and institutional configurations which have evolved and their appropriateness to date. (A summary of the features of each program is given in Appendix C.)

THE SETTING

The Common Framework

All of the settings of our homesteading programs share one basic fact of life—as cities, there is some reasonable doubt that they continue to serve a worthwhile function.[3] While all of the cities we observed have impressively rebuilt their central cores, the graying residential neighborhoods encircling the glittering business districts continue, at best, to pale. The office monuments only partially obscure the fact that the American city faces a crisis of function. In trying to justify their *raison d'etre*, scholars have tended to voice, often with great strain, the cities' unique roles as cultural repositories and communications centers, where face-to-face business transactions can efficiently take place, and where interactions among interdependent economic activities are fostered by density, proximity, and transportation advantages. These statements have currently gained the status of well-worn platitudes.

We should not lose sight of the fact, as Wilbur Thompson has recently reminded us, that we did not build great cities in this country, at least in the classic European image.[4] Manufacturing firms agglomerated in tight industrial complexes and assembled massive labor pools—this is not the same thing as building great cities, the centers of a unique culture. And this occurred during the industrial age; the industrial cities where homesteading is taking place may be anachronisms propped up by tradition in a post-industrial society.

Out of its industrial function, the cities' major historic role in the United States may have been the processing of the successive waves of immigrants to

America, drawn to the opportunities of employment at levels of skill that they could meet.[5] The resultant labor pools provided entrepreneurs with a ready source of cheap labor, and an urban system evolved.

> The concentration of business and jobs, the availability of neighborhood shopping districts and other service areas once made the central city a reasonably attractive and satisfactory place for living and working, particularly for low-income families or persons. These city advantages are less and less persuasive today. Innovations in transportation and communications are making centralness less and less essential. The telephone and the airplane have made wider and wider areas almost as accessible as the inner core of the city. Jobs are relocated outward from the hard core of the city. . . . One of the basic elements of the city's earlier growth, the continual flow of fresh immigrants, has now for the first time been reduced. . . . There is no group to replace the current immigrants into the city as they move upward and outward.[6]

In viewing the city in terms of the great industrial and societal transformations now going on, it is difficult not to conclude that it no longer serves the functions for which it originally came into being. As dislocations and painful adjustments result from these ongoing changes, efforts at keeping the city functioning have multiplied, although their effect has been limited due to their patchwork nature and their adaption to expedience. Given the dynamic nature of the basic shifts taking place, the struggles of those engaged in infusing continued life into the city appear heroic. Nonetheless, the large-scale abandonment of residential parcels may be the terminal effect on the city of our national shift into post-industrialism, and the advent of homesteading may be the last patchwork attempt to maintain an urban residential market.

Program Derivations

While the observations shared many common elements, the purpose of examining the setting of each of the case studies was to answer the basic question of whether homesteading's success or failure was generic to the program itself, or was a one-of-a-kind phenomenon whose fate was intimately tied to its context. While this basic theme was carried out in all sections of the case studies, it was the particular focus of that portion titled "The Setting." And in terms specific to each urban context, we found it was difficult to isolate any unique feature which significantly predominated in the homesteading programs. Most elements of the programs appeared to be substantially independent of the particular actors, unique competences, and distinguishable political, social, and physical milieus.

Certainly, the organizational setting in Baltimore provided fertile soil for the germination of homsteading; nevertheless, this appears to be a replicable feature. Philadelphia, a city of urban dilemmas and contradictions, in contrast, has seen the most stubborn political opposition to homesteading, yet the program moves along in spite of it. Only Newark, continually shaken by failure after program failure, proceeds with a homesteading configuration uniquely molded to the limitations of its civic environment. The many disappointments of Newark have served to temper any thrusts toward programs of a fragile nature which could succumb to the urban traumas permeating the entire city. So they have adopted a free market, "sink or swim" system—a real estate disposal operation proceeding under the guise of the homesteading label. But other than these main contextual constraints of our case observations, it is difficult to suggest that any other unique factor in the setting has yet either blighted or fostered homesteading to a significant degree.

Nevertheless one dimension of the setting which we continually emphasized as necessary for a successful program was the number of potential homesteads adaptable to individual rehabilitation. For example, we originally assumed that the large supply of masonry rowhouses predominating in Baltimore, Wilmington, and Philadelphia provided these cities with a substantial advantage compared to Newark, whose predominant residential configuration is a three-story, wood-framed, six-unit structure, too complex and perhaps too antiquated for suitable homesteading purposes. But upon examining the sequence of events in that city, we found reason to question our initial premises. Providing the impetus for this reevaluation was the apparent success of several immigrant Newark homesteaders in renovating two- and three-family structures to more than habitable status. It is this type of dwelling configuration which enabled large numbers of ethnic immigrants in the first half of the 20th century not only to have adequate shelter but to also build up substantial economic resources. In fact, in a number of New Jersey ethnic communities at present, the two-, three-, and four-family frame structure is still a popular form of housing. It offers the owner-occupant not only a place of residence, but also an economic means of support and parcel maintenance. At the same time, it provides rental quarters to other households under close supervision of the owner-occupant, benefiting not only the tenants, but also the upkeep of the rental property itself. As the *Tenement Landlord* pointed out nearly eight years ago, the best maintained parcels within Newark were those small units whose owner maintained residence within them.[7] Homesteading's general lack of emphasis in regard to this specific residential pattern should well be underscored.

Perhaps historical analogy has led to an overemphasis on individual housing units, equating the single-family dwelling (often attached) to the historical homestead grant, a parcel of land inhabited by a single family. But the western homesteads also provided a means of existence, and not only housing ownership. Thus it may well be that the economic support function of urban homesteading has been underplayed with the separate single-family residential mode given undue focus. The city, however, has always been characterized by interdependence among its parts, and not by individual isolation. The demand for rental quarters in the city could provide the leverage to enable homesteading to shift to a new pattern, one in line with urban economic opportunities and realities. The resultant configuration would be the *small* multifamily homestead.

Moreover, the long standing American dream of single-family homeownership appears to be increasingly out of reach for many of this nation's households; it is an extraordinarily expensive way to live. The devastating effect of inflation on housing costs and buying power has taken a heavy toll on the American dream. Perhaps the stress of homesteading should not fall so heavily on the urban equivalent of this dream. Maybe this is why the current immigrant groups in Newark, not yet imbued with the images of the way Americans are supposed to live, have readily seen the economic advantages of owning and residing in multifamily dwellings, as did their forebearers. This approach could be the true urban equivalent of the historical homesteading pattern, providing a means of income as well as that of residence. While the historical analogue loses somewhat in imagery—and the potency of the image should not be underestimated—this may well be a much more sensible approach than conventional program thrusts for a number of homesteading participants. If the frontier and entrepreneur qualities are really to be fostered by homesteading, then certainly more attention is warranted in regard to small multifamily configurations.

Take-Out Mechanisms

Furthermore, as was indicated in Chapter 3, little thought was given to the idea of "take-out mechanism," the means to recoup investment and equity: no assurance is given the homesteader in any of the settings that he can ever recover in lump financial form the results of his labor. This situation could be moderated somewhat if the homestead evolves into an income-producing property. In this status, the property may not only be more marketable, but the potential current income flow could partially ameliorate the full dependence on the future sale of the parcel to obtain economic return from the initial investment. With the reluctance of financial institutions to readily grant mortgages on inner city realty, this income-producing status of homesteads takes on more than minor importance.

So while the context of each of the observations did not appear to be uniquely critical in determining the success or failure of the homesteading ventures, at least as distinguished from those factors inherent in the programs themselves, the image of the historical antecedents appeared to dominate the program directions in most of the settings. The general ambience of each city in regard to the type of housing homesteaded may well have channeled the programs' formats too narrowly toward the single-family structures, attached and detached.

INSTITUTIONAL FRAMEWORK

The current fashionability of homesteading may simply be the complement of our previous urban failures.[8] A generation of highly institutionalized, centrally directed federal programs has proved at best inconclusive. The number of monuments—office complexes, luxury housing developments, and commercial ventures—has more than been offset by unmarketable tracts of vacant land, the Pruitt-Igoes, and of the decline of adjacent areas overwhelmed by the outflow of problems from the core. While the shortcomings have been rationalized, and perhaps rightly so, in terms of not enough commitment, not enough time, and not enough money, the political forces now behind them possess little clout. These centralized approaches have become indelibly linked to an image of impotency. New thrusts of urban policy indicate a retreat from institutional ventures and the gaps they have left behind.

The noninstitutionalized image of homesteading, then, has contributed greatly to its rapidly rising appeal; it may be the end result of the bankruptcy of the large-scale centralized approach to forestall the demise of the central city. Homesteading then could be interpreted as a last gasp of moribund urban policy. Whether this is actually the case is as yet unclear.

But if homesteading's appeal does in fact stem from its noninstitutional approach, a dilemma arises. As we have seen in our case studies, informal administrative arrangements essentially lead to ineffective programs. While the fledgling efforts examined here suggest that homesteading may yet be a phrase in search of a program, it may be erroneous to assume that any homesteading program will be self-operating. If the sponsoring municipality is truly serious in regard to increased homeownership and homesteading, a sophisticated operational framework is obviously required.

Two approaches readily bound the continuum of alternatives facing any municipality considering homesteading. The first, as evidenced in Newark, is unpretentious, skeletal, and straightforward, but may not provide services necessary to assure the program's success. In such a case, homesteading is probably being misused as a vehicle to get the city out of its fast growing role as receiver-in-bankruptcy. This program is designed to maximize sales of accumulated volumes of housing that have fallen into municipal ownership, thus returning them to tax-paying status. But this is homesteading in public relations terms only. The other boundary is perhaps demonstrated by Baltimore, where a sophisticated institutionalized housing and planning framework will at least test whether the program, given proper resources, can deliver results.

If the approach of Newark is decided upon, no pretensions should be made about its virtues for homesteading per se. If the Baltimore approach is attempted, then it must be administered within a setting that includes substantial support elements if it is to meet the two challenges which really face it—the need for comprehensiveness and for adaptability.

What form should such an approach take? Lacking immediate operational predecessors and a body of empirical and theoretical research to draw upon, most homesteading cities sail into untested waters with at best a fuzzy understanding of the parameters of the task before them. Early hopes quickly undergo revision as the realities of the street fail to yield to untested procedures.

The first experiences have shown that while no one format can work in every situation—the demands of each community are too unique for that—certain tasks must be fulfilled in any program or else it simply doesn't function. How best are these tasks organized?

Baltimore has probably created the best framework of the aforementioned cities, consolidating all of the various city functions directly related to housing under one umbrella agency. This organizational vehicle provides the environment for the homesteading operation. Such a comprehensive agency—encompassing the planning, zoning, inspection, rehabilitation, renewal, acquisition, financing, and housing authority functions—provides a milieu of cooperation and a pool of available services. In such a setting homesteading has available to it the specialized talents which enable it to proceed through its various program elements with maximum speed and effectiveness. Moreover, if homesteading is to transcend its early permutation as a one-shot attempt to deal with abandonment problems, it must become part of a coordinated approach to neighborhood preservation which includes other adjacent rehabilitation and stabilization mechanisms.

We should not lose sight of the fact that homesteading is a process-oriented activity, moving through a series of repetitive cycles. It must perform the same sets of tasks, or variations on them, each time through the cycle. This distinguishes it from a project-based function, geared up to the completion of a one-time-only endeavor, with repetitive tasks kept to a minimum. For example, the acquisition stream of potential homesteads—abandoned and tax-delinquent parcels and HUD foreclosures—flows continuously, if erratically. Its flow must continuously be filtered to secure an adequate supply of potential homesteads. This filtering or inspection function may be initially carried out by a cooperating independent agency, perhaps even with enthusiasm. But it must be done again and again. Will the cooperative enthusiasm maintain itself or will it become an increasingly neglected burden? Multiply this tendency by a number of major functions, and homesteading becomes a one-time-only venture. If it cannot perform its major tasks through its own resource base, then it may well succumb to an ever present bureaucratic malaise.

If homesteading is not imbedded within an umbrella organization, and must stand on its own, it probably will never generate the critical mass of actors to be able to internalize most of its program elements. It will probably have to depend on outside agencies for critical work, agencies which may get a limited payoff for their cooperation. An understaffed, free-standing program agency normally tries to draw in the necessary cooperative services by including the administrative heads of agencies, whose functions the program is dependent upon, on the homesteading board. (More on this strategy in a later section.)

This administrative arrangement lies somewhere along the continuum between the two bounding alternatives, and is typified by a separate homesteading agency established outside the purview of existing operational housing departments or agencies. Such an arrangement leads to perhaps a larger staff than is usually the case when a homesteading system is set up under an existing agency. However, this larger staff still does not permit, at least in terms of our case studies, the internalization of all the necessary program elements. It still must depend upon the cooperation of outside and sometimes competing departments. As a subset of a larger effort, however, the homesteading staff, may have much greater access to cooperative co-workers which enable the overall program to flow much more smoothly.

It should again be emphasized that these generalizations are based on only four observations. Conceivably, the best approach may well be a separate independent homesteading agency internalizing all the activities necessary to carry out all program functions. As yet, no municipality appears willing to devote the resources to try such an organizational arrangement. Lacking such commitments, homesteading must be anchored to the relevant agencies upon whose services the successful homesteading program ultimately hinges.

Enabling Legislation

These institutionalized arrangements often must be codified through enabling legislation, although in cases such as Baltimore the powers previously granted to the umbrella planning and housing agency—The Department of Housing and Community Development—provide for a homeownership development function. Homesteading legally fell under the purview of the latter, and no additional legislation was required, although it may have clarified its distinct role.

The development of enabling legislation can be both a hindrance and a help. All too often the hard-won reforms of yesterday become encrusted, immovable dinosaurs with the passage of time. Yet the stabilizing and unifying characteristics of an enabling act may outweigh the threat of program calcification. Developing a comprehensive yet flexible ordinance should provide the delineation of powers and responsibilities, appropriate bureaucratic interfaces, assigned functions, cooperative arrangements, as well as program limitations, thereby lessening the grounds for legal challenge when theories give way to reality and questions are raised concerning homesteading's precise scope.

The passage of an enabling act should concentrate on matters of program responsibility and organization, avoiding detailed codification of overly restrictive minimal standards and procedural niceties. For example, the inclusion of basic legal requirements for the homesteader's age and civil status are proper, but arbitrary delineations of income parameters, skill requirements, and maximum rehabilitation costs should be avoided.

The legislation should insure adequate staffing and budget for the agency but only in general terms since their full demand will not be known until the program shake-down period is underway. Furthermore, this section obviously is tied to the basic administrative configuration and must be keyed to interorganizational functional relationships as described above.

Moreover, there is often a mismatch between program intentions and the administrative capabilities necessary to transform them to operational status. The legislation is critical in defining the intent of homesteading, but often the program administration is hindered by unfunded budget lines (staff vacancies) and unreleased operating funds. In Philadelphia, for example, funds to fill legislatively mandated staff allocations were delayed and $1.5 million in legislated mortgage guarantees were never released. These realities should serve as a reminder of the gap between legislative intentions and operational capabilities.

Homesteading Board

An important part of the enabling legislation may focus on a homesteading board to serve as the major policy body. Again the administrative structure of the program determines the necessity and scope of such a body. Often such boards appear to be vehicles to secure cooperation from necessary and important parties. In Wilmington and Philadelphia, for example, the homesteading boards serve as major policy bodies. In Wilmington, where the operational staff includes only three part-time professionals, the board consists mainly of city agency heads, whose resources must be drawn upon in order to have any type of homesteading program become or remain operational. Thus a board structured in this fashion is probably appropriate for an effort highly dependent on outside functions. In Philadelphia which has a larger staff but a correspondingly larger area of operation, the board also comprises city officials as well as heads of interested city groups. In this case the program not only is dependent on cooperation from external agencies but also must pay dues to the local neighborhood organizations. As we emphasized earlier, the block council tradition in Philadelphia is a major political force. So in any case homesteading boards are probably useful to gain political clout and insure cooperation of potentially competing agencies by giving them a voice in the program's operation.

Newark and Baltimore have bypassed the board concept (although the latter has an in-house variation). In Baltimore the homesteading program is included within the larger Department of Housing and Community Development, an organization which contains all the necessary services for a comprehensive homesteading program. Thus they do not require a broad-based board to serve as a vehicle to gain commitment of necessary agencies, since such commitment is guaranteed by the basic organizational framework. Newark, in contrast, makes no pretention to providing any substantial services to the program participants. It is a real estate disposal operation and as such comprises the relevant parties geared to that end.

So it appears that homesteading boards must be tailored to their respective settings. But the boards' other functions must be kept in mind: a sounding board for evolving public attitudes toward the concept; a vehicle for satisfying citizen participation demands; and a legislative liaison when changes in the program must be made, as they will during the shakedown period.

EVALUATING THE HOMESTEAD

The two central areas of investigation in determining parcel suitability for homesteading are the physical condition of the structure and neighborhood environmental characteristics. Through the use of a vacant-property management system, Baltimore and Philadelphia and to a lesser degree Newark, present the most sophisticated attempts at evaluating these two determinants. Such abandonment monitoring techniques provide current data on the characteristics of recently abandoned structures and give some indication of the condition of the other units on the block in terms of their inclusion in the system. While these cities' systems could be further refined to include more detailed information, especially regarding the condition of surrounding structures, they provide a firm basis as they now exist for making judgments on the suitability of the structures for habitation. Any effective homesteading effort requires that a system such as this be established, both for suitable site evaluations and as an ongoing attempt to monitor the evolution of abandonment in a city. Appendix A attempts the design of an optimal statewide system.

The mechanics of such a monitoring system require flexibility to adapt easily to the needs of individual localities; however, several of the basic program partitions have wide-spread applicability.

Monitoring Responsibility—To enhance the impact of the system it should be administered by the top level of housing management in the city. This will serve to insure its continuity of operation and insulate it from low-level corruption.

Property Evaluation—This task is best performed by a revitalized Housing Inspection Staff. Evaluation must be ongoing, not a one-time-only process. This can best be achieved by enhancing the local inspection function, not relying on outside consultants or surrogate indicators. Philadelphia experimented with use of water meter readings as a short-term measuring device but found the accuracy was inferior to that of the regular housing inspection function.

Reporting System—A computerized system allows for quick updating and rapid retrieval of information—both necessities if the information contained in the system is to be of any relevance.

Once prospective parcels have been identified, on-site inspection of the premises should be made to evaluate its homesteading potential. The evaluation and actions should focus on: 1) ascertaining physical conditions, particularly in terms of the condition of major utility systems; 2) insuring the property is secured from weather and vandalism; 3) determining initial estimates of rehabilitation costs; and 4) assessing the immediate neighborhood environment, i.e., the structural condition of neighboring structures, the spatial arrangements of conflicting land uses, and the viability of neighborhood groups. Minor problems, such as abandoned automobiles and uncollected trash, may have relevance as indicators of a more major deterioration in the socioeconomic fabric of the community. Exogenous factors, such as the perceptions of local lending institutions about the area and the level of city services provided in relation to other areas of the city, must also be assessed.

To date, most homesteading cities have admitted their lack of success in evaluating the environment which surrounds the homestead, making this one of the areas most in need of increased competency. It may be necessary to classify urban neighborhoods as to their stage of decline—as described in Chapter 2—before any prospective homestead is evaluated. While this may lead to the redlining of the worst areas, such market realities cannot yield to the morality of the times if effective employment of program resources is to be achieved.

The individual parcel in question may be determined adaptable to resident rehabilitation only if preceded by major structural work. If this work is completed by a centralized repair operation under the aegis of the local municipality, an idea advanced by the City of Newark, the homestead supply would increase with the city either absorbing the cost or passing it onto the homesteader in the form of a fee at the time of selection or when financing is secured. The argument against such a program is that it would involve the municipality too deeply in the actual rehabilitation work. While increased involvement no doubt would result in correcting major defects before homesteading occurs, the city could considerably shorten the rehabilitation period, thereby lessening the burdens of the transition period for the homesteader.

Baltimore offers another approach for increasing the sophistication with which a parcel's homesteading potential is evaluated. Under the aegis of a special committee comprising representatives from all the city's revitalization programs, each vacant property is evaluated in terms of its worth and in relation to the needs of the community surrounding it. Should abandoned properties permeate the immediate area, demolition might be suggested. Should only one or two abandoned buildings be present, homesteading and public or private rehabilitation emerge as alternatives. On any single block under study by this committee, one unit may be included in a large-scale city rehabilitation program, another homesteaded, two abandoned structures acquired, and one demolished. Pruning mechanisms—for removing "diseased" properties—rehabilitation at a wide scale, and homesteading are viewed as complementary public actions. The advantage of this system is its comprehension of neighborhood decline as a complex process requiring flexible and wide-ranging responses, if there is to be any progress in combating it.

This forced interfacing of all the varous agencies affecting the city's housing stock makes a great deal of sense and may form the central element of any effective property evaluation system. Again, its success in Baltimore may be due to the inclusion of all functions related to housing within a single administrative structure. The end product of the homestead evaluation procedure should be the indentification of a unit which is both physically and fiscally suited to rehabilitation and which is situated in an environment that will permit the homesteader to break the cycle of abandonment which engulfed the owner before him.

SELECTION OF HOMESTEADER

The key factor in the homesteader selection process should be the design of a mechanism which maximizes the opportunities for program success while remaining true to the objectives established for the program. The degree to which these two, often conflicting and diametrically opposite, requirements can be successfully melded determines the long-term validity of the homesteading concept.

Maximizing the opportunities for success have tended to revolve about the inclusion in the program of low-risk households, usually accomplished through the specification of minimum selection criteria. Each of the case observations require that applicants be at least of the age of majority and usually the head of a family.

Opposition has been raised to the formal requirements that homesteaders be members of a stable family unit and possess either the financial ability or manual skills necessary to satisfactorily rehabilitate their parcel. By the imposition of these prerequisites, critics believe, the program is, in effect, making those most in need of public housing—the poor who often live in "incomplete" family units—ineligible.[9]

While requirements that the applicant be "18 years old or head of a household" or "21 years old or head of a family" do not preclude female-headed or "incomplete" families from participating in homesteading, a basic misconception of the program's potential exists if it is believed that homesteading offers an alternative to public housing for the poorest members of our society. As our analyses of the financial constraints burdening the typical homesteader show, homesteading is not, and without massive government aid cannot be, truly a housing program for low-income persons.

The focus in selecting homesteaders, given present program limitations, must be to encourage financially and socially stable families to risk urban homeownership, and to insure they have at least a fighting chance for economic survival. The lessons of our earlier heritage must be applied in this instance.

The first settlers west were not the poor and the indigent but rather middle and lower-middle class families who could afford to equip themselves, albeit often inadequately, for the rigors of frontier life. Likewise today only the more economically stable members of society have the wherewithal to try the challenge of the inner city frontier.

While implicitly recognizing the latter philosophy, the moderation that the sponsoring jurisdictions have demonstrated in the legal requirements placed on homestead applicants has been admirable. By keeping the detailed specifications simple the program is readily available to the maximum number of persons feasible.

Each of the cities, except Newark, attempts to evaluate its respective candidates in terms of their ability to handle the often complex rehabilitation responsibilities and the burdens of homeownership. While the assessment mechanisms are crude—usually based solely on statements made by the prospective homesteader—the practices tend to become increasingly refined as experience is gained. Newark in contrast has taken a "Social Darwinist" philosophy in establishing candidate suitability, relying on the common sense of the applicants to sift themselves out if they feel they are unable to handle the responsibility. While many persons have been purchasing homesteads in Newark, it is too early to measure the effects of this loose-to-nonexistent selection process on the eventual disposition of abandoned parcels in that city.

Another approach to maximizing program effectiveness would be the careful evaluation and selection of homesteaders in terms of their financial abilities. Each city but Newark does try to match homesteaders with parcels whose rehabilitation costs are commensurate with their resources, but distinct formal methods of analysis have yet to be synthesized. By the use of pro forma operating cost statements, as we have attempted to operationalize them, even stronger assessment processes could be developed. This would go a long way in assessing the abilities of households to homestead a parcel.

But the latter should not evolve into a straight-jacket. In viewing several homesteads undergoing major rehabilitation work, it was evident that some of the more successful were using a distinctly unconventional approach. The latter involved the substantial construction skills of the principals involved, who felt their skills had to be exercised full-time in order to complete the task at hand. This had the obvious result of interrupting the normal income flow. These same observations have revealed the occurrence of distinct employment-rehabiliation patterns, with the homesteader successively moving through repetitive cycles of capital accumulation and reconstruction tasks. After saving the money for a particular stage of rehabilitation, the homesteader terminates employment and invests the fruits of his labor in the parcel. When the immediate work element is finished, the homesteader returns to the labor force, again accruing resources eventually to be poured back into the homestead.

A second scenario enabled the new parcel owner to expend his efforts full time on the structure's resucitation, by letting the secondary household members serve as the principal means of economic support. Both of these seemingly chancy approaches appear to be working, mainly on the basis of the yeoman efforts of the parties involved. Thus credence is added to the claim of flexible eligibility criteria to insure such hearty individuals are not precluded from proving their mettle.

In developing such selection procedures, it is necessary to clearly comprehend the objectives of that program. Both Philadelphia and Wilmington express the desire that homesteading serve as a means of bringing homeownership to people who are unable to afford it under the requirements of present housing market conditions. This is where the fundamental dilemma arises. An increase in the minimum criteria to the point where low-income and moderate-income persons are ruled out of participation would seriously violate one of the central objectives of their programs. The attempt to bring homeownership to economic groups which heretofore could not afford it is admirable but must be tempered by the economic realities of present conditions. While low-income homeownership may be a desired goal, the placement of such a burden on homesteading may cause it to topple from the weight of great expectations.

A much more consistent objective may be the return of properties to the tax rolls through rehabilitation of structures by persons with the economic wherewithal to do so—mainly persons with at least modest incomes. Once the basic program is operationalized, further outgrowths can be attempted, such as assisting low-income familites in achieving homeownership. As we have stressed previously, the highly visible success stories are indispensible at first, necessary to establish the program's validity. Only after solid entrenchment can the broadening of the program be considered.

A final issue in evaluating and selecting participants is the process used to attract them to the program. The employment of local media resources as an advertising medium appears as an effective device for drawing a sufficient number of applicants. Other procedures might include: rehabilitation of a sample unit to demonstrate the possibilities inherent in homesteading, Sunday tours of the prospective homesteads, and open house tours of some of the previously homesteaded parcels to further publicize the concepts' viability and potential.

FINANCIAL ASSISTANCE

Homesteading's first image, as we have discussed earlier, focuses on the independent, frontier associations drawn by historical analogy. But the dilemmas engendered by needed support mechanisms, institutional and legislative encumberances, and market realities soon predominate in the day-to-day operations of a modern homesteading program. The manifold complexities of modern urban society fail to yield to the simplified visions of the program's initial press releases. For those intimately involved in the operationalization of the homesteading concept, the experience becomes a rapid-fire education in the once-foreign languages of building codes, fiscal systems, and financial packaging. Politicans and urban planners must quickly grasp the precise terminology of these institutionalized formulas, about code enforcement standards, fast taking mechanisms, marginal service costs, title encumberances, first lien positions, balloon mortgages, debt service charges, carrying costs, and insititutional redlining. Concurrently, program technicians have been force-fed the language of politics which, while considerably less elegant, is equally precise in its own right; it is measured not in interest rate subsidies but in what the public will bear and how they will react at the ballot box. And at no point has the education been more traumatic than when the programs turn to the financial institutions to provide rehabilitation monies.

As pointed out earlier, a major contextual element causing the initial abandonment of the prospective homesteading property was the lack of adequate financing to assist in both parcel rehabiliation and the provision of a vehicle for leveraging other funds through second mortgages. When the former owner was denied the wherewithal to repair or, more importantly, use his parcel as collateral for other investment purposes, interest in the property declined fast. It is essential that any homesteading program be aware of this fact and provide some form of financial assistance that at a minimum insures that rehabilitation monies will be available at terms low enough to attract sufficient households into the program.

Each city has faced this need, with resolution more successful in some than others. The variety in their approaches affords a mosaic of alternatives from which a homesteading city can draw a model closest to its needs and the realities of its socioeconomic and political climate.

The experimental nature of the early homesteading programs has led to a wide variety of financing packages. Wilmington has endeavored to draw the participation of local lending institutions in providing homestead rehabilitation loans by guaranteeing a substantial proportion of the loans' face value. Philadelphia has drawn support from interested citizen groups for the initial start up costs (seed and construction monies) and the Pennsylvania Housing Finance Agency for long-term financing. Newark, under a previously existing program and the proposed city mortgage scheme, would provide subsidies and grants to borrowers of loans negotiated with local lending institutions and the city. Baltimore has established, through bonding, a special housing rehabilitation loan fund which keeps the rehabilitation financing process entirely in-house.

Each program offers unique advantages as well as considerable drawbacks, and the determination of the program which best suits the needs of a given city depends on the objectives that city has established for its program. With that understanding behind us, some comparisons between programs can be made.

Cost to the Homesteader

The most basic objective of a homestead loan program is the provision of adequate financing for parcel rehabilitation at a cost the homesteader can afford. The results of each of the loan programs in this regard are as varied as the cities from which they come. The following exhibit presents the impacts of alternative interest rates and term periods. However, it should be emphasized that due to the different payback periods, the annual costs should be viewed with caution. Overall costs can only be compared by conversion to present worth configurations, as was done in each of the case studies.[10] (See Exhibit 8-1.)

Assuming the standard home improvement terms at 12 percent interest for five years, a $7,000 loan would cost the homesteader $1,942 annually, and assuming an 8 percent inflation rate, would realize a present worth of $7,760. All of the programs provide a substantial reduction of such costs. Both in terms of the effective interest rate and the length of the loan, Philadelphia's utilization

EXHIBIT 8-1
FINANCING COSTS INCURRED BY HOMESTEADERS ON A $7,000 LOAN

City	Terms	Annual Cost	Present Worth[1]
Wilmington	9% for 15 years	$ 907	$7,776
Philadelphia	3½% for 30 years	381	4,267
Newark			
HDRC	10% for 5 years	1,440	5,590
Municipal Loan[2]	8% for 10 years	1,043	7,714
Baltimore	6% for 20 years	610	5,989

1. The present worth determination is explained in the finance sections of
    each of the case studies.
2. The Newark Municipal Loan is computed via the "balloon" principle. After
    5 years, the loan is refinanced at an annual payment of $1,306 for an
    additional 5 years.

of the Pennsylvania Housing Finance Agency's program appears as the most beneficial to the homesteader. The lease lucrative proposition exists in Newark, as would be expected.

One serious drawback with the Newark HDRC and Wilmington programs is the existence of a maximum loan ceiling. While the need for some form of a limit certainly cannot be refuted, the present levels may be unrealistically low. In Newark, the HDRC limits is $7,500, which may not permit any kind of substantial rehabilitation to occur; the $10,000 ceiling imposed in Wilmington, though substantially above Newark, is still inadequate in the view of some program administrators.

Cost to the City

While the impact of the financing vehicle on the homesteader is of primary importance, the scope and solvency of that financing vehicle is also of major concern.

Wilmington, through the consortium of banks established to lend to homesteaders, has created a program which depends entirely on private institutional support to finance the loans. This approach, relieving the city of any revenue commitment other than an allocation of $50,000 to assure 40 percent of the loans' value on default, is one of chief factors in making this a sound approach for securing homestead capital in cities of small size or of limited resources. The drawback of this approach is that most financial institutions, since they are absorbing the loss in interest on the loans, are unwilling to handle a large volume of homesteads. Wilmington was only able to extract participation by proposing that no more than three parcels would be assigned to any one bank over a year's period; therefore, with agreement secured from only eight lenders, the maximum number of homestead loans per year cannot exceed 24. This may be interpreted as simply a public relations effort with maximum visibility and minimum exposure on the part of participating financial institutions.

Philadelphia has established a two-level system of financing which permits equity buildup in the property before long-term financing is granted. By issuance of what is in effect a construction loan, the homesteader can begin to improve his property and demonstrate the value of the unit to satisfy long-term financial requirements. Moreover, through use of the Pennsylvania Housing Finance Agency's special pool of monies, the homesteader is given very lucrative terms on his mortgage, superior to any of the programs here examined. One question which might be raised is the strength and durability of the Housing Finance Agency's commitment. This makes the Philadelphia effort, like Wilmington's, somewhat weakened by the same factor which absolves it from financial commitment—dependence on outside capital.

Newark, as of yet, has no program designed to aid the homesteader. The use of HDRC monies is a possibility, but to date there has been little interaction between these programs. The other possibility of a balloon-type city mortgage has yet to be operationalized. It has been demonstrated that homesteaders in Newark face the most difficult financial challenge to their solvency, and a better financing vehicle, either through a modified HDRC or in terms of the city mortgage, is in order.

Baltimore, through its REAL program, has floated a $3,000,000 bond issue, out of which loans can be made to a fair number of homesteaders. The control of this money by the city administration allows flexibility in its disbursements should future conditions warrant. The loan ceiling of $17,400 allows wide latitude in the amount which can be granted to the homesteader. The "in house" nature of the REAL program and its use by other rehabilitation efforts in the city seems to indicate it would be most applicable to larger communities where both adequate bonding capabilities and staff are available to effectively operate the program.

Each of these programs, just as with each of the loans available to the homesteaders, works best in the proper context, making the delineation of an "ideal" program pointless. By assessing the particular characteristics and demands of a given community in terms of these examples, some guidance should be found as to the financing vehicle most amenable to that community. Moreover, it may be possible to pyramid these efforts if a large-scale effort is desired—for example, to take what the reluctant financial institutions will give, add in the participation by State Housing Finance Agencies, and maximize municipally granted mortgages. A successful homesteading effort must attempt to exploit these sources to their fullest extent.

SPECIAL TAX CONSIDERATIONS
AND COST-REVENUE IMPLICATIONS

The burden of establishing a homestead claim in the urban context is without precedent in terms of the historical homestead analogies—the strains are particularly great during the initial years of settlement when various institutional requirements must be grappled with. The applied standards of rehabilitation are then faced; the sometimes hectic pace of rehabilitation must be maintained in order to satisfy the residency requirements; and ultimately the carrying costs of these activities must be met. What contribution can the sponsoring municipality play here? Given the conventional market scene, the mechanisms most easily manipulable by a political body, and most directly relevant, are special assessment or property appraisal techniques. These appear to be indispensible elements of support.

In most cities the disincentive pressure exerted by the threat of increased assessments on improvements or rehabilitation has deterred all but the most stubborn residents from reinvesting in their parcels. The free distribution of homesteads serves as a strong initial "carrot" for increased central city homeownership. However, the ever present "sticks," i.e., tax burdens, must be converted to yield more long-range support in order to secure continued faith in the program once the initial glow disappears.

In three of the four cases, the need for property tax adjustments are explicitly recognized, despite the promulgation of homesteading's virtue of bringing properties back onto the tax rolls. Wilmington, Philadelphia, and Baltimore all have a direct or indirect form of abatement which substantially lowers the tax burden during the first five years of occupancy. (See Exhibit 8-2.) The savings to the homesteader should be evident—an 86.7 percent property tax deduction in Wilmington, 48.3 percent in Philadelphia, and 40 percent in Baltimore. These savings must be interpreted as a form of financial assistance since they can be applied to the rehabilitation costs experienced during the early stages of homesteading. The only city to deviate from the pattern of granting special tax considerations to homesteaders is Newark. As we have emphasized earlier, Newark is a city on the brink. Its program administrators saw little merit in special tax considerations given homesteading's main objective in their setting of additional property tax revenues. The continual despair of program failure has forged the hard-nosed belief that those unable to bear the financial burdens of homesteading should not be lured by initially lower costs only to be trapped later. The logic of this viewpoint may be unassailable given the unparalleled fiscal straits of the city. No doubt there is validity in the attempt by the Newark officials to avoid seduction and entrapment of homesteaders into parcels which are beyond their means. However, the gauntlet of high costs facing the Newark homesteader may make the program short-lived indeed. The question which must be answered is whether Newark would be better off with three homesteads under partial taxation or with three abandoned structures. The long-term valuation of adjacent parcels—which are inextricably linked to whether their neighboring structures are abandoned—should be fitted into this equation.

Diametrically opposite to Newark's policy is Wilmington's, which provides substantial assistance to the homesteader in maintaining an initial claim. Instead of adopting the more moderate approach of staggering or delaying upward property assessments for various rehabilitation improvements, the value of the improvement actually serves to decrease the assessment on the parcel. Homeowners can realize significantly reduced tax bills by virtue of improving their properties; the benefits surpass those of programs buffering upward reassessment by a graduated approach.

It is also significant that Wilmington does not limit this special mechanism only to homesteaders but offers it to all city residents willing to improve their residential properties. The spark of neighborhood revitalization need not require the creation of a homestead in the area but can be complementary to such an effort.

To facilitate a more gentle transition into the burdens of homeownership during the first crucial years of high costs, homesteading jurisdictions should consider adopting a special assessment procedure similar to Wilmington's which would encourage homeowners to improve their properties by lowering their assessment in proportion to the value of their improvements.

While the operation of such reforms lessens the homeowner's burden, the complementary impact worsens a city's cost-revenue posture. This latter issue

EXHIBIT 8-2
A COMPARISON OF VARIOUS
TAX ABATEMENT PROCEDURES OVER TIME

City	Type of Abatement
Baltimore[1]	The city holds title until the first two years of residence are completed. For that reason no property taxes are paid on the parcel during that period. With the transfer of the title the owner pays full taxes, with assessments based on the value of surrounding properties.
Wilmington[2]	Owner may deduct 1.5 times the value of improvements from his original assessment for five years.
Philadelphia[3]	The value of improvements are added to the assessment in graduated steps over a 5 year period. 0 percent of value the first year; 20 percent the second year; 40 percent the third year; 60 percent the fourth year and 80 percent the fifth year and full assessment is reached the sixth year.
Newark[4]	No special tax considerations are given in Newark.

1. See Exhibit 4-2; Assessed Value = $8,000; Tax Rate = .0609; Unabated Tax = .0609 ($8,000)
2. See Exhibit 5-2; Initial Assessment = $12,120; Value of Improvements = $7,000; Tax Rate = .03727; Unabated Tax = .03727 ($12,120)

Amount of Property Tax Collected Annually						*Estimated*	*Difference Between Abatement*	
Year					*Total*	*Unabated*	*and Full Tax*	
1	*2*	*3*	*4*	*5*	*Tax*	*Tax*	Absolute/Percent	
$0	$0	$487	$487	$487	$1,461	$2,436	$ 975	40%
$60	$60	$60	$60	$60	$ 300	$2,259	$1,959	86.7%
$167	$224	$282	$339	$396	$1,408	$2,722	$1,314	48.3%
$697	$697	$697	$697	$697	$,3485	$3,486	0	0

3. See Exhibit 6-2 and 6-4; the total tax differs from that presented in Chapter 6 since the latter employs the average assessment on the six year base; Initial Assessment = $3,500; increases by $1,200 per year; Tax Rate = .04775; Unabated Tax = .04775 ($9,500)
4. See Exhibit 7-2; Assessed Value = $10,536; Tax Rate = .0662; Unabated Tax = .0662 ($10,536)

raises three vexing questions:

1. Properties which were paying no taxes are returned to the property tax rolls, but at what cost in terms of municipal services?

2. Furthermore, how significant are the kind of losses we estimate will occur should the programs expand to a significant degree?

3. Does the city see homesteading as a means of revenue or rehabilitation? The conception of the program as either will determine its attitude towards alternative cost-revenue postures.

In all of the case studies, the cost-revenue estimations painted a gloomy picture, though the deficit amount varied greatly. Wilmington was the most adversely affected, exhibiting a $1,474 deficit per unit. Baltimore's was of similar magnitude, $1,148. Newark, in contrast, showed a deficit of *only* $803 per unit. There is a direct inverse relationship between the amount of revenue raised and the application of special assessment and taxation procedures in the jurisdiction. Wilmington, which has the lowest tax yield because of its extremely generous abatement procedure, also has the highest deficit of costs versus revenues. Not surprisingly, Newark, which grants no assessment abatements, shows the minimal deficit posture. At the same time, it has the highest taxing rate in the sample grouping of cities. All this sounds logical enough and quite reasonable.

But what of our three basic questions?

Perhaps we can partially answer them in reference to the following example. We will assume Baltimore as our representative area. The total number of abandoned units in this setting is approximately 5,000. Let us assume that all 5,000 of these units are homesteaded. What will be the effect on the fiscal structure of the city? Exhibit 8-3 attempts to make this determination. Each homestead generates $292.32 in revenues and requires municipal expenditures of $1,440.91 to service it. Thus a substantial deficit exists on a per unit basis. (See Exhibit 4-4 for the derivation of these parameters.)

Each unit is assumed to be assessed at an average value of $8,000.00, as was the case in Chapter 4. If 5,000 units are homesteaded, the service costs which the municipality must bear amount to over $7,204,550, while at the same time the added assessments approach $40,000,000. These additions thus change the general parameters in Baltimore. The total assessed valuation would rise by the aforementioned amount and the municipal and school property taxes levied would also rise by an amount equivalent to the costs necessary to service the 5,000 units. Given this new level of expenditures and a new total assessed valuation, we can determine the revised tax rate upon entrance of these units

EXHIBIT 8-3

COST-REVENUE IMPACT OF LARGE SCALE HOMESTEADING

Baltimore General Parameters

Total Assessed Valuation	$3,034,500,000
Municipal and School Property Tax Rate	
per $100 Assessed Valuation	$6.09
Municipal and School Property Taxes	
(6.09 x $30,345,000)	$184,801,050
Revenues Per Homestead (Annually)[1]	$292.32
Property Tax Costs Per Homestead	$1,440.91
Assessment Per Unit (Average)[2]	$8,000.00

Assume 5,000 Units Homesteaded

Revenues Added Annually	
(5,000) ($292.32)	$1,461,600
Costs Added Annually	
(5,000) ($1,440.91)	$7,204,550
Assessed Value Added	
(5,000) ($8,000.00)	$40,000,000
Revised Total Assessed Valuation	$3,074,500,000
Revised Municipal and School Property Taxes	$192,005,600
Revised Tax Rate	
($192,005,600/$3,074,500,000)	6.25
Percent Tax Rate Increase	
(6.25–6.09)/6.09	2.62%

1. See Exhibits 4-4 and 8-2.

2. Average assessment based on a sample of homestead units.

into the municipal fiscal system. The tax rate thus rises to about $6.25 per $100 assessed valuation, up from the previous $6.09, an increase of 2.62 percent. Thus it would cost the average taxpayer an increase of $.16 per $100 assessed valuation. While this does represent substantial costs to Baltimore, it does not represent an inordinate amount.

Several qualifications also present themselves. First, as explained in Appendix B, we are using an average cost approach. That is, we are assuming the costs of added residents and school children as multiples of existing per capita and per pupil averages. Using this methodology, we are surely overestimating such service costs, since substantial slack capacity probably remains in most municipal service and educational delivery systems. But since we must assume that they do generate some costs, it is probably not inappropriate to represent them the way we have. These limitations, however, should be kept in mind. Additionally, this basic equation should not ignore the potential long-term effects of abandoned buildings on the property values of adjacent properties. If the units were not homesteaded, certainly they would stand as negative influences in maintaining residential and ratable stability in a neighborhood area. In contrast, if they are homesteaded, it is conceivable that property values and assessments can be maintained or even increased if deterioration of an area is halted. In the latter case, the overall increase in assessed valuation may negate the effect of the increased service costs, thereby maintaining a stable tax rate. On the other hand, if the units are not homesteaded and no additional service costs are generated, it is always possible that the blighting effect of the abandoned units will reduce adjacent valuation, thereby necessitating an increased tax rate to offset the declining ratable base. Overall then, the expansion of homesteading programs to the degree we have examined here will not engender losses of such magnitude that the municipality cannot absorb them.

The issue then becomes not only one of program objectives, but also the long-term effects of the program alternatives. Even Newark's approach to homesteading, where the sole goal is to bring properties back onto the tax rolls, has no empirical or theoretical basis indicating it is the soundest from a mere dollars-and-cents perspective in the long run. Clearly, its effort is not one which will foster low-income ownership or comprehensive neighborhood renewal, but it may—and there is no evidence to date that this is the case—achieve the stated objective of bringing parcels back onto the tax rolls. Most cities, however, view the program more as a rehabilitative program and therefore face immediate deficits in their cost-revenue posture. We believe that while turning abandoned properties into revenue-producing entities is necessary, the greater goal of the program must be parcel and neighborhood renewal, which in the long run offers the potential of cost-revenue solvency. If the city must face a substantial revenue loss for the first few years, the long-range benefits of urban neighborhood stabilization may forestall or halt its eventual demise and the traumatic loss of even more revenues.

Minimum Income Thresholds

Another important relationship predicated upon the property tax assessment procedure is the linkage to the minimum income threshold necessary to bear the costs of homeownership. While the financing rate plays a very large role here, certainly the impact of reduced assessment cannot be underestimated. Wilmington, for example, facing the greatest loss in revenue, also has the lowest income threshold level, $8,400, while Newark, least impacted by the cost-revenue deficit, shows a $15,000 annual income required to meet the carrying costs of their homesteaded units. Again this is partially a function of financing rates along with the alternative configurations of assessments. Even allowing for some leeway in costs due to variances in the cost of living in the different metropolitan areas, the gap between these two cities is still substantial.

Again the lack of a national urban housing policy is evident. By accommodating homesteaders, local governments incur significant service and school costs, as has been demonstrated. While there are usually payments made by the homesteaders, the amount of revenue received by the local governments is most often considerably less than the full taxes on such property if there was no abatement. The result is that these localities, which assist their citizens in obtaining adequate safe and sanitary dwelling units, carry a disproportionate share of the burden of state and federal housing policy. Therefore, in the ideal it may be desirable for the state and federal government, in recognition of the increased financial burden those municipalities assume in undertaking a homesteading program, to assist the localities by compensating them for the loss in revenue they experience during the tax abatement period of the homestead's existence. However, the will and wherewithal to accomplish this may just not be there.

SUPPORTIVE SERVICES

In an early "thinkpiece" on urban homesteading, George Sternlieb first emphasized the need for special services to help adjust in the transition to homeownership and to counter the environmental hazards, which are endemic to homesteading settings, if residency is to be more than a temporary phenomenon.[11] As experience has borne out, most homesteading jurisdictions have come to the same conclusion. In all of the case examples, the sponsoring administrations provide a basic clean-up and securing of the parcel, to insure the unit will not deteriorate further in the interim period between time of application and residency. Detailed rehabilitation estimates are concurrently provided in every city but Newark, which makes token efforts in this regard. Philadelphia has coordinated its homesteading program with city rodent control and lead paint removal programs, further improving the parcel before the homesteader moves in.

The hazards and fears of closing on a property are alleviated by the internalization of the title transfer process in Philadelphia, Wilmington, and

Baltimore. Other services in those cities include provision of a list of approved contractors and generally close supervision of all reconstruction work, accomplished principally through the programs' control of rehabilitation monies. One functional area in which development has been slow in most programs, and would be required if low-income residents entered the programs in large numbers, is homeownership counseling services. Sternlieb has proposed that such efforts be fasioned in a manner analogous to the Morrill Act, which established land grant universities to assist the earlier homesteading populations. This format would be particularly relevant if the present small homesteading programs become part of national housing policy.

Services designed to improve the neighborhood environment have been neither as numerous nor successful. At the most basic level there should be a major upgrading of city services to the homestead area. Because the parcels are widely scattered, improvement should be made not only to upgrade conditions for the homesteader but to emphasize neighborhood preservation by demonstrating the cities' commitment to the area.

Wilmington's special tax assessment practice for improvements offers an example of how a general program could be structured to aid in upgrading neighborhood conditions. Its inducement to home improvement should provide a major upgrading in the physical quality of the housing stock. This programmatic format of general application may well be an indispensible corollary to successful homesteading. Other programs aimed at improving the neighborhood environment could include improved street lighting, a minipark system, and greater access to public transportation—in short, any program designed to increase the residential utility of a neighborhood. The whole area of supportive services has received less attention than it warrants, especially in terms of the neighborhood environment, making it one of the areas with the greatest potential for improvement.

A FINAL WORD

Urban homesteading is entering into the most critical phase of its existence. While it has done much to dramatize the plague of abandonments infecting America's cities, its slow and often tortuous evolution toward operational program status has almost exhausted the potency of its historical analogy, the original impetus for its initiation. Despite the cynicism which is following in the wake of unfulfilled expectations, the experiences of the past few years have produced important lessons, many of them obvious. Homesteading is not a program which by itself can halt or reverse the long-standing trends buffeting the American city; it is, however, one of the few positive initiatives taken in regard to the snowballing abandonment process. And it is not a program which can simply send courageous but naive participants unaided into an urban wilderness characterized by hostile social, economic, and institutional elements. The difficulties facing present day homesteaders may well equal or exceed those of their forebearers. Substantial support is indispensable if any long-term success is to be obtained; even then, it will be a long struggle. Significant achievements can be made, but only with a real commitment by local governments, neighborhood institutions, and the society at large.

As George Sternlieb has stated: ". . . We are asking many things of the homesteader, and a successful program has a considerable award to our society as a whole. Is our society willing to pay for these elements?"[12]

NOTES

1. Donald A. Krueckeberg and Arthur L. Silvers, *Urban Planning Analysis: Methods and Models* (New York: John Wiley & Sons, Inc., 1974), Chapter I.

2. *The New York Times*, June 9, 1975, p. 30.

3. See James W. Hughes, *Suburbanization Dynamics and the Future of the City* (New Brunswick, N.J.: Center for Urban Policy Research, 1974).

4. Wilbur Thompson, "Economic Processes and Employment Problems in Declining Metropolitan Areas," in George Sternlieb and James W. Hughes, eds., *Post-Industrial America: Metropolitan Decline and Inter-Regional Job Shifts* (New Brunswick, N.J.: Center for Urban Policy Research, Rutgers University, forthcoming).

5. George Sternlieb, *The Tenement Landlord* (New Brunswick, N.J.: Rutgers University Press, 1966) p. xiii.

6. *Ibid.*

7. *Ibid.*, p. xvii.

8. Again this paragraph paraphrases the ideas of George Sternlieb. See: George Sternlieb, "The Myth and Potential Reality of Urban Homesteading," a paper presented at Confer-In 1974, American Institute of Planners, October 14, 1974.

9. *Design and Environment*, Vol. 5, No. 2, Summer 1974, p. 15.

10. The present worth is that present sum, at a given interest rate, which is sufficient to cover specified future payments or series of payments. This concept is more fully explained in each of the case studies. The lower the present worth for a given loan face value, the more advantageous the loan to the borrower.

11. George Sternlieb, "Towards an Urban Homesteading Act," *Papers Submitted to Subcommittee on Housing Panels*, Committee on Banking and Currency, House of Representatives 92nd Congress, First Session, June 1971.

12. Sternlieb, "The Myth and the Potential of Urban Homesteading," p. 9.

Urban Homesteading

Appendices

Bibliography

Appendix A

Abandonment: Operational Definition And Monitoring System

INTRODUCTION

Urban homesteading is a program which was devised principally to recycle abandoned housing back into the housing supply system. It is a response to the growing presence of abandoned residential parcels which have appeared in many of this nation's urban areas. It is the supply of abandoned housing then, which becomes a major focus of any urban homesteading program. Thus, the starting point for the latter must be an inventory of such structures. This leads us to the very important question: What is an abandoned building? Municipalities and larger governmental units must come to grips with this question as part and parcel of any homesteading endeavor. For example, before a municipality can give out such buildings to be homesteaded, it must take title to such properties, a process which may necessitate having the building declared legally abandoned. This requires certain information about the parcel which should be provided at the same time such structures are inventoried. Consequently, it is very important that a precise definition of abandonment be obtained as a first step in the ultimate disposition of housing for homestead programs.

This appendix provides a survey of abandonment definitions with the goal of constructing both an operational and legal definition of the phenemonon. The vantage point which is taken is from the statewide level. This has been done to facilitate a program established by state governments, so that their constituent municipalities will be acting in accordance with a standardized format. However, this does not limit the usefulness of the definition as it is presented for use solely by municipal officials. Included in this presentation, originally constructed for the Commonwealth of Pennsylvania, is a method for funding a consistent local monitoring system as a function of the larger statewide effort. Such a large-scale effort should enable the magnitude of the abandonment phenomenon to be gauged, with all participating subunits employing consistent measurement criteria, and thereby setting the stage for any type of homestead effort or method of parcel disposition once the title to such structures is obtained. We will first begin with a survey of various definitions of abandonment.

THE TASK OF MEASUREMENT

Abandonment can be defined at several levels of complexity; the most difficult to construct is one which is both simple and *operational*. The latter is critical if a standard reporting system is to be designed to survey current and future housing abandonment at the statewide or other level. The definition must therefore be easy to apply in a number of different contexts by a number of different agencies with individuals of varying abilities and skills. However, to achieve a general, operation definition it is first necessary to examine the more extensive interpretations of the abandonment phenomenon to isolate those elements which are reasonably measurable. Moreover, such an inventory of definitions may be useful in justifying what is and what is not being measured.

Most of the common definitions of housing abandonment are socioeconomic in nature, that is, they attempt to describe or define abandonment as a social and economic phenomenon. While these must be rated satisfactory to their designed end, they often lack the *objective criteria* necessary for active field survey work. They also lack the unambiguity necessary for an operational legal definition. But their survey is useful in that they contain many of the necesasary elements essential for a legal and/or operational definition. The first part of this appendix reviews, then, the *socioeconomic interpretations* of abandonment, out of which a series of measurable elements are extracted.

How do these conceptualizations compare to actual on-line attempts in the field to inventory abandoned residential units? The Baltimore, Maryland system is subsequently examined, since its computerized vacant house survey may represent the current limits to the state of the art in terms of existing *operational procedures.*

The third avenue of investigation involves *legal definitions of abandonment* which have been utilized, in the case of New York specifically, for taking of abandoned buildings under the police power—such a survey system should provide the basic building blocks of data for direct action by localities. Objective criteria utilized in a legal definition should be included in any operational definition so that post-survey efforts—such as declaring a building legally abandoned as part of a taking mechanism—can be carried out as efficiently as possible. Thus a basic parameter for any survey structure should be the utility of the gathered data for subsequent action programs.

Based upon these three considerations (and after the problems of longitudinal accounting are reviewed) an operational definition is constructed, a survey form is proposed, and the general outlines of local measurement and a funding mechanism are suggested. Again, the proposed system attempts to be so structured not only to gather data for statewide purposes, but also to stimulate more responsive actions at the local level and to improve their capacity to deal with the abandoned housing problem.

A SURVEY OF SOCIOECONOMIC DEFINITIONS

As a starting point, abandonment is viewed as a condition in which buildings are vacant of tenants; commonly this is coupled with the virtual disappearance of the owner either *de jure* or *de facto*.[1] This is the end result or final step in a chain of housing market relationships which result in the decreasing value of a building until it is below the level of economic viability. The two critical stages in the process are:

1. A lack of willingness by the owner to make future investments in a property because of declining revenue potential. This results in *psychological* abandonment.

2. This is soon followed by tenant departure, service termination, and vandalization, thereby completing the process through *physical* abandonment.

The essential act of abandonment is the owner's decision to stop maintaining and financially supporting a structure. When owners believe their structures have become liabilities rather than assets, they make such conclusions. As properties become sources of potential and actual loss rather than income, owners decide that it is in their best interest to abandon them, giving up all future gains and losses, as well as the difficulties such properties generate.

Abandonment usually occurs at about the point that the owner starts to experience a negative cash flow. The abandonment decision can come several months before, or as much as a year after this point is reached. The market for such properties is almost nonexistent and owners find it nearly impossible to sell them. Thus, not only do owners suffer a net cash loss, but they also lose their equity investment in the property. The lack of a market also means that most creditors, including tax collectors and mortgagees are discouraged from taking action.[2]

But such decisions, which are the key acts of abandonment, are obviously not publicly announced to municipal authorities. Thus, we cannot measure abandonment by monitoring these decisions directly, but only by observing the consequences of these actions. We must try to identify the key measurable indicators which are generated by the owner's abandonment decisions. According to the aforementioned definition, the owner's act is soon followed by tenants' departure and the building's simultaneous or subsequent vandalization and deterioration due to service termination.

So two critical defining elements of abandonment appear to be tenant departure and service termination due to noneconomic viability of the residential parcel.

An Expanded Format

The Urban League broadens the definition somewhat:

When a landlord no longer provides services to an occupied building
and allows taxes and mortgages to go unpaid, it is clear that the
building is uninhabitable by all but desperation standards. We
consider such buildings to be finally abandoned. On the other hand,
when a building is temporarily unoccupied or is to be demolished for
another socially or economically useful purpose, it cannot be
considered finally abandoned.[3]

The added measurable elements brought forth by this definition are
unpaid taxes and mortgages, the former probably being the easiest to identify by
a municipal government unit.

The above factors are also contained in another widely employed
definition of housing abandonment:

1. A reduction in maintenance procedures.

2. Permitting the structure to become tax delinquent.

3. The virtual abandonment of all reinvestments for maintenance
    usually coupled with increased tax delinquency.

4. The cessation of vital services to the structure, particularly
    utility elements and heating.

5. The landlord arranging through a paper sale to avoid any level
    of legal liability for the structure.[4]

The reduction or elimination of maintenance operations which probably
precede the final abandonment of a parcel and the subsequent cessation of vital
service elements, particularly utilities and heating, *manifest themselves clearly in
the declining physical conditions of the structure.* In fact, one national survey of
housing abandonment employed such surrogate indicators to measure the extent
of the phenomenon. In this survey, Linton, Mields, and Coston defined
structures as abandoned if they were unoccupied and

a. Vandalized (e.g., doors and windows knocked out, walls
    kicked in, paint sprayed mischievously on exterior, wiring and
    fixtures stripped, gutters stripped).

b. Boarded up (i.e., openings into buildings secured by nailing
    closures over them).

c. Deteriorated (an intermediate state of disrepair).

d. Dilapidated (having one or more critical defects in sufficient number to require extensive repair on building).

e. Unmaintained grounds (a combination of trash and garbage accumulation, uncut grass or weeds, broken fence).[5]

This working definition employed by Linton, Mields, and Coston was related to the problem of wasted housing resources. They saw complete vacancy and derelict physical condition as the basic characteristics of standing structures most clearly representing a waste of housing resources. Derelict meant that buildings were, in varying degrees, deteriorated, dilapidated, vandalized, and unmaintained. This operational definition was used in visual surveys of abandonment in four observation cities—Chicago, St. Louis, Oakland, and New Orleans.

Thus vacated structures characterized by uninhabitable physical condition has been one criterion used to establish housing abandonment, *utilizing the condition of the structure as the indicator of service termination and owner abandonment.* This approach certainly has the simplicity necessary for a wide-ranging survey effort. But does it measure the total problem?

If we move to a more general socioeconomic definition which was employed in Newark, N.J.,[6] that is, an abandoned building is one which has been removed from the housing stock for no apparent alternate profitable reason and for which no succeeding use occurs on the land, we find the above approaches do not take into account those buildings that have been demolished due to the owner's fear of continued economic loss and therefore have also ceased to perform their shelter function.

Nor do they take into account those buildings demolished for reasons of hazard (by public action) with no replacement economic use forthcoming. In this case, private demolitions for reasons of commercial gain are not considered abandonments, nor are structures which are removed from the housing supply as part of either a scheduled urban renewal program or a planned transportation project. Thus the comprehensive Newark survey took into account the following elements in determining residential abandonment:

1. housing vacancy, and

2. service termination; or

3. demolished buildings which were removed not for any other socially or economically useful purpose.[7]

The approach includes all those structures which have ceased to provide basic housing services, either standing without alternative use or actually removed from the existing stock (demolished) for reasons other than private economic or public reuse. Accordingly, abandonment may or may not occur before local municipal records indicate tax delinquency, or may not occur before the owner, via paper sale, absolves himself from complete responsibility for the building.

How important is it to take demolitions into account? The operational definition in the Newark survey yielded the following assessments over the period 1967-71:

		Number	Percent
1.	Observed as vacant and open in violation of fire inspection standards.	652	25.5
2.	Observed as vacant and secured meeting fire inspection standards.	820	32.1
3.	Observed initially as vacant and subsequently removed from housing stock by non-urban renewal demolition or fire.	1,081	42.3
4.	Total gross residential abandonment.	2,553	100.0

Since these are four-year totals, the demolished category may appear to be much more of a significant element than were one-year summary tabulations undertaken. If the latter were the case, many of the demolished buildings would initially have been tabulated when they were vacant and standing. Then, if they were subsequently demolished, their status would be so recorded at the next inventory. In any case, a record keeping system designed for use over time must be cognizant of the possible shifts in status of abandoned buildings.

Summary of Measurable Elements Extracted
from Socioeconomic Interpretations

The following elements appear to constitute the operational indices contained in the previous abandonment definitions:

1. Tenant vacancy: this can be qualified to include occupancy by tenants not paying rent.

2. Service termination
    a. utility elements and heating
    b. declining physical condition
        1) Vandalized (e.g., doors and windows knocked out, walls kicked in, paint sprayed mischievously on

exterior, wiring and fixtures stripped, gutters stripped).

2) Boarded-up (i.e., openings into buildings secured by nailing closures over them).

3) Deteriorated (an intermediate state of disrepair).

4) Dilapidated (having one or more critical defects in sufficient number to require extensive repair on building).

5) Unmaintained grounds (a combination of trash and garbage accumulation, uncut grass or weeds, broken fence).

3. Tax delinquency; OR

4. Public demolition for hazard

5. Private demolition with no succeeding use occurring on the lands.

AN OPERATIONAL SYSTEM: THE CITY OF BALTIMORE APPROACH

Recognizing the difficulties of defining and isolating abandoned housing per se, the Department of Housing and Community Development in Baltimore avoids this terminology completely; instead it has disaggregated unoccupied structures into two categories, unoccupied and vacant.[8] Unoccupied units are those lacking tenants, but for all intents and purposes are still on the market. Vacant units, in contrast, are generally absent of tenants, but not always, and are either:

1. Open to casual entry, with doors open or broken; or

2. Have had major appliances removed; or

3. Have had their major utilities removed.

The above determinations are made both by a drive-by approach and actual entrance into the structure. (These criteria are similar to but appear more precise than the aforementioned Linton, Mields, and Coston definition.) Subsequent analysis of city records categorizes the status of the building into five types:

1. Private Ownership

2. Private Ownership to Be Acquired

3. Ownership by Mayor-City Council

4. Demolition scheduled by Mayor-City Council

5. Acquisition by the Housing Authority-City of Baltimore

Most likely, abandoned units would be included under private ownership, but not all such units would be privately owned.

Exhibit A-1 presents the Vacant House Survey Sheet of the Baltimore Department of Housing and Community Development. The numbers in parentheses correspond to the column number on an 80-column computer card; hence 35 spaces remain for additional information if the scope of this system is expanded, particularly in regard to the disposition of the parcel over time. Moreover, additional structural information would be desirable, such as whether the house is frame or masonry, and the like. But while lacking in some detail, the Baltimore approach is a good building block upon which to design a survey, since it is an *operational* system which has been successfully implemented.

The block, lot, planning area, and district codes associated with Baltimore building and planning records take up the first 14 columns of this computerized record. Unfortunately, the planning areas and districts do not correspond to census tracts and hence are unique local codes. Street address is alloted the next 22 spaces. Structural characteristics are then recorded—land use, number of stories, estimated number of dwelling units, and type of structure—in columns 37 through 41. The condition of the building and the quality of the block are then recorded. Status and legal condition of the parcel conclude the recorded elements of the computerized system. Physical condition information is recorded on the form, but is not keypunched; this data is used to prepare required forms for additional departmental actions, such as vacant house and code enforcement notices.

The information so recorded is highly amenable to summary tabulations, which is an important consideration in terms of large-scale accounting procedures. Exhibit A-2 presents an illustration of one of the summary tabulations constructed by the Baltimore Housing and Community Development Department from the vacant house survey sheets. Cross-tabulated are the condition of the building by the quality of the block, by the type of structure and by ownership; the type of structure by the quality of the block; and ownership by the quality of structure and by the type of structure. A number of other cross-tabulations and descriptions could be isolated to provide additional information, particularly if the vacant house survey sheets were expanded in scope.

As can be seen from the exhibit, almost half of the vacant buildings are in private ownership with no plans for public taking at the time of the survey, while another 20 percent are owned by the city without plans for disposition. The latter probably includes a number of parcels acquired through tax foreclosures and the like; these two categories in total probably account for a

EXHIBIT A-1
BALTIMORE DEPARTMENT OF HOUSING AND COMMUNITY
DEVELOPMENT VACANT HOUSE SURVEY SHEET

BLOCK(1-5)	LOT(6-9)	AREA(10-11)	DIST.(12-14)	STREET ADDRESS(15-35)

USE   (Check one box only)   36

Residential ☐   1   Mixed-residential ☐   2   commercial ☐   3

NO. OF STORIES (37-38) | **EST. D/U (39-40)**

TYPE STRUCTURE (41)

Detached – – – – – – – – – ☐ 1

Semi-detached – – – – – – – ☐ 2

Row – – – – – – – – – – ☐ 3

CONDITION OF BUILDING (42)

Good – – – – – – – – – –☐ 1

Fair (Needs some attention – – –☐ 2
    but habitable)
Poor (Needs extensive work – – –☐ 3
    to be made habitable)
Very Poor (Beyond – – – – –☐ 4
    rehabilitation)

QUALITY OF BLOCK (43)

Good (No other vacants; – – – –☐ 1
    minor main. needed)
Fair (No other vacants;– – – –☐ 2
    some work needed)
Poor (Other vacants or – – – –☐ 3
    major work needed)

STATUS OF BUILDING (44)
Private ownership – – – – – –☐ 1

Private ownership to be – – – – ☐ 2
    acquired
Ownership by Mayor-City Council –☐ 3

Demolition scheduled by Mayor- – –☐ 4
    City Council
Acquisition by Housing Authority - –☐ 5
    City of Baltimore

LEGAL CONDITION (45)

Unoccupied; no notice – – – – – – ☐ 1
    needed
Has vacant house notice – – – – – ☐ 2

Vacant house notice to – – – – – ☐ 3
    be issued

PHYSICAL CONDITIONS   ** A **

Missing walls – – – – – – – – – – Δ

Defective roof – – – – – – – – – Δ

Open to public – – – – – – – – – Δ

Windows or doors broken – – – – – – Δ

Fire in the structure – – – – – – – Δ

Rubbish & debris inside – – – – – – Δ

Grounds unsanitary– – – – – – – – Δ

Windows & doors locked – – – – – Δ

Vacate notice posted – – – – – – Δ

Condemnation posted– – – – – – – Δ

All 1st floor openings covered– – – – Δ
    with solid material

INSPECTOR'S REMARKS   ** B **

_____

_____

_____

_____

INSPECTORS SIGNATURE   ** C ** | DATE OF INSPECTION   ** D **

EXHIBIT A-2
VACANT HOUSE ANALYSIS
BALTIMORE DEPARTMENT OF HOUSING AND COMMUNITY DEVELOPMENT

	Quality of Block			Type of Structure			Ownership					Totals
	Good	Fair	Poor	Detached	Row	Semi-Detached	Private No Plans	Private To Be Acq.	M&CC No Plans	M&CC To Be Demo.	HABC[2]	
Condition of Building												
Good	24	4	6	6	24	4	32	1	1	0	0	34
Fair	143	319	762	65	1,126	33	876	34	261	23	30	1,224
Poor	90	305	2,618	67	2,878	68	1,478	283	861	320	71	3,013
Very Poor	5	14	700	16	697	6	162	150	203	195	9	719
Quality of Block												
Good				57	192	13	219	3	37	0	3	262
Fair				59	544	39	489	19	111	13	10	642
Poor				34	3,989	59	1,840	446	1,178	525	97	4,086
Type of Structure												
Detached							127	4		8	4	154
Row							2,333	463		528	105	4,725
Semi-Detached							88	1		2	1	111
TOTAL							2,548	468		538	110	

Total Buildings Vacant: 4,990

1. M && CC indicates ownership by the Mayor and City Council.
2. HABC indicated ownership by the Housing Authority of the City of Baltimore.
Source: Computer tabulation provided by the Baltimore Department of Housing and Community Development.

good deal of the abandoned structures within the city with a number sprinkled throughout the remaining categories.

LEGAL DEFINITIONS

The previous conceptualizations arise from a social and economic interpretation of the abandonment phenomenon. How have these been codified into law? We present two examples of the determination of housing abandonment as they appear, respectively, in the Michigan and New York statutes. The former perhaps is least useful, since it is designed for purposes of mortgage foreclosure rather than efficient field measurement. The latter, in contrast, is part of a legal mechanism to enable the reclamation of an abandoned building while it is still salvageable. It is an operational definition in that it is statutory and makes possible the judicial recognition of building abandonment.

The Michigan law sets up the following requirements in order for abandonment to be conclusively presumed:

(a)   Within 30 days before the commencement of foreclosure proceedings hereunder, the mortgagee mails by certified mail, return receipt requested, to the mortgagor's last known address a notice that the subject mortgage is in default and that the mortgagee intends to foreclose it.

(b)   Before commencement of foreclosure proceedings, the mortgagee executes and causes to be duly recorded in the county where the premises are located an affidavit which states:

(i)   That the mortgagee has mailed to the last known address of the mortgagor a notice of default and intention to foreclose pursuant to subdivision (a) and that the mortgagor has not responded to the notice.

(ii)   That the mortgagee has made a personal inspection of the mortgaged premises and that the inspection does not reveal that the mortgagor or persons claiming under him are presently occupying or intend to occupy the premises.

(c)   The mortgagee mails by certified mail, return receipt requested, a copy of the affidavit recorded pursuant to subdivision (b) to the mortgagor at his last known address before commencement of foreclosure proceedings.

(d)   The mortgagor, his heirs, executor, administrator, or any person lawfully claiming from, or under 1 of them, before expiration of the period of redemption, does not give a written affidavit to the mortgagee and record a duplicate original in the county where the premises are located stating that the mortgagor or persons claiming under him is occupying or intends to occupy the premises.[9]

Since this definition is predicated upon mortgage foreclosure, its use in terms of an operational survey is limited. It was constructed basically for the purpose of fast mortgage foreclosure proceedings and not as a strict legal definition of a socioeconomic phenomenon, nor as an instrument to enable a municipality to deal with the abandoned building problem.

The New York law, in contrast, was designed to convey an abandoned multiple dwelling to New York City, the prime mover behind the law. The certification procedure is as follows, with department referring to that agency of the city responsible for the enforcement of the state's multiple dwelling law:

1. The department may make a finding that a multiple dwelling is abandoned if:

    (a)   In the case of an occupied dwelling, the owner has failed for a period of at least three consecutive months either to demand rent or institute summary proceedings for nonpayment thereof, and the department finds that the dwelling has become a danger to life, health or safety as a result of the owner's failure to assume his responsibility for its condition. Such failure may be shown by such facts as an owner's failure to make repairs, supply janitorial service, purchase fuel or other needed supplies, or pay utility bills.

    (b)   In the case of a vacant dwelling, it is not sealed or continuously guarded as required by law, and either of the following facts exists:

    (i)   A vacate order of the department or other governmental agency currently prohibits occupancy of the dwelling; or

    (ii)   The tax on such premises has been due and unpaid for a period of at least one year.

2. When the department finds that a multiple dwelling is abandoned within the meaning of this article, it may make and file among its records, a certification containing such finding and the facts on which it is based.[10]

The legislation containing this definition was enacted at the request of New York City to obtain title to an abandoned building while it still is salvageable. After a building is declared abandoned, the courts can vest title to the city, providing the owner or other lien holder does not contest the action, or does not bring the building up to housing code specifications as directed by court order, or does not demolish the building.[11]

Thus abandoned buildings can be obtained by the city by using the police power and by basing actions on nuisance law. An underlying concept is that abandoned buildings constitute a nuisance and a public emergency, because they "are hazardous to human life, health, safety and morals, have a deleterious effect on the community as a living environment, and attract vandals and other criminals."

The definition itself, as can be seen above, is divided into two parts, recognizing the fact that an abandoned building can be either occupied or vacant. If it is occupied, the failure by the owner to demand rent or institute summary proceedings for payment for three consecutive months, or the failure to assume his responsibility for its condition (with what constitutes this failure being spelled out above), the structure can be found abandoned. If the building is vacant, and is not sealed (under existing law, a vacant building must be sealed or continuously guarded), either tax delinquency for a period of one year or a vacate order in effect are conditions for declaring the structure abandoned.

SOME LONGITUDINAL COMPLEXITIES

If we are to design a comprehensive inventory scheme, we must be able to account for the situations illustrated in Exhibits A-3 and A-4. In the example, a total of six units constituted the housing stock at the start of year one. During the year, two units were abandoned, one of which was demolished after, say, fire damage and vandalism. At the end of the year, five standing buildings remain, one of which is abandoned, as well as one demolition, which had been abandoned that year. Thus the year's abandonment totals two, comprising one standing and one demolished.

During Year Two, one standing building was abandoned. Thus for that accounting period, one abandonment was experienced. The total abandoned inventory now comprises two vacant standing and one demolished for a total of three.

Year Three introduces an added complexity. Not only was an additional structure abandoned, but one structure which had been abandoned the previous year was demolished during the current accounting period. Moreover, one previously abandoned building had been, say, renovated, returning it to the usable stock. Thus for Year Three, only one new abandoned structure is reported, for a total three-year inventory of three abandoned units. Also tabulated is the previously abandoned structure demolished this year and the reused dwelling. The total abandoned inventory now consists of one structure standing and two demolished.

This type of accounting system not only records a current year's activity (or whatever length recording period is desired), it also takes into account

EXHIBIT A-3
OPERATIONAL APPLICATION OF THE SURVEY TECHNIQUE

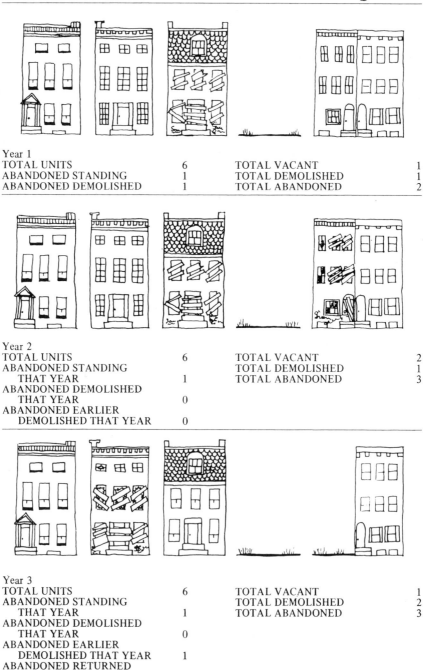

Year 1

TOTAL UNITS	6	TOTAL VACANT	1
ABANDONED STANDING	1	TOTAL DEMOLISHED	1
ABANDONED DEMOLISHED	1	TOTAL ABANDONED	2

Year 2

TOTAL UNITS	6	TOTAL VACANT	2
ABANDONED STANDING THAT YEAR	1	TOTAL DEMOLISHED	1
		TOTAL ABANDONED	3
ABANDONED DEMOLISHED THAT YEAR	0		
ABANDONED EARLIER DEMOLISHED THAT YEAR	0		

Year 3

TOTAL UNITS	6	TOTAL VACANT	1
ABANDONED STANDING THAT YEAR	1	TOTAL DEMOLISHED	2
		TOTAL ABANDONED	3
ABANDONED DEMOLISHED THAT YEAR	0		
ABANDONED EARLIER DEMOLISHED THAT YEAR	1		
ABANDONED RETURNED TO STOCK	1		

EXHIBIT A-4

FLOW CHART OF AN OPERATIONAL APPLICATION OF THE SURVEY TECHNIQUE

YEARLY HOUSING INVENTORY:

Year 1	
Total Units	6
Abandoned Standing	1
Abandoned Demolished	1

Year 2	
Total Units	6
Abandoned Standing This Year	1
Abandoned Demolished This year	0
Abandoned Previous, Demolished This Year	0

Year 3	
Total Units	6
Abandoned Standing This Year	1
Abandoned, Demolished This Year	0
Abandoned Previous, Demolished This Year	1
Abandoned, Returned To Stock	1

CUMULATIVE HOUSING INVENTORY:

Year 1	
Abandoned Standing	1
Abandoned Demolished	1
TOTAL ABANDONED	2

Year 2	
Abandoned Standing	2
Abandoned Demolished	1
TOTAL ABANDONED	3

Year 3	
Abandoned Standing	1
Abandoned Demolished	2
TOTAL ABANDONED	3

changes in status of abandoned buildings over time, recording their eventual demolition or reuse.

AN OPERATIONAL DEFINITION

Combining the legal and operational components of the previous definitions of housing abandonment enables a field operational definition to be constructed. The major elements are presented in Exhibit A-5.

A field survey using this definition would first be confronted with what appears to be an unoccupied or vacant building (no distinction is made between the unoccupied and vacant terms). If the structure is not sealed or secured and appears open to casual entry from an exterior survey but upon entry it is found that major appliances have been removed (or services terminated or major utilities removed), the structure would also be considered abandoned. These categories include vacant structures wherein a process of owner disinvestment appears distinctly underway in terms of the declining physical condition of the structure. But owner disinvestment does not have to begin by withdrawing or holding back resources from the structure itself. Before this step is taken, the owner may stop paying his property taxes as a first step in disengaging from the parcel. Consequently it is possible for a building to be vacant and delinquent in taxes, but still in habitable or better condition, and in the process of being abandoned. Thus vacant buildings identified by survey, which are not subject to the above physical deficiencies (and this is probably a very small number), should be checked against municipal tax delinquency records. Those delinquent should be counted as abandoned.

The second major type of building situation the survey should confront would be that which visually indicates only partial occupancy (or full occupancy with abandonment by the owner indicated through inhabitants' complaints). This category is much more relevant to municipalities containing large numbers of multifamily structures, rather than those characterized by rowhouses. In any case, if the physical condition of the building should indicate the owner's disengagement from the parcel—deterioration and dilapidation and termination of services—rent questions should be addressed to the remaining residents. If the owner has failed to demand rent for three months, as specified in Exhibit A-5, the structure should be reported abandoned. Or if physical condition does not indicate the owner's withdrawal, but clearly rent payments have stopped (again this should be a very small number), a check of tax delinquency records should again be made; those delinquent should be classified as abandoned.

The final category would come from municipal demolition records. If the structure was declared a public hazard, condemned, and demolished, most likely the structure was abandoned by its owner and should be tabulated as such.

An abandonment survey sheet including this definitional framework is presented as Exhibit A-6.

EXHIBIT A-5

OPERATIONAL CATEGORIES OF ABANDONED RESIDENTIAL BUILDINGS

---

1. *Observed Vacant and*

   a) *Not Secured: Open to Casual Entry with Doors Open or Broken*

   or

   b) *Major Appliances Removed*

   or

   c) *Services Terminated or Major Utilities Removed*

   or

   d) *Not Sealed and Tax Delinquent*

2. *Observed Partial Occupancy (or Occupancy with Complaint)*

   a) *The Owner Has Failed to Demand Rent for Three Months or Failed to Institute Summary Proceedings for Payments (Non-Rent Paying Tenants)*

   and

   b) 1. *Services Terminated or Major Utilities Inoperable*

   or

   2. *Physical Deterioration and Dilapidation*
      a) *Vandalized*
      b) *Critical building defects*
      c) *Unmaintained grounds*

   or

   c) *Tax Delinquent*

3. *Demolished Publicly for Hazard (condemned and demolished)*

EXHIBIT A-6

ABANDONMENT SURVEY SHEET

	Item	*Column*	
1.	Block Number	(1– 5)	_____
2.	Lot Number	(6– 9)	_____
3.	Other Area I.D.	(10–14)	_____
4.	Street Address	(15–36)	_____
5.	Structure Status	(37–39)	_____

    A.   Observed Vacant   (37)   _____

        a)   Not secured. Open to Casual Entry with Doors Open or Broken [1]

        b)   Major Appliances Removed [2]

        c)   Services Terminated or Major Utilities Removed [3]

        d)   Not Sealed and Tax Delinquent [4]

    B.   Observed Partial Occupancy (38) (or Occupied Complaint)   _____

       No Rent Paid or Demanded for Three Months

              and

        a)   Services Terminated or Major Utilities Removed [1]

        b)   Physical Deterioration or Dilapidation [2]

        c)   Tax Delinquent [3]

EXHIBIT A-6

ABANDONMENT SURVEY SHEET (Cont'd.)

C. Demolished Publicly for Hazard (39)   _____

    a) Yes [1]

6. Use   (40)   _____

A. All Residential [1]

B. Mixed-Residential [2]

7. Number of Stories   (40–41)   _____

8. Estimated Number of
    Dwelling Units   (42–44)   _____

9. Type of Structure   (45)   _____

A. Detached [1]

B. Semi-detached [2]

C. Row [3]

D. Multifamily [4]

10. Construction   (46)   _____

A. Frame [1]

B. Masonry [2]

11. Condition of Building   (47)   _____

A. Good [1]

B. Fair (Needs some attention but habitable) [2]

C. Poor (Needs extensive work to be made habitable) [3]

D. Very Poor (Beyond rehabilitation) [4]

EXHIBIT A-6

ABANDONMENT SURVEY SHEET (Cont'd.)

---

12.   Quality of Block   (48)   _____

   A.   Good (No other vacants; minor
        maintenance needed) [1]

   B.   Fair (No other vacants; some
        work needed) [2]

   C.   Poor (Other vacants or major
        work needed) [3]

13.   Date Surveyed   (49—54)

   A.   Month   (49—50)   _____

   B.   Day   (51—52)   _____

   C.   Year   (53—54)   _____

14.   Date Resurveyed (or Entry
      Date of Parcel Disposition) (55—60)   _____

   A.   Month   (55—56)   _____

   B.   Day   (57—58)   _____

   C.   Year   (59—60)   _____

15.   Disposition   (61)   _____

   A.   Demolished [1]

   B.   Rehabilitated [2]

   C.   Homesteaded [3]

THE PROPOSED SYSTEM: MEASUREMENT AT THE
LOCAL LEVEL AND FUNDING MECHANISM

A statewide abandonment reporting system is highly dependent on several critical elements. First, and probably most important, is the quality of the individuals and agencies actually carrying out the fieldwork and providing the basic building blocks of data.[12] Most successful monitoring efforts are functions of unique, capable, and strong local organizations. Second, abandonment reports are often subsystems of larger housing inspection efforts, and if the latter are of high quality, then the abandonment element is often of similar caliber. Moreover, a host of other inspections do take place in an urban area for a number of purposes, and certainly abandonment counts can be an important ancillary function. And third, the system must be ongoing, with strong built-in continuities to the local scene.

The above elements would tend to rule out the use of outside consultants, since the latter would probably represent just the opposite qualities to those specified in terms of ongoing long-term familiarity. For better or worse, a statewide system must be tied to local inspection efforts. But as experience has shown, expanding duties, responsibilities, and work loads, without commensurate increases in resources, manpower, or funding, does not stimulate the involved parties to their best efforts. If the state wants its constituent urban areas to monitor abandonment in a fashion that is amenable to statewide aggregation, and to stimulate programmatic accounting at the local level, then it must be prepared to offer incentives in some fashion. It will have to offer direct aid if the municipality agrees to carry out the required survey procedures and to report units meeting the prescribed abandonment description.

The Funding Mechanism

How would such a funding mechanism work? Ideally, monies could be allocated on a per-abandoned-unit basis; this appears satisfactory for the long run but it is of little utility for the base year of implementation. The funding approach for the initial startup could be on a size criterion, that is, a per unit allocation applied to the total number of units in the jurisdiction. This may be suitable as a starting point, but such a scheme would tend to overfund areas with little abandonment and underfund those with an extensive problem. Consequently, the base year resource allocation procedure should be refined somewhat. Areas with high abandonment potential could be isolated by a state, using leading indicators of abandonment and various census materials.[13] In the case of Pennsylvania, for example, we assumed such areas accounted for 10 percent of the census tracts in the state (all SMSAs are tracted); therefore, about 10 percent of the housing units in metropolitan and urban areas—300,000 to 400,000 units—were encompassed. It is not unreasonable to suggest that these units could be surveyed from the street, and the abandoned units subsequently tabulated, at an initial cost of $2 per unit. Thus a survey in Pennsylvania would cost in the vicinity of $700,000 with the funds apportioned to the municipalities in proportion to the number of their units in potentially high abandonment areas.

Given this base-line data, serious problem areas can be more definitively isolated, enabling more efficient, in-depth, and/or cheaper overall monitoring in subsequent accounting periods or years. While the actual survey costs for abandoned unit identification would tend to decline, the cost of follow-up accounting, and recordkeeping on disposition, status and the like would tend to go up. Given the tabulations established in Year One, funding could be based for each record period on the number of abandoned units, in total, of the previous record period. For example, if the base year in our example established a total of 70,000 abandoned units spread throughout all areas of the state, then, if $10 per unit were allotted, a total $700,000 would again be dispersed for both monitoring and recordkeeping of previously abandoned units. This would enable a continuous audit to be maintained of the disposition of abandoned units by program and by resources expended if the units were returned to the housing supply.

Thus the costs associated with setting up a statewide abandonment system are not inconsequential, but such a system is a necessary adjunct to an admittedly inadequate federal census. States must amplify their data bases if they are to monitor the housing supply system within their boundaries. Moreover, the impetus of the infusion of state funds for local action in response to the abandoned housing problem may well be consequential. The entire system of definition, measurement, accounting, and disposition monitoring cannot but help to insure a greater awareness and competence at the local level.

Ancillary Support Requirements

Thus we are recommending that the internal staffs of local municipalities actually be the building blocks of any statewide system of monitoring housing abandonment. While the deficiencies and inadequacies of building or housing inspection agencies have often been voiced, an economical approach outside of these bodies does not appear feasible. Moreover, in any abandonment response program, housing inspection plays a key role. For example, if a municipality obtains title to a building and wants to make a decision on its disposition—demolition or rehabilitation representing the bounding choices—it must have adequate information on the cost of rehabilitation, of meeting building codes or code enforcement standards, and the like. It must also have follow-up monitoring if the structure is, for example, homesteaded; in programs of any type long-range recordkeeping is a vital feedback mechanism.

It may well be that states will have to provide the dynamic to improve local building inspection and monitoring efforts. This may require an intensive training effort as well as a direct infusion of funding. Monitoring in and by itself cannot be considered an end, but a starting point for public policy responses. The talents necessary to implement the monitoring are analogous to those which must underlie ameliorative programs. For example, a homesteading program depends upon successful estimates of the costs of rehabilitation necessary to eliminate code violations and create a satisfactory residential environment. Decisions on demolition or "go/no-go" are hazardous indeed without an effective data base on rehabilitation costs and the ultimate cash flow requirements of the parcel. This requires a good bit of sophistication and knowledge at the local level.

The latter requirements must be considered in conjunction with the abandonment survey needs. They may well generate a program package beyond that envisioned by an isolated survey technique. *Surveying, measuring, appraising, costing, and recordkeeping are a bundle of interrelated functions which must be carried out at the municipal level or else response actions will be decidedly inferior.*

States can provide guidance and technical support to local program operators by providing a centralized staff whose functional responsibility would include abandonment monitoring and accounting, building inspection procedures, costing, and appraising—the skills which underlie the definition of the abandonment problem and which provide the data base to select and initiate action programs. The guidance and technical support functions should include recommended procedures and approaches, direct training and educational efforts for local officials, the provision of expertise, and direct assistance by having state staff members work directly at the local level. Additional financial support could be designed to provide the wherewithal to implement the innovative programs necessary to deal with abandoned housing.

NOTES

1. George Sternlieb, Robert W. Burchell, James W. Hughes, and Franklin J. James, "Housing Abandonment in the Urban Core," *Journal of the American Institute of Planners*, September 1974, p. 321.

2. U.S. Department of Housing and Urban Development. *Abandoned Housing Research: A Compendium* (Washington, D.C.: U.S. Government Printing Office, 1973), p. 8.

3. National Urban League, *The National Survey of Housing Abandonment* (New York: The Center for Community Change, 1971), p. 1.

4. George Sternlieb, *Some Aspects of the Abandoned Housing Problem,* mimeograph (New Brunswick, N.J.: Center for Urban Policy Research, 1970).

5. Linton, Mields and Coston, *A Study of Abandoned Housing and Recommendations for Action by the Federal Government and Localities,* mimeographed (Washington, D.C., 1971).

6. George Sternlieb and Robert W. Burchell, *Residential Abandonment: The Tenement Landlord Revisited* (New Brunswick, N.J.: Center for Urban Policy Research, Rutgers University, 1973), p. 277.

7. *Ibid.*

8. This concept of vacancy, unfortunately, conflicts with the vacant definition of the U.S. Bureau of the Census:

A housing unit is vacant if no one is living in it at the time of enumeration, unless its occupants are only temporarily absent. In addition, a vacant unit may be one which is occupied entirely by persons who have a usual residence elsewhere.

New units not yet occupied are classified as vacant housing units if construction has reached a point where all exterior windows and doors are installed and final usable floors are in place. Vacant units are excluded if unfit for human habitation; that is, if the roof, walls, windows, or doors no longer protect the interior from the elements, or if there is positive evidence (such as a sign on the house or in the block) that the unit is to be demolished or is condemned. Also excluded are quarters being used entirely for nonresidential purposes, such as a store or an office, or quarters used for the storage of business supplies or inventory, machinery, or agricultural products.

See: U.S. Bureau of the Census, *Census of Housing: 1970, Vol. 1, Housing Characteristics for States, Cities, and Counties*, Appendix B, (Washington, D.C.: U.S. Government Printing Office, 1972).

9. Michigan Statute § 600.3241.

10. New York Annotated Code Title 49½ § 1972.

11. Previously, the city could obtain title through its taxing power (i.e., it could foreclose outstanding tax liens, proceeding against the building, after a statutory redemption period if it is delinquent in taxes) or it could condemn and demolish, but the owner would retain title to the land with the demolition cost entered as a lien.

12. For example, the Fire Department of the City of Newark, New Jersey maintains a superb data file on abandoned structures in that city. The Baltimore Department of Housing and Community Development has implemented an effective monitoring system whose results are eventually computerized. These success stories may not be due to structure and process per se, but just as much to the high caliber of individuals administering and guiding their agency's endeavors.

13. See George Sternlieb and Robert Burchell, *Residential Abandonment* and George Sternlieb, *et al.*, "Housing Abandonment in the Urban Core."

Appendix B

A Cost-Revenue Methodology

Cost-revenue analysis for each of the homesteading programs is undertaken in the case studies. They are all constructed according to the following format.

The introduction of residential development or new households into a municipality brings with it both a demand for services funded through the municipal treasury, and a revenue source based upon the tax rate and the residential unit's valuation. A first task in any municipal cost-revenue investigation is the problem of defining both educational and noneducational costs and determining the appropriate charging methods. These are subject to a variety of interpretations and approaches, principally revolving around the difference between marginal and average costing.

MARGINAL VS. AVERAGE COSTING

The basic question is whether the additional residents and pupils brought into a municipality by new residential development should be charged with just those additional dollars associated with their advent (this is called the marginal cost approach), or should be charged a cost based upon a multiple of what the municipality is now spending on an average per capita and per pupil basis.[1] The latter computation often puts a proposed development to its stiffest test—this is known as the average cost methodology. The difference between the two approaches can best be illustrated by an example.

Assume a municipality with 100 pupils spends $100,000 per year in school property taxes, or $1,000 per pupil. Assume also that there are 15 empty spaces in the school system. A new program is proposed which would generate 10 additional pupils. What would be the impact on the municipality? According to the marginal cost approach, the proposed housing or households would cause little increase, if any, in educational costs since the pupils can be added into the vacant spaces in the school system. Under the average cost approach, the 10 additional students would be assumed to cost a multiple of the existing $1,000 per pupil expenditure, or $10,000. So quite different results are obtainable depending on the charging method employed. Two further illustrations with reference to the following exhibit may help clarify the distinction:

Case I. Assume a municipality with a population of size A and a service infrastructure of level X. The average cost per capita (or per pupil in the case of educational expenditures) is equal to X/A. If new residential development generates an increase in population A-B, two different estimates of their costs are obtained according to the marginal cost or average cost procedures. Under the marginal cost approach, the added population causes little appreciable increase in expenditures due to the slack capacity in the existing level of municipal facilities. Under the average cost methodology, the increment in population growth A-B, is multiplied by the average cost per capita of the existing population level X/A. This changing level is represented by the dashed line in Exhibit B-1.

Case II. Alternatively at population size B, the slack capacity of the municipal facilities is fully exploited and the system becomes saturated. Any increase in population, say B-C, will necessitate an increase in infrastracture (i.e., a new school) to level Y. In the marginal costing procedure, this small population increase, B-C, causes a vast increase in costs attributable to a *very* marginal population growth. This stands in marked contrast to Case I, where the large population increase A-B was not attributed with any increased costs. The average cost methodology is again represented by the dashed line. This latter approach thus attributes the increase in expenditures to all the previous growth, and not simply to the "straw which broke the camel's back."

Furthermore, the marginal cost method would replicate this pattern of cost assignment when facilities expand to a new plateau at level Z as population growth E-F is experienced.

Thus, in order to evaluate servicing costs suitable for long-range planning purposes, an average costing approach may serve as an appropriate methodology. Educational and municipal service delivery systems do not, or at least should not, rise and fall with the addition or demise of housing projects. Even in urban areas, an unsaturated system which is not planning for eventual replacements is living off capital and will probably have to accept further expenditure sooner or later. Similarly the saturated system should not blame the last straw for the total costs of expansion, but rather accept the phenomenon as, at most, accelerating the facts of life. There are unquestionably deviations from these generalizations. For example, older cities sometimes have school systems deserted by their earlier users, and similar conditions could arise in older suburbs. For these cases, detailed, long-run marginal analysis may justify the costs of its preparation. For the great bulk of situations, however, average costing is probably more useful—at least as a takeoff place for immediate impact studies.

Another minor issue also arises in regard to school costs. Should the total expenditure per student be employed as the basic cost, regardless of revenue source, or simply that expenditure the municipality makes in terms of the property tax mechanism? Again for immediate impact studies, the direct

EXHIBIT B-1

MARGINAL VS. AVERAGE COSTING

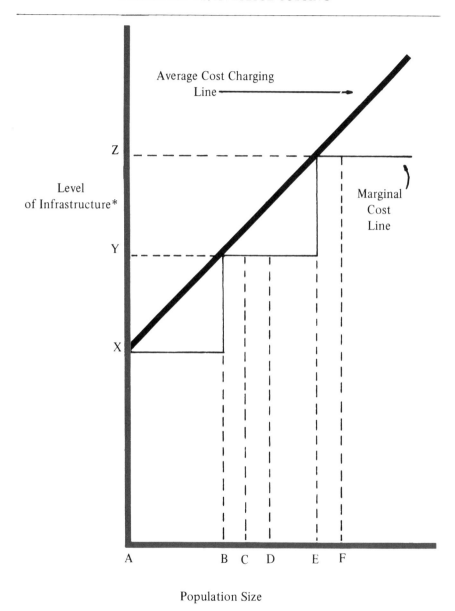

Population Size

*Level of municipal and educational facilities required to service population size.

property tax cost implication has probably the most conceptual clarity and is the most useful. This is the cost that directly impacts the local resident.

To generate the basic building blocks of cost, then, an average cost methodology is used where the cost of service is defined as that expenditure which must be financed through the property tax system.

METHODOLOGY: EDUCATIONAL COSTS-RESIDENTIAL SECTOR

The basic format of constructing modular educational cost units for a municipality involves the comparison of the income which the community derives from the specific residential configuration with the educational tax levies required to service it.[2] This approach necessitates, first of all, estimates of the school children generated by each type of dwelling unit. These are presented in Exhibit B-2.[3]

The impact variables and demographic characteristics can be summarized as follows:

1. Public School Children Per Dwelling Unit x School Property Taxes Levied Per Student = Local Educational Costs Per Dwelling Unit

2. Assessed Valuation Per Dwelling Unit x School Property Tax Rate = Revenue Generated

3. Educational Surplus or Deficit = 2 - 1

METHODOLOGY: NONEDUCATIONAL COSTS-RESIDENTIAL SECTOR

In order to calculate the property tax portion of noneducational costs assignable to occupied units, total household size rather than the number of school children in the unit becomes the important multiplier. Total household size as a result of various residential and bedroom configurations is presented in Exhibit B-2.

Using the total household figure (persons per unit), a similar methodology is employed to calculate noneducational costs as was the case for educational expenditures. Once again the income derived from a particular residential configuration is compared to the cost it generates.[4]

The approach may be summarized as follows:

1. Persons Per Dwelling Unit x Municipal Property Tax Levied Per Capita = Local Municipal Costs Per Dwelling Unit

EXHIBIT B-2
APPROXIMATE UNIT DEMOGRAPHIC CHARACTERISTICS

Public School Children Per Unit

Number of Bedrooms	Urban Garden Apartment	Urban Rehabilitation	Suburban Garden Apartment	Suburban Townhouse
1	.028	.012	.046	------
2	.525	.333	.344	.220
3	1.423	1.871	1.310	.655
4	------	------	------	1.026

Total Household Size

Number of Bedrooms	Urban Garden Apartment	Urban Rehabilitation	Suburban Garden Apartment	Suburban Townhouse
1	1.80	1.90	1.90	----
2	2.90	2.70	2.81	2.68
3	3.70	3.90	----	3.35
4	----	----	----	3.71

Source: George Sternlieb, *et al., Housing Development and Municipal Costs* (New Brunswick, N.J.: Center for Urban Policy Research, Rutgers University, 1973), and George Sternlieb, James W. Hughes, and Lawrence Burrows, *Housing in Newark* (New Brunswick, N.J.: Center for Urban Policy Research, Rutgers University, 1974).

2.   Assessed Valuation Per Dwelling Unit x Municipal Property
     Tax Rate = Revenue Generated

3.   Surplus or Deficit = 2 - 1

In the case study evaluations, the above approach is employed. The demographic characteristics are assumed equivalent to those of Exhibit B-2. The specific parameters integral to the methodology—costs per pupil or person, tax rates, and the like—were obtained directly from the municipality.

NOTES

1. See George Sternlieb, *The Garden Apartment: A Municipal Cost-Revenue Analysis* (New Brunswick, N.J.: Bureau of Governmental Research, Rutgers University, 1964), for a further discussion of this issue.

2. See George Sternlieb, Robert W. Burchell, James W. Hughes, *et al. Housing Development and Municipal Costs* (New Brunswick, N.J.: Center for Urban Policy Research, Rutgers University, 1973) for a further discussion of this methodology.

3. See George Sternlieb, James W. Hughes, and Lawrence Burrows, *Housing in Newark,* mimeograph (New Brunswick, N.J.: Center for Urban Policy Research, Rutgers University, 1974) for socio-demographic characteristics of new residents in rehabilitated units. Other urban area household characteristics are revealed in George Sternlieb and James W. Hughes, *Housing and People in New York City* (New York: Housing and Development Administration, 1972).

4. Further analysis of residential impact in urban areas is presented in George Sternlieb and James W. Hughes, "Profiling the High Rent Center City Market," *Real Estate Review*, Fall 1973. Other cost conceptualizations and attitudes toward fiscal impacts are analyzed in James W. Hughes, ed., *New Dimensions of Urban Planning: Growth Controls* (New Brunswick, N.J.: Center for Urban Policy Research, Rutgers University, 1974).

PROGRAM ADMINISTRATION	WILMINGTON	BALTIMORE
Administrative Framework	The Homesteading Board comprises six agency heads responsible for major policy and program administration. These officials are selected by the Mayor.	Homesteading is part of the comprehensive Department of Housing and Community Development and is directly associated with the Home-ownership Development Division. A board composed of six city officials intimately involved with the provision of services to the program oversees its administration.
Number of Persons and Function of Homesteading Staff	Staff responsible for day-to-day operations is composed of a homesteading program director and a staff of two. The staff is part-time, focusing also on urban renewal.	The staff is responsible for the daily operation of the program. It consists of eight people divided among three programmatic functions: promotion-selection; post-lease, construction, work-writeup; specifications, financing, and progress monitoring.

PROGRAM CONTEXT

Number of Abandoned Homes	2,000 units.	5,004 units.

Appendix C

Summary Matrix of Homesteading Programs

PHILADELPHIA	NEWARK	PROGRAM ADMINISTRATION
Philadelphia's program is headed by a Homesteading Board composed of eleven members. Unlike the other case cities, Philadelphia's Board is not composed of city officials but rather representatives of various segments of the general public. Relevant city agencies do sit as ex officio members, however.	The Real Estate Commission, composed of the Tax Collector who serves as chairman, tax assessor, a representative from Newark Economic Development Corp., a City Councilman and the Planning Officer, serves as the City's homesteading board.	*Administrative Framework*
Positions for twelve staff have been made. Presently eight persons have been hired. Their duties run from program administration, community coordination, rehabilitation monitoring, and financial assistance.	The staff numbers six, the Real Estate Officer, the Secretary to the Real Estate Commission, and four clerical workers. They, along with assistance from the Tax Collector's office, handle the day-to-day administration of the program.	*Number of Persons and Function of Homesteading Staff*
		PROGRAM CONTEXT
24,000 units.	5,000 units.	*Number of Abandoned Homes*

(Continued)

PROGRAM CONTEXT (Cont'd.)	WILMINGTON	BALTIMORE
Number of Those Units Suitable for Urban Home-steading, Owned by the City	50 units.	Because of recent inclusion of many city condemnations the potential stock is quite high—1,300 to 1,500 units.
Number of Units Home-steaded To Date	28	136
The Average Cost of Rehabilitation	$6,000-$10,000	$10,000-$15,000
Condition of Neighborhoods Where Homestead-ing is Occurring	While early homesteading sites were chosen with little regard for sur-rounding neighborhood conditions, the city is moving rapidly towards a position of not home-steading in those areas experiencing severe deterioration.	Increasing sensitivity to neighborhood conditions is evidenced in scattered site selections. Baltimore has also homesteaded an entire block of parcels and sig-nificant numbers of units in other areas. This com-prehensive treatment pro-cess goes to the heart of the problem of overwhelming neighborhood conditions.
HOMESTEADER SELECTION		
Necessary Charac-teristics of homesteader	Applicant must be 18 years or older, head of a family, citizen or regis-tered alien, with "proven financial know-how and ability to rehabilitate an existing dwelling."	Applicant must be 18 or the head of a household, be or declare intention to become a citizen, and have "proven financial ability and/or building trade skills."
Minimum Residency Requirement	3 years.	2 years.

PHILADELPHIA	NEWARK	PROGRAM CONTEXT *(Cont'd.)*
Less than 25 of the 250 vacant buildings owned by the city are thought suitable. The prime source of sites has been recent HUD foreclosures, circumventing the heavy dependence on tax sale properties found in the other case cities.	Because of the constant inflow of new tax delinquent properties and the outflow through sale at the bi-monthly auctions no fixed amount is possible to estimate.	*Number of Those Units Suitable for Urban Homesteading, Owned by the City*
30	77	*Number of Units Homesteaded To Date*
$6,000-$10,000	Estimates run from several thousand dollars for still occupied and sound buildings to $15,000 and up, depending on condition.	*The Average Cost of Rehabilitation*
While early homesteads were scattered throughout several target neighborhoods, more recent awards have been on a concentrated basis in neighborhoods carefully scrutinized to insure they don't overwhelm the homesteader in an environment of decay.	All neighborhoods in the city have had homesteads since they are granted wherever tax delinquent properties of a modest size are present.	*Condition of Neighborhoods Where Homesteading is Occurring*
		HOMESTEADER SELECTION
Applicant must be 21 or the head of a family, be or declare intention to become citizen, and have "proven financial ability and/or building trade skills."	Must be 18 years of age and have the financial ability to make the necessary payments.	*Necessary Characteristics of homesteader*
5 years.	5 years.	*Minimum Residency Requirement*

(Continued)

HOMESTEADER SELECTION (Cont'd.)	*WILMINGTON*	*BALTIMORE*
Preference Given to Low Income Applicants	No weight is given to any applicant because of his socioeconomic status.	Each case is decided on its individual merits, but no set policy favoring those of a lower economic status has been adopted.
Preference Given to Applicants From the Immediate Neighborhood.	Yes.	Yes.
Minimum Income Requirement	No dollar amount, however, homesteader must have sufficient means to cover the cost of the rehabilitation loan.	No dollar amount, however, homesteader must have sufficient means to cover the cost of the rehabilitation loan.
Maximum Period to Bring Structure Up To Code Standards	18 months.	18 months.
Mandatory Date for Commencement of Rehabilitation	None has been established.	Within 6 months.
SUPPORTIVE PROGRAMS		
Special Financing	A special loan agreement between the city and a consortium of eight local banks has been established whereby each bank has agreed to make up to three loans to homesteaders at 9¾ percent interest for a term of 10 to 15 years. This would lower the cost and assure the availability of much needed capital.	The city has established a $3,000,000 loan fund—REAL— which lends money (up to $17,400) at 6 percent (for 20 years).

PHILADELPHIA	NEWARK	HOMESTEADER SELECTION (Cont'd.)
Preference is given, should the applicant meet all other selection criteria.	No preference is given to applicant because of his socio-economic status due to the straight bid mechanism.	*Preference Given to Low Income Applicants*
Yes.	No.	*Preference Given to Applicants From the Immediate Neighborhood.*
No dollar amount, however, homesteader must have sufficient income to cover the cost of the rehabilitation loan.	The ability to make the required payments is the only income threshhold.	*Minimum Income Requirement*
2 years.	11 months.	*Maximum Period to Bring Structure Up To Code Standards*
60 days after award of property.	30 days	*Mandatory Date for Commencement of Rehabilitation*
		SUPPORTIVE PROGRAMS
Through a special two stage financing procedure the homesteader receives the needed rehabilitation monies at 1 to 7 percent interest for a 20-25 year term. The initial "equity loan" is made by the program from a special fund and serves as a construction loan allowing the homesteader to establish equity in the parcel. This amount is later refinanced through the Pennsylvania Housing Finance Agency once equity has been established, on a long term basis at low interest.	Presently no assistance is offered.	*Special Financing*

•

(Continued)

SUPPORTIVE PROGRAMS (Cont'd.)	WILMINGTON	BALTIMORE
Special Tax Considerations	For a five year period following parcel improvement 1.5 times the value of that improvement may be deducted from the initial assessment thereby drastically lowering the property taxes to less than pre-rehabilitation levels.	No specific tax abatement program has been adopted, but because the city holds title to the property for the first two years, the homesteader is technically a leasee and pays no property taxes. Reassessments on rehabilitated properties will be in line with surrounding property values.
Special Services	Each homesteader is assigned to one of the Homesteading Board members who acts as his spokesman in the administrative structure of the city. This "buddy system" facilitates direct communication and clear lines of responsibility for the program's participants.	The city provides assistance in the form of special rehabilitation counseling with the aim of making the homesteader his own competent general contractor. Major improvements in basic city services have been instituted, increasing the city's supportive framework to the homesteader.
Parcel Improvements Undertaken by the Homesteading jurisdiction	No programs have been established other than to "clean and seal" the potential homestead sites.	No programs have been established other than to "clean and seal" the potential homestead sites.

PHILADELPHIA	*NEWARK*	
Under a special assessment procedure the reassessment for the value of the improvements is spread over a five year period with 20 percent increases annually.	No special tax considerations are in operation and, because the owner may not use his purchase price as a grounds for a decrease in taxes, many homes are assessed far above their sale price.	*Special Tax Considerations*
The program provides home-ownership counseling to the homesteader to make him better able to handle the burdens of homeownership. Neighborhood environmental problems such as abandoned automobiles and accumulation of trash are treated in conjunction with other city agencies.	None.	*Special Services*
All parcels are "cleaned and sealed" by the city, as well as treated for rat infestation and lead paint.	Where major structural work is necessary to make a property saleable, the city will do the work and include the costs in the minimum bid required.	*Parcel Improvements Undertaken by the Homesteading Jurisdiction*

Appendix D

Examples Of Relevant Ordinances And Agreements

*AN ORDINANCE AUTHORIZING THE
PHILADELPHIA HOMESTEAD PROGRAM*

Authorizing the Mayor of the City of Philadelphia to create and appoint members of a Board to be known as The Urban Homestead Board whose purpose shall be to administer programs in Homesteading and Reclamation of City-owned ground and dilapidated properties to proper applicants for the purpose of requiring the ground and/or existing structures to be built upon and/or rehabilitated and used for housing purposes, under certain terms and conditions.

Whereas, The City of Philadelphia has become owner of certain properties and ground through abandonment, tax liens, gifts and other legal processes; and

Whereas, Many of these properties are located in areas which are blighted, unoccupied, dilapidated and/or economically unproductive; and

Whereas, In most instances, private or governmental development of the said vacant ground or structures located thereon is economically unfeasible; and

Whereas, These City-owned ground and structures constitute a high percentage of total land area which cannot be readily used or sold by the City; and

Whereas, The constant abandonment and forfeiture of unproductive ground and structures are creating a severe problem for the City of Philadelphia in creating blighted, unsightly and ghetto areas; therefore

*THE COUNCIL OF THE CITY OF
PHILADELPHIA HEREBY ORDAINS:*

Section 1. The Mayor of the City of Philadelphia is hereby authorized to create and appoint, from a list, supplied by the Council of the City of

Philadelphia, containing at least three (3) names for each position as recited in Section 2 hereof, exclusive of the ex-officio appointments, members of a Board to be known as The Urban Homestead Board, whose purpose shall be to administer programs in homesteading and reclamation of City-owned ground and dilapidated properties in accordance with this ordinance.

Section 2. The Urban Homestead Board shall be composed of eleven members, who shall be appointed by the Mayor of the City of Philadelphia in the manner stated in Section 1 hereof, who shall also have the power to appoint a chairman of the Board. At least one (1) member shall be selected from each of the following groups: Architects, Contractors, Building Trades Council, Clergymen, representatives of Savings and Loan Associations, the General Public and (2) from City Council as designated by the President of City Council. The Deputy Managing Director for Housing, the Executive Director of the Redevelopment Authority, and the Executive Director of the Philadelphia City Planning Commission shall serve on the Board ex officio. The Mayor shall appoint the Board within sixty (60) days of the signing of this ordinance.

Section 3. The members of the Board shall receive no compensation and shall by majority vote elect a secretary of the Board from its members.

Section 4. The members of the Board shall serve for a term of three (3) years. So that the terms of the members of the Board shall continue to be staggered, the initial appointments to the Board excepting the Council members and ex-officio members shall be made as follows: Two (2) for one (1) year, two (2) for two (2) years; two (2) for three (3) years.

Section 5. The Board shall prepare regulations to implement the purpose and spirit of urban homesteading and reclamation as here envisioned, said regulations shall become effective after approval by the Law Department of the City of Philadelphia.

Section 6. The Board is empowered and has the duty and responsibility to: A. Compile and maintain a catalogue of all City-owned vacant structures and vacant ground, and determine whether said structures and ground are appropriate for inclusion in homesteading programs. In carrying out this responsibility, the Board shall utilize the aid and assistance of other relevant City agencies, which City agencies shall cooperate with the Urban Homestead Board.

B. With the cooperation of the Department of Collections, shall recommend to the City Solicitor and the City Solicitor shall institute sheriff foreclosure proceedings against certain vacant ground and structures to obtain title in the City's name for prompt transfer to successful homestead bidders.

C. Recommend to the Department of Licenses and Inspections and the Department of Licenses and Inspections shall institute public nuisance proceedings against certain deteriorated and blighted structures for demolition.

D. Recommend to the Department of Licenses and Inspections and the Department of Licenses and Inspections shall exempt homesteaders, who are rehabilitating existing structures, from the enforcement of sections 200 through 206 of Title 7 of the housing code for two years.

E. Approve applicants for participation in programs in homesteading and reclamation after certifying that an applicant:

1. Is twenty-one years of age or head of a family;

2. Is a citizen of the United States or has legally declared his/her intentions to become such;

3. Has proven financial ability and/or building trade skills to build on or rehabilitate approved ground or structure to building and housing code standards;

4. Has contractually agreed to build on approved ground or rehabilitate approved structures to building and housing code standards, beginning said building or rehabilitation no later than sixty days after title has been acquired; and

5. Has covenanted to live in and occupy said structure for a period of not less than five years.

F. Assist applicants in submitting bids for approved ground or structures. Said bids shall be in compliance with requirements of City Charter. The considerations of said bids shall include: (a) a contractual agreement to build or rehabilitate structure according to a plan to be submitted and approved prior to title passing to the applicant, commencing said building or rehabilitation not later than sixty (60) days after acquiring title; (b) a covenant to live-in and occupy said structure for five years; and (c) a sum of money in an amount not less than one dollar ($1.00).

G. With the cooperation of the Department of Public Property, recommend for approval by City Council the acceptance of the best bids for applicants.

H. Aid and assist applicant in applying for necessary financial assistance to complete the rehabilitation of the assigned ground and structure.

I. Obtain a reevaluation and reassessment of the approved ground and structures as to present values before conveyance of title to homesteader.

J. Recommend for approval and certification by City Council exemptions of homesteaders from paying real property tax on assessed valuation of improvements to ground and structures in accordance with Act No. 34 of the General Assembly of the Commonwealth of Pennsylvania dated January 1, 1971.

K. Recommend to City Council the establishment of various Community Homesteading Areas and such areas shall not be established except by ordinance of City Council and to appoint Councils in various homesteading areas, consisting of local community and civic organizations and indigenous community leaders to promote, assist, and advise the Board on homesteading programs in their respective area.

Section 7. The Urban Homestead Board is empowered to hire staff and obtain aid and assistance from other City agencies to implement its programs and policies.

Section 8. The amount of five hundred thousand (500,000) dollars specified in the Capital Program and Capital Budget shall be for the use of this

Board, and other funds, not specifically appropriated to this Board for its use, shall be from funds now or hereafter appropriated to the Office of Managing Director.

Ordinance approved by the Mayor: July 20, 1973.

AN ORDINANCE AUTHORIZING
THE BALTIMORE REAL LOAN PROGRAM

An Ordinance to authorize the Mayor and City Council of Baltimore (pursuant to Chapter 157 of the Acts of the General Assembly of Maryland of 1972), to issue and sell its certificates of indebtedness to an amount not exceeding Two Million Dollars ($2,000,000), the proceeds derived from the sale of the same to be used for the cost of issuance, including the expense of engraving, printing, advertising, attorneys' fees, and all other incidental expenses connected therewith, and the remainder of such proceeds shall be used to make or contract to make financial loans to the owners of buildings or structures located within the boundaries of Baltimore City, which are used or occupied for residential purposes, for or in connection with rehabilitating or improving said buildings or structures; to guarantee or insure financial loans made by third parties to the owners of buildings or structures located within the boundary lines of Baltimore City, which are used or occupied for residential purposes, for or in connection with rehabilitating or improving said buildings or structures, and for doing any and all things necessary, proper or expedient in connection with or pertaining to any or all of the matters or things hereinbefore mentioned; conferring and imposing upon the Commissioners of Finance of Baltimore City certain powers and duties: PROVIDING WHEN THE POWER AND AUTHORITY VESTED IN THE MAYOR AND CITY COUNCIL OF BALTIMORE BY THIS ORDINANCE SHALL BECOME OPERATIVE; authorizing the submission of this ordinance to the legal voters of the City of Baltimore, for their approval or disapproval, at the General Election to be held in Baltimore City on Tuesday, the 7th day of November, 1972, and providing for the expenditure of the proceeds of said certificates of indebtedness in accordance with the provisions of the Charter of the Mayor and City Council of Baltimore, and by the municipal agency designated in the annual Ordinance of Estimates of the Mayor and City Council of Baltimore.

Whereas, by Chapter 157 of the Acts of the General Assembly of Maryland of 1972, the Mayor and City Council of Baltimore is authorized to create a debt and to issue and sell its certificates of indebtedness (hereinafter called "bonds") as evidence thereof, to an amount not exceeding two Million Dollars ($2,000,000), in the manner and upon the terms set forth in said Act, the proceeds thereof, not exceeding the par value of said certificates of indebtedness, to be used for or in connection with making, guaranteeing, or insuring financial loans for rehabilitating or improving residential properties in Baltimore City, as authorized by said Act; and

Whereas, Funds are now needed for said purposes; therefore

Section 1. Be it ordained by the Mayor and City Council of Baltimore, That the Mayor and City Council of Baltimore acting by and through the Commissioners of Finance of said municipality, be and it is hereby authorized and empowered to issue bonds of the Mayor and City Council of Baltimore to an amount not exceeding Two Million Dollars ($2,000,000), from time to time, as the same may be needed or required for the purposes hereinafter named and said bonds shall be sold by said Commissioners of Finance from time to time and at such times as shall be requisite, and the proceeds derived from the sale of said bonds shall be used for the purposes hereinafter named, provided that this ordinance shall not become effective unless it shall be approved by a majority of the votes of the legal voters of Baltimore City cast at the time and place hereinafter designated by this ordinace.

Section 2. And be it further ordained, That said bonds shall be issued in denominations of not less than One Thousand Dollars ($1,000.00) each, but may be in sums of One Thousand Dollars ($1,000.00) or any suitable multiple thereof, to be redeemable in ten (10) yearly series on the Fifteenth day of October in each of the years and in the amounts as set forth in the following schedule:

Each of the Years	Amount in Each of the Years
1976 through 1985, both inclusive	$2,000.00

Said bonds, when issued, shall bear interest at such rate or rates as may be determined by a majority of the Commissioners of Finance by resolution at such time or times when any of said bonds are issued, the interest to be payable semi-annually on the Fifteenth day of April and the Fifteenth day of October, in each year after issuance, during the respective periods that the series in which said bonds are issued may run.

Section 3. And be it further ordained, That a majority of the Commissioners of Finance of the Mayor and City Council of Baltimore be, and they are hereby, authorized to pass a resolution or resolutions, from time to time, to determine and set forth any or all of the following:

(a) The form or forms of the bonds representing the debt, or any part thereof, authorized to be issued under the provisions of this ordinance at any particular time, including any interest coupons to be attached thereto; the provisions, if any, for the issuance of coupon bonds; the provisions, if any, for the registration as to principal of any coupon bonds; and the provisions, if any, for the conversion and reconversion into coupon bonds of any fully registered bonds or coupon bonds registered as to principal; the place or places for the payment of principal and interest of said bonds; and the date of said bonds issued at any particular time, and the right of redemption of said bonds by the City prior to maturity; and

(b) The time, place, manner and medium of advertisement of the readiness of the Commissioners of Finance, acting for and on behalf of the Mayor and City Council of Baltimore, to receive bids for the purchase of the bonds authorized to be issued hereunder, or any part thereof; the form, terms and conditions of such bids; the time, place and manner of awarding bonds so bid for, including the right whenever any of the bonds authorized by this ordinance are offered for sale and sold at the same time as other bonds of said corporation, to establish the conditions for bids and awards and to award all of said bonds on all or none basis; and the time, place, terms and manner of settlement for the bonds so bid for.

Section 4. And be it further ordained, That: (a) All premiums resulting from the sale of any of the bonds issued and sold pursuant to the provisions of this ordinace shall be applied first to defray the cost of issuance thereof and the balance, if any, shall be applied to the payment of interest on any of said bonds becoming due and payable during the fiscal year in which said bonds are issued and sold or during the next succeeding fiscal year.

(b) The debt authorized by the provisions of this ordinance, and the bonds issued and sold pursuant thereto and their transfer, and the principal and interest payable thereon (including any profit made in the sale thereof), there shall be and remain exempt from any and all State, county and municipal taxation in the State of Maryland.

(c) All bonds issued and sold pursuant to the provisions of this ordinance shall be sold at public sale to the highest responsible bidder or bidders therefor after due notice of such sale, but the Mayor and City Council of Baltimore, acting by and through the Commissioners of Finance thereof, shall have the right to reject any or all bids therefor for any reason, and thereafter reoffer such bonds at public sale as aforesaid or at private sale, provided that if such bonds be offered at private sale they shall be offered for sale and sold for not less than par and accrued interest.

Section 5. And be it further ordained, That until all of the interest on and principal of any bonds issued pursuant to the provisions of this ordinace have been paid in full, the Mayor and City Council of Baltimore shall levy and impose an annual tax on each One Hundred Dollars ($100.00) of assessable property in the City of Baltimore at a rate sufficient to produce revenue to pay all interest on and principal of all bonds theretofore issued and outstanding or authorized to be issued and outstanding, payable in the next succeeding year.

Section 6. And be it further ordained, That this ordinance shall be submitted to the legal voters of the City of Baltimore, for their approval or disapproval, at the General Election to be held in Baltimore City on Tuesday, the 7th day of November, 1972.

Section 7. And be it further ordained, That prior to the date of the election hereinbefore mentioned, notice shall be given to the public of the amount of money which the Mayor and City Council of Baltimore is authorized to borrow, and the general purposes for which such borrowed funds may be expended, under the terms and provisions of this ordinance, and the time when the election hereinbefore mentioned is to be held; and such public notice shall be given in such manner and by such means or through such media and at such time or times as may be determined, from time to time, by a majority of the

Commissioners of Finance.

Section 8. And be it further ordained, That the actual cash proceeds derived from the sale of the bonds authorized to be issued under the provisions of this ordinance, not exceeding the par value thereof, shall be used exclusively for the following purposes, to wit:

(a) So much thereof as may be necessary, in addition to the premiums realized from the sale, if any, for the cost of issuance, including the expense of engraving, printing, advertising, attorneys' fees, and all other incidental expenses connected therewith; and

(b) The remainder of such proceeds shall be used to make or contract to make financial loans to the owners of buildings or structures located within the boundaries of Baltimore City, which are used or occupied for residential purposes, for or in connection with rehabilitating or improving said buildings or structures; to guarantee or insure financial loans made by third parties to the owners of buildings or structures located within the boundary lines of Baltimore City, which are used or occupied for residential purposes, for or in connection with rehabilitating or improving said buildings or structures, and for doing any and all things necessary, proper or expedient in connection with or pertaining to any or all of the matters or things hereinbefore mentioned.

Section 9. And be it further ordained, That the expenditure of the proceeds derived from the sale of the bonds authorized to be issued under the provisions of this ordinance shall be in accordance with the provisions of the Charter of the Mayor and City Council of Baltimore, and by the municipal agency designated in the annual Ordinance of Estimates of the Mayor and City Council of Baltimore.

Section 10. AND BE IT FURTHER ORDAINED, THAT THE POWER AND THE AUTHORITY VESTED IN THE MAYOR AND CITY COUNCIL OF BALTIMORE UNDER THE TERMS AND PROVISIONS OF THIS ORDINANCE SHALL BECOME OPERATIVE UPON THE ADOPTION OF THE AMENDMENT TO THE CONSTITUTION OF MARYLAND PROPOSED BY HOUSE BILL 758, AS ENACTED BY THE 1972 SESSION OF THE GENERAL ASSEMBLY OF MARYLAND, BY THE QUALIFIED VOTERS OF THE STATE OF MARYLAND AT THE GENERAL ELECTION TO BE HELD ON TUESDAY, THE SEVENTH DAY OF NOVEMBER, 1972.

Ordinance approved by the Mayor: June 15, 1972.

AN AGREEMENT BETWEEN THE CITY OF WILMINGTON AND LOCAL LENDING INSTITUTIONS TO PROVIDE REHABILITATION FINANCING

WHEREAS The City of Wilmington (City) has amended the City Code by adding a new Chapter 33 A entitled "Homestead Program" for the purpose of making available to proper applicants city-owned ground and reclaimable dwellings on condition that such applicants construct on or rehabilitate such property to conform to City code standards and thus return said property to the tax rolls, and

WHEREAS City is desirous of providing a satisfactory private program for the best available financial assistance to participants in the said Homestead Program for the purpose of enhancing and accelerating the success thereof, and

WHEREAS Wilmington City Housing Corporation (WCHC) is desirous of assisting in the establishment of the private program hereinbefore mentioned for the same purpose noted above, and

WHEREAS Artisans' Savings Bank, Bank of Delaware, Delaware Trust Company, Farmers Bank of the State of Delaware, First Federal Savings and Loan Association, Home Federal Savings and Loan Association, Wilmington Savings Fund Society and Wilmington Trust Company (Banks) consider the said need for financial assistance to qualified Homestead Program participants (Homesteaders) to be a most worthwhile one in view of the anticipated resultant revitalization of the community,

NOW THEREFORE City and Banks and WCHC hereby cause to be set their respective seals to the following agreement dated July 1, 1974.

FIRST: One official employed by one of the Banks will be recommended by Banks annually to the Mayor of City for appointment to the Homestead Board in an advisory capacity, eligible to attend all meetings of the said Homestead Board.

SECOND: One of the Banks will be designated as the Contact Bank on the effective date of this agreement. The Contact Bank designation will rotate annually on each anniversary of this agreement in the same order as that in which mortgages are placed as noted in Section Fifth. The Contact Bank will hold all guarantee deposits, receive all approvals and disapprovals on mortgage applications, and send and receive all correspondance regarding this agreement and matters pertaining thereto.

THIRD: City will forward to the Contact Bank eight copies of each of (i) a fully completed Application for Wilmington Homestead Program form indicating the amount and term of the mortgage desired, (ii) a report by City's Department of Licenses and Inspections (L & I) detailing all repairs and replacements together with the cost thereof required to bring the property for which application is being made to within City's Building Code Standards and (iii) a complete description of the property for which application is being made for any prospective Homesteader whom City has previously determined is qualified to be a recipient of a Homestead within the purview of the Homestead Program and who has indicated to City that he wishes to apply for a conventional mortgage from Banks, (iv) an approval for guarantee of such application by WCHC.

FOURTH: Banks will review the applications referred to in Section Third above and within one week of receipt thereof from Contact Bank must indicate approval or disapproval to the Contact Bank. Approval by at least six of the eight banks listed above is required for acceptance of any application under this agreement.

FIFTH: Contact Bank will notify City within one week after receipt of all approvals or disapprovals mentioned in Section Fourth above Banks' decision to approve or disapprove the mortgage application. City will then notify the Homesteader who in the case of approval, will then have thirty days in which to notify City that he wishes to proceed with the financing as approved; City will then notify Contact Bank which will commit the mortgage for the bank following the most recent previously assigned mortgagee in the following rotation with the first mortgage committed under this agreement to be committed for number one.

1. Farmers Bank of the State of Delaware
2. Delaware Trust Company
3. First Federal Savings and Loan Association
4. Bank of Delaware
5. Artisans' Savings Bank
6. Wilmington Trust Company
7. Home Federal Savings and Loan Association
8. Wilmington Savings Fund Society

Exceptions to the above order are as follows:

A. In any case where a mortgage is committed by a bank and is not taken within sixty days of commitment for that bank, said bank shall then become the next bank in rotation with the regular rotation to thereafter continue as if such interruption had not been made.

B. In any case where a bank incurs any loss of principal and/or interest subsequent to the final disposition of a Homestead mortagage under this agreement on its next one regular position in rotation.

SIXTH: Under no circumstances will the rotation revolve more than three times in any one calendar year nor will any individual bank be required to accept more than three mortgages under this agreement in any one calendar year. Each calendar year's rotation will begin with the bank following the last bank to be assigned a mortgage in regular rotation in the previous calandar year after giving consideration to the exceptions noted in Section Fifth.

SEVENTH: The following limitations and standards will apply to loans made under this agreement:

A. Interest rate is to be 9% simple interest per annum on the unpaid, outstanding blance.

B. (i) Loans granted in amounts up to and including $6,500. shall be amortized in 120 or less equal monthly payments (which shall include principal and interest).

(ii) Loans granted in amounts greater than $6,500. to the maximum allowable under this agreement shall be amortized in 180 or less equal monthly payments (which shall include principal and interest).

(iii) No loan granted under this agreement shall exceed $10,000.

C. No loan shall be made under this agreement, the final maturity date of which shall be subsequent to the applicant's seventieth anniversary of birth.

D. No service charges will be made except that a late charge may be made upon any monthly payment which is not paid within fifteen days of the date due; such late charge may not exceed two percent of the total amount of the monthly payment due including escrow amounts.

E. Each monthly payment shall include an additional sum (escrow) equal to one twelfth of the annual cost of all real estate taxes and fire insurance. Such sum shall be held by the mortgagee in a non-interest bearing account for the purpose of paying said taxes and insurance only.

F. The Homestead must be insured against fire under a standard Fire and Extended Coverage Insurance policy issued by an insurance company acceptable to the majority of Banks in an amount not less than the outstanding amount of the mortgage and naming the mortgagee as beneficiary.

G. The Homestead must be insured against risks during the construction period under a standard Builders Risk Insurance policy issued by an insurance company acceptable to the majority of Banks in an amount not less than the outstanding amount of the mortgage and naming the mortgagee as beneficiary.

H. The fee title to the Homestead must be insured under a standard Title Insurance policy issued by an insurance company acceptable to the majority of Banks in an amount not less than the outstanding amount of the mortgage and naming the mortgagee as beneficiary.

I. During the construction (rehabilitation) period, the loan shall be on a monthly interest only payment basis.

J. The funds will be advanced only for the amounts actually charged to the Homesteader and directly the result of rehabilitating the subject Homestead or fees involved in settling the mortgage. These funds will be advanced not more frequently than twice per calendar month upon presentation by L and I of (a) bills for materials and labor (other than that of the Homesteader and other volunteer labor) actually utilized in the rehabilitation of the subject Homestead together with the Homesteader's check properly drawn to the order of the materialmen and/or contractors submitting the aforesaid bills and (b) a certification by an authorized official of L and I that the Homestead has been inspected and that materials and labor for which the bills in (a) above are presented have been properly installed or utilized in the rehabilitation of the Homestead and that such materials and labor have been in accordance with the City Building Code Standards.

Upon receipt of aforementioned bills, checks and certificates, funds to cover said checks will be deposited by the mortgagee into the Homesteader's checking account on which such checks have been drawn, and the mortgagee will then mail the said checks. The above mentioned checking account must be maintained at one of the Banks signing this agreement.

EIGHTH: The following acts shall each be considered an act of default under this agreement and shall be specified in each mortgage accepted by a lender under this agreement:

A. Any breach of or failure by the mortgagor to fully comply with the conditions of Section Fourth of the Homestead Act, as amended.

B. Any voluntary reconveyance by the mortgagor to the City of homestead premises prior to mortgagor's full compliance with the conditions of

Section Fourth of the Homestead Act, as amended.

C. Any failure by the mortgagor to pay the mortgagee any interest and/or principal, late charges, or escrows for property taxes and hazard insurance when the same are due and payable, if such failure is not remedied within thirty days after any such due date.

D. The failure to maintain at all times a policy of fire and extended coverage insurance on the building on the mortgaged premises for the full insurable value thereof, with first mortgagee clause naming the mortgagee, and to deposit the original of such policy with the mortgagee. The term "extended coverage" shall include flood insurance if, and to the extent, required under the provisions of the national Flood Disaster Act of 1973 and Regulations adopted thereunder.

E. Any failure to perform or observe any other of the terms, conditions or obligations of the mortgage or obligation secured thereby.

F. Discovery of any material misrepresentation or misstatement furnished to Banks, or any one of them, by or on behalf of the Homesteader or City.

G. Entry of judgement, execution process or additional liens against the Homestead or Homesteader.

H. Substantial uninsured damage to the Homestead.

NINTH: If any act described in Section Eight occurs, the mortgagee may, at its option, declare the mortage in default. All the mortgagee's rights and remedies hereunder are cumulative and no waiver, either expressed or implied, of any default shall affect any later default.

TENTH: In the event any Bank, as mortgagee, elects to declare all sums owing under any mortgage granted under the provisions of this agreement and held by it to be due and payable in full by reason of any event of default set forth in Section Eighth above and specified in such mortgage, such Bank shall notify this City in writing of such election, specifying the default or defaults, with a copy thereof being sent to WCHC, and the City, within thirty days after receipt of such notice, shall:

(a) Cause such mortgage to be fully reinstated by curing or causing to be cured all specified defaults and effecting the payment of all sums required to the date of reinstatement; or,

(b) Exercise its right of reversion or secure a voluntary reconveyance of the property, free of all liens excepting the lien of said mortgage, and free of the possession of the defaulting mortgagor.

ELEVENTH: In the event the mortgage is reinstated as provided in sub paragraph (a) of Section Tenth above, the effect shall be as though no default had occurred and all provisions of the agreement as to subsequent defaults, guarantees, or otherwise shall continue in full force and effect as to such mortgage.

TWELFTH: In the event the City regains title to said property as provided in sub paragraph (b) of Section Tenth above, the City may, at its election:

(a) Within Twenty days after regaining title to said homestead property, submit to the Contact Bank an application from a proposed substitute

Homesteader willing to assume the mortgage and the obligation secured thereby, and such application shall be submitted and processed as provided in Sections Third, Fourth and Fifth above, excepting that if such application is approved, settlement, including the execution of a written assumption agreement, shall be completed within thirty days after approval of the application to assume the mortgage. Any such application shall demonstrate the ability of the applicant to complete any work required to bring the property to City Code requirements, including the ability of the applicant to provide for any costs of such work in excess of mortgage funds, if any, remaining to be disbursed; or,

(b) Within thirty days after any application under (a) above is rejected or within thirty days after the City acquires title as aforesaid if no application is made under (a) above, the City may notify the mortgagee Bank that the City (or one of its agencies acceptable to Banks) has elected to assume the payment of the mortgage indebtedness in accordance with its terms, in which event such notice shall be accompanied by a payment of all delinquent interest and principal and a written assumption agreement with the approval of the City Solicitor endorsed thereon, with provision that the City may convey such property at any time to a grantee or grantees who will assume the mortgage, with release of the City from its assumption, provided such grantee or grantees are first approved by Banks. Such conveyance may be under the Homestead Program or otherwise (with the prior approval of Banks) and, if under the Homestead Program, such approval and assumption shall be processed as in sub paragraph (a) above.

THIRTEENTH: In the event the City fails to comply with (a) or (b) of Section Tenth above or to effect an assumption by a new Homesteader or an assumption by the City pursuant to (a) or (b) of paragraph Twelfth above, the Mortgagee Bank may, on written notice to both the City and WCHC:

(a) Assign the defaulted Mortgage to WCHC and file a claim against the Guaranty Fund established in accordance with Section Fifteenth below for forty percent of either (i) the total amount advanced under the said mortgage or (ii) the principal amount due and owing it under the aforesaid Mortgage, whichever is less; or,

(b) Foreclose on the mortgage and bid competitively at such foreclosure sale up to a sum equivalent to property taxes and assessments due and owing, principal, interest, costs, counsel fees and other sums due to owing the Mortgagee in foreclosure. In the event the mortgagee is the successful bidder, it shall assign such bid to WCHC or otherwise provide for title to be conveyed to WCHC and, in such event, the mortgagee shall file a claim against the Guaranty Fund established in accordance with Section Fifteenth below for forty percent of all principal amounts owing it under said defaulted mortgage or forty percent of the total amount advanced under the said mortgage, whichever is less. In the event the aforesaid foreclosure sale is confirmed to a third party bidder, the claim against the Guaranty Fund mentioned above shall be restricted to any deficiency of sums owing on said mortgage after crediting any proceeds received by the mortgagee from the Sheriff's Sale or forty percent of the principal amount then owing under the said morgage, whichever is less.

FOURTEENTH: Claims against the Guaranty Fund shall be presented to the Contact Bank and shall specify the amount claimed and the basis thereof under this Agreement. Such claim shall be in duplicate and a copy thereof shall be mailed by the Contact Bank to WCHC. Ten days from the date of mailing of the copy of the claim to WCHC, the Contact Bank shall forthwith pay the claim from the Guaranty Fund. Upon rotation of the Contact Bank, any pending, unpaid claims shall be transferred to the successor Contact Bank for payment thereby.

FIFTEENTH: With the signing of this agreement WCHC hereby agrees that it shall deposit in an account with the Contact Bank in the name of WCHC as trustee of the Guaranty Fund under this agreement an amount equal to forty percent of the total committed amount of each and every mortgage committed under this agreement at the time of the recording of each mortgage. The balance in such account will bear interest at the maximum rate permitted to be paid by law on regular savings accounts. Amounts so deposited may not be withdrawn except as hereinafter provided. These deposits are for the purpose of providing Banks with a partial guarantee for loans made under this agreement in keeping with the joint efforts of City and Banks to enhance the success of the Homestead Program. These deposits may be used to repay any defaulted mortgage in the manner hereinbefore described in Sections Thirteenth and Fourteenth above. Withdrawals from the Guaranty Fund shall be made only for the following purposes:

A. To pay claims against the Guaranty Fund under the provisions of Sections Thirteenth and Fourteenth above; provided, that no such claim on any particular mortgage shall exceed forty percent of the face amount of such mortgage.

B. To transfer the Guaranty Fund to a successor Contact Bank.

C. Upon full payment and satisfaction of a mortgage without claim against the Guaranty Fund, the amount of the Guaranty deposited with respect to such mortgage shall be refunded to WCHC.

D. Upon payment of a claim against the Guaranty Fund on a particular mortgage where such claim is less than the amount of Guaranty allocable to such mortgage, the balance remaining of such allocated amount shall be refunded to WCHC.

E. Annually, on June 30, the Contact Bank shall refund to WCHC that portion of the Guaranty Fund which on June 15 of the then subject year exceeded forty percent of the principal balance owing on June 15 of the then subject year on all mortgages outstanding on said June 15 under this agreement.

SIXTEENTH: It is understood and agreed that no waiver, forebearance, modification or extension allowed or granted by any mortgagee Bank to any Homesteader shall in any manner affect or diminish the Guaranty provided for under Section Fifteenth and WCHC hereby consents to any such waiver, forebearance, modification or extension so long as it does not increase the principal indebtedness or increase the interest rate or change the final maturity date of the mortgage.

SEVENTEENTH: Notices to the City hereunder shall be addressed to the Secretary of the Homestead Board, City of Wilmington, Public Building, Wilmington, Delaware 19801, notices to the Banks hereunder shall be addressed to the named Contact Bank at its principal office in the City of Wilmington, attention Vice President, Mortgage Division. Notices to WCHC shall be addressed to the Chairman of the Wilmington City Housing Corporation, 1213 Walnut Street, Wilmington, Delaware 19801.

EIGHTEENTH: Nothing in this agreement contained shall be construed to restrict the right of any mortgagee Bank to avail itself of any applicable remedies by reason of any default by a Homesteader mortgagor, whether during the construction (rehabilitation) period or thereafter, including the filing of a claim against the Guaranty Fund and receipt of payment therefrom as provided in this agreement.

NINETEENTH: It is mutually agreed that in the event Bank or Banks, including commercial banks, savings banks, and savings and loan associations, having offices in the City of Wilmington, not initially parties to this agreement, elect to participate in this agreement, they may become party to this agreement by executing a supplementary Agreement subscribing to all the terms and conditions of this agreement, with provision for their rotation as a Contact Bank under Section Second and as a mortgagee Bank under Section Fifth Subject only to the delivery of a signed copy of any such supplementary agreement to each of the then parties to this agreement. Such supplementary agreement shall have the same force and effect as if such new Bank participant had executed this agreement initially.

TWENTIETH: This agreement shall not be effective until endorsed by the City Solicitor, which endorsement shall constitute an opinion by such Solicitor that all the terms and conditions of this agreement are valid and effective in so far as they pertain to the obligations hereunder of the City of Wilmington, its Homestead Board and the Wilmington City Housing Corporation, excepting that there are currently legal restrictions on the ability of the City and the WCHC to assume the payment of mortgages under the optional provisions of Section Twelfth, Part (b).

TWENTY-FIRST: This agreement shall be construed in accordance with the laws of the State of Delaware. References to Homesteader or other terms used in the Homestead Program shall have the meaning as defined in said Program.

TWENTY-SECOND: This agreement shall not be altered or changed orally, but only by an agreement in writing signed by all the parties hereto.

TWENTY-THIRD: This agreement shall be subject to annual review by Banks, and within thirty days prior to each anniversary, Banks, or any one of them, may withdraw from participation in this agreement by indicating such interest in writing to each party then participating in this agreement; provided, that withdrawal shall not affect the rights and remedies available to any Bank hereunder with respect to mortgage loans made by it hereunder, including loans to be made by it under outstanding commitments, all of which shall be entitled to the rights, remedies and guaranty applicable to mortgage loans, it being understood and agreed that the obligations of the City and the WCHC hereunder shall continue with respect to all mortgage loans made hereunder until the same are fully paid and satisfied.

TWENTY-FOURTH: This agreement shall be binding upon and shall inure to the benefit of the parties hereto, their respective successors and assigns.

Bibliography

Akre, M.J. "Urban Homesteading: Once More Down the Yellow Brick Road." *Environmental Affairs*, Vol. 3, No. 3, 1974, pp. 563-594.

Arnold, Joseph L. *The New Deal in the Suburbs: A History of the Greenbelt Town Program, 1935-1954*. Columbus: Ohio State University Press, 1971.

Baltimore Department of Housing and Community Development Home Ownership Development Program, *The Settler* (bi-monthly newsletter). July/August 1974.

Baltimore Department of Housing and Community Development Home Ownership Development Program. *Urban Homesteading Awards Socio-Economic Data*. Mimeographed. Baltimore: Homeownership Development Program, 1974.

Berry, M.F. "Homesteading: New Prescription for Urban Ills," *HUD Challenge*, Vol. V, No. 1, January 1974, pp. 2-5.

Borsodi, Ralph. *Flight From the City: An Experiment in Creative Living on the Land*. New York: Harper Brothers Publishing Co., 1933.

Boston, City of. *Ordinances of 1973, Chapter 13, Section 7*. Boston: City of Boston, Massachusetts, 1973.

Brant, A. *Urban Homesteading – Interim Report I*. Mimeographed. Detroit: Division of Research and Analysis, Detroit Common Council, 1973.

Brewster, John. "The Relevance of the Jeffersonian Dream Today." In *Land Use Policy and Problems in the United States,* ed. by Howard Ottoson. Lincoln, Nebraska: University of Nebraska Press, 1964.

Bronson, Gail. "The Old Homestead-Abandoned Houses Are Given Free to People Willing to Restore Them." *Wall Street Journal*, September 21, 1973, p. 1.

Brophy, Paul C. *Urban Homesteading: Prospects for the Pittsburgh Area*. Pittsburgh: ACTION-Housing, Inc., 1974.

Brown, Dee. "Settlement of the Great Plains." *American Historian*, June 1974, pp. 4-11.

Burchell, Robert, Hughes, James W., and Sternlieb, George. *Housing Costs and Housing Restraints: The Realities of Inner City Housing Costs.* New York Life Insurance Association of America, 1970.

Busler, Joseph. "Homesteading Rush Around Corner." *Courier-Post* (Camden, N.J.), November 12, 1974, p. 7.

Campbell, Kenneth. "City Homesteading Opens New Frontier." *The Boston Globe*, July 29, 1973.

Chamberlain, G.M. "Homesteading Offers Antidote for Urban Blight." *American City*, Vol. 89, January 1974, p. 60.

"Cities' Attitudes Towards HUD Homesteading Giveaway is Cool." *Housing and Development Reporter*, Vol. 2, No. 3, July 1, 1974, p. 93.

Clark, Palmer S. *Memorandum: Homesteader Selection Criteria.* Mimeographed. Baltimore: Department of Housing and Community Development, November 1, 1974.

Clawson, Marion. *The Land System of the United States.* Lincoln, Nebraska: University of Nebraska Press, 1968.

Coleman, Joseph E. "Address before the Common Council of Detroit." Detroit: August 21, 1973.

Coleman, Joseph E. "The New Frontier in our Cities." *Focus,* Vol. 3, No. 1, November 1974, pp. 4-5.

Coleman, Joseph E. *Urban Homesteading, A Plan for Developing Our New Frontiers.* Philadelphia: The Author, undated.

Conkin, Paul. *Tomorrow a New World: The New Deal Community Program.* Ithaca, New York: Cornell Universtiy Press, 1959.

Crooks, Douglas. "Urban Homesteading: A Land Reform Idea that Works in Cities." *People and Land*, Summer 1974, p. 21.

Dickman, S. "Homesteaders Diverse as Early Counter-Parts." *The Evening Sun* (Baltimore), February 14, 1974, p. 28.

Division of Planning, Baltimore Department of Housing and Community Development. *Design Guide: Exterior Residential Rehabilitation.* Baltimore, Maryland: Department of Housing and Community Development, 1974.

"Does Homesteading Offer Investment Opportunities." *The Mortgage and Real Estate Executives Report,* Vol. 7 No. 6, May 15, 1974, pp. 1-2.

Drewes, Chris W. "Homesteading 1974: Reclaiming Abandoned Houses on the Urban Frontier." *Columbia Journal of Law and Social Problems*, Spring 1974, pp. 416-455.

Dror, Yehezkel. *Public Policy Making Re-examined.* San Francisco, California: Chandler Publishing Company, 1962.

Federal Writer's Project. *Delaware: A Guide to the First State.* New York: Hastings House, 1938.

Federal Writer's Project. *Maryland: A Guide to the Old Line State.* New York: Oxford University Press, 1940.

Federal Writer's Project, *New Jersey: A Guide to its Present and Past.* New

York: The Viking Press, 1939.

Federal Writer's Project, *Pennsylvania: A Guide to the Keystone State.* New York: Oxford University Press. 1940.

Friedman, Shelly S. "Philadelphia's Urban Homesteading Act: A Poor Beginning Toward Reoccupying the Urban Ghost Town." *Buffalo Law Review,* Vol. 23, No. 3, Spring 1974, pp. 735-763.

"From Plows to Pliers—Urban Homesteading in America." *Fordham Urban Law Journal,* Vol. 2, Winter 1974, pp. 273-304.

Frump, Bob. "Homesteaders in a Bind." *The Morning News* (Wilmington, Del.), September 2, 1974, p. 17.

Frump, Bob. "Will Maloney Homestead Stampede or Fizzle." *The Evening Journal* (Wilmington, Del.), May 17, 1973, pp. 1, 16.

Fulmer, Eugene, and Stumpf, Jeri. *A Report on Homesteading: An Approach to the Housing Problem and Analysis of House Bill 1703 (P.N. 3121).* Mimeographed. Harrisburg: The Majority Caucus Research Staff, May 29, 1974.

Gates, Paul. "The Homestead Act: Free Land Policy in Operation 1862-1935." In *Land Use Policy and Problems in the United States,* ed. by Howard Ottoson. 2nd ed. Lincoln, Nebraska: University of Nebraska Press, 1964.

"Ghetto Homesteaders," *Time,* August 13, 1973, p. 6.

"Give Homesteading a Chance to Show What It Can Do." *The Philadelphia Inquirer,* March 15, 1975. p. 6-A.

Grant, Eugene L., and Grant, Ireson W. *Principles of Engineering Economy.* New York: The Ronald Press Company, 1964.

Harris, Marshall. *Origin of the Land Tenure System in the United States.* Ames, Iowa: Iowa State College Press, 1953.

Hibbard, Benjamin. *The History of the Public Land Policies.* Madison, Wisconsin: University of Wisconsin Press, 1965.

Holt, Marjorie S. "Extensions of Remarks." *Congressional Record,* September 19, 1973, pp. E5888 - E5889.

Home Ownership Development Program, *Urban Homesteading Awards Socio-Economic Data.* Mimeographed. Baltimore, Maryland: Home Ownership Development Program, Department of Housing and Urban Renewal, November, 1974.

Homesteading as an Option. Mimeographed. Wilmington, Delaware: Urban Homestead Board, 1973.

"Homesteading Big City Fashion." *Realtor,* Vol. 41 No. 1, January 7, 1974, pp. 3A, 8A.

"Homesteading in '73: City Houses for $1." *U.S. News and World Report,* Vol. 75, November 15, 1973, pp. 43-44.

"Homesteading Plan is Worth the Effort." Editorial. *The Philadelphia Inquirer,* October 4, 1973, p. 11.

Hoover, Edgar M., and Vernon, Raymond. *Anatomy of a Metropolis,* New York:

Doubleday-Anchor, 1962.

"Hope for Housing." Editorial. *New York Times,* November 23, 1973, p. 34.

Hospitality House, Inc. *Urban Homesteading for Washington, D.C.* Washington, D.C.: Hospitality House, February 16, 1974.

"Houses for-a-Dollar Plan Faltering." *The Philadelphia Inquirer,* March 10, 1975.

Housing Association of Delaware Valley, *A Consumer's Guide to Urban Homesteading in Philadelphia.* Philadelphia: Housing Association of Delaware Valley, 1974.

"Housing Buyers Ignore Newark Trouble," *New York Times,* September 14, 1974, p. 33.

Housing and Community Development Act of 1974, Public Law 93-383, 88 Statutes 633. Washington, D.C.: U.S. Government Printing Office, 1974.

Hoyt, Homer. *The Structure and Growth of Residential Neighborhoods in American Cities.* Washington D.C.: Federal Housing Administration, 1939.

Hughes, James W. (Ed.) *New Dimensions of Urban Planning: Growth Controls.* New Brunswick, N.J.: Center for Urban Policy Research, Rutgers University, 1974.

Hughes, James W. *Suburbanization Dynamics and the Future of the City,* New Brunswick, New Jersey: Center for Urban Policy Research, Rutgers University, 1974.

Hughes, James W. *Urban Indicators, Metropolitan Evolution, and Public Policy.* New Brunswick, New Jersey: Center for Urban Policy Research, Rutgers University, 1973.

Husock, Howard. "The Sexiest Political Idea of the Year." *The Boston Phoenix,* Vol. 11 No. 4D 2, October 1973, pp. 3, 5.

King, Wayne, "Homesteaders Combating Urban Blight." *New York Times,* September 16, 1973, pp. 1, 34.

Kravitz, Jeffrey S., and Chiv, Nancy K. "Adverse Possession of Abandoned Urban Housing." *Loyola of Los Angeles Law Review,* Vol. 7 No. 1, February 1974, pp. 30965.

Krueckeberg, Donald A., and Silvers, Arthur L. *Urban Planning Analysis: Methods and Models.* New York: John Wiley and Sons, Inc., 1974.

Le Duc, Thomas. "History and Appraisal of U.S. Land Policy to 1962." In *Land Use Policy and Problems in the United States,* ed. by Howard Ottoson. 2nd ed. Lincoln, Nebraska: University of Nebraska Press, 1964.

Lewis, Arthur M. "The Worst American City." *Harpers,* January 1974, p. 67-71.

Linton, Mields, and Coston, *A Study of Abandoned Housing and Recommendations for Action by the Federal Government and Localities.* Mimeographed. Washington, D.C.: Linton Mields, and Coston, 1971.

Listokin, David. *The Dynamics of Housing Rehabilitation: Macro and Micro Analyses.* New Brunswick, New Jersey: Center for Urban Policy Research, Rutgers University, 1973.

Maloney, T.C. "Homesteading, Twentieth Century Style: Program Begun in

Wilmington, Delaware," *American City,* Vol. 89, March 1971, pp. 41-42.

Marcus, Matityahu, and Taussig, Michael. "A Proposal for Government Insurance of Home Values Against Locational Risk." *Land Economics,* November 1970, pp. 404-413.

Maslow, Jonathan. "Harlem Housing: The New Homesteaders." *Ramparts,* August 1974, pp. 12-15.

McKenzie, Roderick D. "The Ecological Approach." In *The City,* ed. by Robert E. Park, Ernest W. Burgess, and Roderick D. McKenzie. Chicago: University of Chicago Press, 1925.

Michner, James. *Centennial,* New York: Random House, 1974.

"Minneapolis Considers Homesteading Program." *Housing and Development Reporter,* Vol. 2, No. 5, July 29, 1974 p. 212.

National Homestead Act of 1973, H.R. 10373, 93rd Congress, 1st Session. Washington, D.C.: U.S. Congress, 1973.

National Urban Coalition. *Urban Homesteading: Process and Potential, An Exploration into Options for Urban Stabilization,* Washington, D.C.: National Urban Coalition, 1974.

National Urban League. *The National Survey of Housing Abandonment,* New York: The Center for Community Change, 1971.

New York City Public Housing Authority. "Annual Tenant Characteristics Summary." Unpublished. New York: N.Y.C. Public Housing Authority.

Newark Real Estate Commission. "Newark West Ward Ho!" Listing booklet for the April 1974 Auction. Newark: Newark Real Estate Commission, 1974.

Oliphant, A. "Can Urban Homesteading Be an Idea Whose Time Has Come?" *Planning,* February 1973, p. 3.

"$1 Home Program Slowed." *The Sun* (Baltimore, Maryland), October 27, 1974, p. 15.

Pfeiffer, Sophie Douglass. " 'Go Urban Young Man!' — American Homesteading, 1862-1974." *Historic Preservation,* July, September 1974, pp. 16-22.

"Philadelphia Awards First Houses to Urban Homesteaders," *HUD Challenge,* Vol. V, No. 9, September 1974, p. 15.

Philadelphia Pensylvania City Ordinance 543. June 20, 1973.

Philadelphia Pensylvania City Ordinance, 909A. December 14, 1973.

Philadelphia Urban Homesteading Office. *Summary Characteristics of Philadelphia's First Homesteaders.* Mimeographed, Philadelphia: Urban Homesteading Office, 1974.

Priest A.R., and Turvey, R. "Cost-Benefit Analysis: A Survey." *Economic Journal,* No. 75, 1965, pp. 683-735.

Profile of Philadelphia's first 20 Homesteaders. Mimeographed. Philadelphia: Urban Homesteading Office, 1974.

Public Affairs Counseling. *HUD Experimental Program for Preserving the Declining Neighborhood: An Analysis of the Abandonment Process.* San Francisco, California: Public Affairs Counseling, 1973.

Real Estate Research Corporation. *Possible Program for Counteracting Housing Abandonment.* Chicago, Illinois: Real Estate Research Corporation, 1971.

"Rhode Island Passes Homesteading Bill." *Housing and Development Reporter,* Vol. 2, No. 2, July 17, 1974, p. 69.

Robbins, Roy M. *Our Landed Heritage: The Public Domain, 1776-1936.* 3rd ed. Lincoln, Nebraska: University of Nebraska, 1962.

Robinson, D., Jr., and Weinstein, J.I. "Urban Homesteading: Hope . . . or Hoax?" *Journal of Housing,* August-September 1973, pp. 395-396.

Rose, Jerome G. *The Legal Advisor of Home Ownership.* Boston: Little, Brown and Company, 1964.

Rosskam, Edwin. *Roosevelt, New Jersey: Big Dreams in a Small Town and What Time Did to Them.* New York: Grossman Publishers, 1972.

Rother, Steve. "Urban Homesteading: It May Be a Way to Reclaim Abandoned City Dwellings." *New Jersey Municipalities,* January 1974.

Scott, Mel. *American City Planning Since 1890.* Berkeley and Los Angeles, California: University of California Press, 1969.

Select Committee of the House Committee on Agriculture, *Hearings on the Farm Security Administration, 78th Congress, 1st Session, 1943-1944.* Washington, D.C.: U.S. Government Printing Office, 1944.

"Stay East, Young Man," *Architecture Plus,* November 1973, pp. 20-21.

Sternlieb, George. *The Garden Apartment: A Municipal Cost-Revenue Analysis.* New Brunswick, N.J.: Bureau of Governmental Research, Rutgers University, 1964.

Sternlieb, George. "The Myth and Potential Reality of Urban Homesteading." Paper presented at Confer-In 1974, American Institute of Planners.

Sternlieb, George. *The Tenement Landlord.* New Brunswick, N.J.: The Rutgers University Press, 1969.

Sternlieb, George. *Towards an Urban Homestead Act.* Mimeograph. New Brunswick, New Jersey: Center for Urban Policy Research, 1972.

Sternlieb, George. "Toward an Urban Homesteading Act." *Papers Submitted to the Subcommittee on Housing Panels,* Committee on Banking and Currency, House of Representatives, 92nd Congress First Session, June 1971, pp. 366-371.

Sternlieb, George. *The Urban Housing Dilemma: The Dynamics of New York City's Rent-Controlled Housing.* New York: Housing Development Administration, 1972.

Sternlieb, George, and Burchell, Robert. *Residential Abandonment: The Tenement Landlord Revisited.* New Brunswick, New Jersey: Center for Urban Policy Research, 1973.

Sternlieb, George and Hughes, James W. "Analysis of Neighborhood Decline in Urban Areas." A policy paper prepared for the U.S. Department of Housing and Urban Development. New Brunswick, New Jersey: Center for Urban Policy Research, Rutgers University, 1973.

Sternlieb, George and Hughes, James W. *Housing and People in New York City.* New York: Housing and Development Administration, 1972.

Sternlieb, George, and Hughes, James W. "Profiling the High Rent Center City Market." *Real Estate Review,* Fall 1973.

Sternlieb, George, Hughes, James W., and Burchell, Robert. "Housing Abandonment in the Urban Core." *Journal of the American Institute of Planners,* September 1974.

Sternlieb, George, Hughes, James W., and Burrows, Lawrence. *Housing in Newark.* New Brunswick, New Jersey: Center for Urban Policy Research, Rutgers University 1974.

Sternlieb, George, et al. *Housing Abandonment in Pennsylvania.* New Brunswick, New Jersey: Center for Urban Policy Research, Rutgers University, 1974.

Sternlieb, George, et al. *Housing Development and Municipal Costs.* New Brunswick, New Jersey: Center for Urban Policy Research, Rutgers University, 1973.

Stevenson, George M. *The Political History of the Public Lands: From 1840 to 1862.* 2nd ed. New York: Russell and Russell, 1967.

"St. Louis Homestead Plan Now Entering Second Year." *Journal of Housing,* May 1974 p. 228.

Tatro, Nick. "Homesteading Continues with Mixed Success." *Sunday Times Advertiser* (Trenton, N.J.), March 23, 1975, p. 5.

U.S. Bureau of the Census. "Housing Characteristics for States, Cities, and Counties." In *Census of Housing: 1970,* Vol. 1. Washington, D.C.: U.S. Government Printing Office, 1972.

U.S. Bureau of the Census. *Census of Population and Housing: 1970, Census Tracts Final Report PHC(1)-196 Newark, N.J. SMSA.* Washington, D.C.: U.S. Government Printing Office, 1971.

U.S. Bureau of the Census. *Census of Population and Housing 1970, Census Tracts, Final Report PHC(1)-159 Philadelphia, Penna. SMSA.* Washington, D.C.: U.S. Government Printing Office, 1971.

U.S. Bureau of the Census. *Census of Population and Housing: 1970 Census Tracts, Final Report PHC(1)-191 Baltimore, M.D. SMSA,* Washington, D.C.: U.S. Government Printing Office, 1971.

U.S. Bureau of the Census. *Census of Population and Housing: 1970 Census Tracts, Final Report PHC(1)-234 Wilmington, Delaware, SMSA.* Washington, D.C.: U.S. Government Printing Office, 1971.

U.S. Bureau of the Census. "Mobility of the Population of the United States: March 1970 to March 1973." *Current Population Reports,* Series P-20, No. 262. Washington, D.C.: U.S. Government Printing Office, 1974.

U.S. Department of Housing and Urban Development. *Abandoned Housing Research: A Compendium.* Washington, D.C.: U.S. Government Printing Office, 1973.

"Urban Homestead Plan: A Bright Promise for the City." Editorial. *The Philadelphia Inquirer,* July 22, 1973, p. 6-H.

"Urban Homesteading." *Architectural Forum,* Vol. 139, December 1973, p. 75.

"Urban Homesteading." *Municipal Attorney,* Vol. 14, No. 10, October 1973, pp. 196, 216.

"Urban Homesteading." *Philadelphia Inquirer,* January 12, 1974.

"Urban Homesteading: A Boon for Blacks." *Ebony,* Vol. 29, January 1974, pp. 108-109.

"Urban Homesteading: Saving Old Housing is the Name of the Claim." *Savings and Loan News,* Vol. 95, January 1974, pp. 50-54.

"Using Homesteaders to Restore the City." *Business Week,* September 1, 1973, pp. 22.

Van Allsburg, Mark. "Property Abandonment in Detroit." *Wayne Law Review,* Vol. 20, No. 3, March 1974, pp. 845-888.

Wedemeyer, Dee. "Urban Homesteading." *Nation's Cities,* Jan. 1975, pp. 19-20.

White, Anthony G. *"Urban Homesteading: A Bibliography.* Council of Planning Librarians Exchange Bibliography Number 719. Monticello, Ill.: Council of Planning Librarians, 1975.

Wilmington, Delaware, City of. *Wilimington Code, Chapter 33A.* Wilmington: City Council, 1973.

Wilmington, Delaware, City Ordinance 081. June, 1972.

Wilmington Homesteading Board. *Homesteading As an Option.* Mimeographed. Wilmington: Wilmington Homesteading Board, Summer 1973.

Wilmington Homesteading Board. *Regulations of the Wilmington Homestead Board.* Mimeographed. Wilmington: Wilmington Homestead Board, May 1974.

Winslow, J.B. "Urban Homesteading: Little to Lose and A Lot to Gain." *American City,* October 1974, p. 71.

Yarmolinsky, Adam. "Reassuring the Small Homeowner." *The Public Interest,* No. 22, Winter 1971 pp. 106-10.

Zevin, Rona, and Jaffee, Jan. *Urban Homesteading—The First Steps—Identification of Goals and Objectives.* Mimeographed. Philadelphia: Urban Homesteading Office, 1973.